INDOCTRINATING THE YOUTH

INDOCTRINATING THE YOUTH

Secondary Education in Wartime China and Postwar Taiwan, 1937–1960

Jennifer Liu

University of Hawai'i Press
Honolulu

© 2024 University of Hawai'i Press

All rights reserved

Printed in the United States of America

First printed, 2024

Library of Congress Cataloging-in-Publication Data

Names: Liu, Jennifer, author.

Title: Indoctrinating the youth : secondary education in wartime China and postwar Taiwan, 1937–1960 / Jennifer Liu.

Description: Honolulu : University of Hawai'i Press, [2024] | Includes bibliographical references and index.

Identifiers: LCCN 2023029711 (print) | LCCN 2023029712 (ebook) | ISBN 9780824895570 (hardback) | ISBN 9780824897000 (epub) | ISBN 9780824897017 (kindle edition) | ISBN 9780824896997 (pdf)

Subjects: LCSH: Zhongguo guo min dang—Influence. | Education and state—China—History—20th century. | Education and state—Taiwan—History—20th century. | Communist education—China—History—20th century. | Communist education—Taiwan—History—20th century. | Education, Secondary—China—History—20th century. | Education, Secondary—Taiwan—History—20th century.

Classification: LCC LC94.C6 L58 2024 (print) | LCC LC94.C6 (ebook) | DDC 379.51/0904—dc23/eng/20230801

LC record available at https://lccn.loc.gov/2023029711

LC ebook record available at https://lccn.loc.gov/2023029712

Cover photo: Girls attending the first Three People's Principles Youth Corps summer camp on August 1, 1939, after Chiang Kai-shek's personal order dated May 30, 1939. Courtesy of the Central News Agency (Taiwan)

University of Hawai'i Press books are printed on acid-free paper and meet the guidelines for permanence and durability of the Council on Library Resources.

*For my parents, Frank Liu and Ellen Liu,
and my husband Lane Demas*

Contents

Acknowledgments	ix
Note on Romanization	xiii
Abbreviations	xv

Introduction	1
1. The Relocation of Middle Schools during the Sino-Japanese War, 1937–1945	15
2. The Three People's Principles Youth Corps on the Mainland, 1938–1947	35
3. The China Youth Corps in Taiwan, 1952–1960	73
4. Military Training and Instructors, 1953–1960	108
5. Civics Textbooks and Curricular Standards, 1937–1960	132
Epilogue	153

Notes	163
Bibliography	195
Index	213

ACKNOWLEDGMENTS

I have incurred many debts on this project. First and foremost, I would like to express my deepest appreciation to Ken Pomeranz for mentoring me to become a historian and guiding me in formulating and writing this book. I have been blessed by his intellectual generosity and support through the years. I am also grateful for Jeff Wasserstrom and Guo Qitao's constructive feedback on this project's early versions. I have also been lucky to have Michael Fuller as my classical Chinese teacher. As an undergraduate at UCLA, I took my first Chinese history class with Richard von Glahn, which sparked my interest in the subject.

This book would not have been possible without generous funding from the National Central Library's Center for Chinese Studies Research Grant for Foreign Scholars in Taipei and the Fulbright in Taiwan. The University of California, Irvine's Humanities Center Research Grant; Summer Dissertation Fellowship; Center for Asian Studies grants; International Center for Writing and Translation grant; UCI History Department's Travel Fellowship; the Peking University–UC Irvine Exchange Scholar program; and the University of California's Pacific Rim mini-grant also contributed financial assistance. The Association for Asian Studies provided the China and Inner Asia Council small grant as well. Central Michigan University's Summer Faculty Scholar grant and Faculty Research and Creative Endeavors grants gave me opportunities to conduct further research in China, Taiwan, and US libraries.

I relied on numerous institutions, their staff, and other individuals for this research. I am grateful to the staff at the Second Historical Archives in Nanjing, Jiangsu Provincial Archives, Shanghai Library, National Library in Beijing, Chongqing Municipal Archives, Academia Sinica libraries, Academia Historica, the National Institute for Compilation and Translation and the National Institute of Educational Resources and Research (Taiwan; now merged as the National Academy for Educational Research), National Central Library (Taipei), China Youth Corps headquarters, the Hoover Institution Library and Archives, Stanford University East Asian Library, and the Library of Congress. I also greatly appreciate the interlibrary loan services at UC Irvine and CMU for their assistance.

x   Acknowledgments

I thank Nanjing University's Hu Cheng and Qiong Liu for facilitating access to the Second Historical Archives. At Academia Sinica's Institute of Modern History, Hu Kuo-tai provided great insight on wartime education and generously shared materials, while Yu Chien-ming and Peter Zarrow imparted their knowledge of oral interviews and education, respectively. Lien Ling-ling also introduced me to her colleagues. At National Central Library's Center for Chinese Studies, Jane Liau and Yi-chun Yeh were welcoming hosts. I would also like to thank Rui Wang at the CMU Library. Moreover, I am deeply grateful for the former China Youth Corps staff and members, as well as secondary school administrators and students who took the time to share their experiences, thoughts, and opinions with me.

I have had the privilege of sharing parts of my research at conferences and invited talks and benefited from the audience and discussants posing thoughtful questions and helpful feedback. At the Association of Asian Studies annual meetings, I received insightful comments from co-panelists and the discussants Denise Ho, Fabio Lanza, and Kristen Stapleton. I also thank Russ Crawford, Jack Neubauer, and Yi-chun Yeh for opportunities to speak at Northern Ohio University, National Chengchi University, and the National Central Library's Center for Chinese Studies in Taipei. Wang Liangqing imparted his knowledge of the Three People's Principles Youth Corps. I would like to extend special thanks to my supportive colleague and friend Doina Harsanyi for hosting my talk on the CMU campus. To all those who have aided the preparation and publication of this book at the University of Hawai'i Press—especially my editor Masako Ikeda—I am very grateful. Anonymous readers provided detailed and constructive feedback.

Portions of this volume have appeared in previous publications, and I am thankful to their publishers for permission to reuse them here. Parts of chapter 1 were previously published as "Defiant Retreat: The Relocation of Middle Schools to China's Interior, 1937–1945," *Frontiers of History in China* 8, no. 4 (December 2013): 558–583. A version of chapter 4 was published as "Anticipating Invasion: Military Training in Taiwan's High Schools, 1953–1960," *Twentieth-Century China* 37, no. 3 (October 2012): 204–228.

At UC Irvine, I benefited from the scholarly community and friendship of April Anderson, John Augustine, Nicole Barnes, Casey Christensen, Maura Cunningham, Pierre Fuller, Nuan Gao, Miri Kim, Claire Li, Kate Merkel-Hess, Xia Shi, Chloe Tai, Wensheng Wang, Michael Wert, Xinjie Yang, and Jie Zhao. At my home institution, CMU, I thank my chairs Mitch Hall and Greg Smith, and my colleagues, especially Doina Harsanyi, Brittany Fremion, and Tara McCarthy for their friendship and support. My students continue to inspire me with their curiosity, discussions, and passion for history.

This book is inextricably tied to my family. The riveting stories I heard about my four grandparents' courageous survival in the Second Sino-Japanese War and their subsequent retreat to Taiwan first inspired it. My parents' childhood and education in Taiwan also sparked my curiosity to research and write about the subject. I thank my parents and brother Harry for their love, unwavering support, and encouragement to explore the past. My father deserves my utmost gratitude for helping me translate some difficult Chinese texts. I also owe Lane Demas a tremendous debt. I thank him for accompanying me on research trips to Taiwan and across the US, painstakingly editing the full manuscript multiple times, and cooking almost every family meal. And last, but not least, I am wonderfully blessed with Drexler and Olivia, who are the source of all my happiness and joy.

Note on Romanization

Most Chinese names and other words in this book have been rendered into the internationally accepted pinyin system of romanization. Guomindang (GMD) is used instead of Kuomintang (KMT) because the text covers the GMD's years on the mainland and GMD is now commonly used. However, in some cases better-known alternative romanizations are used, such as Chiang Kai-shek (rather than Jiang Jieshi), Chiang Ching-kuo (rather than Jiang Jingguo), and Sun Yat-sen (rather than Sun Zhongshan). Quotes from original sources using titles and authors of referenced works remain in their original spellings. This was done to maintain accuracy and preserve the integrity of previous authors' work.

Abbreviations

CCP	Chinese Communist Party
CYC	China Youth Corps
CYL	Communist Youth League
DRC	Development and Relief Commission
GMD	Guomindang, also Chinese Nationalists and Kuomintang (KMT)
GPWD	General Political Warfare Department
MND	Ministry of National Defense
MNDPD	Ministry of National Defense Political Department
MOE	Ministry of Education
MRA	Moral Re-Armament Assembly
PRC	People's Republic of China
ROC	Republic of China
SQT	Sanqingtuan, which is the abbreviation for the Sanmin zhuyi qingniantuan, also translated as the Three People's Principles Youth Corps
SSGA	student self-governing association

Introduction

> Young people are the future masters of our country... we
> must emphasize party indoctrination in education to unify
> youth ideology so they may understand entirely that our
> principles will bring true happiness to the race and nation.
> —*Chiang Kai-shek (1930)*

During the Second Sino-Japanese War (1937–1945), Hou Yongqing, a representative of Wusheng county in Sichuan, reported that Jingren Middle School's refugee students destroyed Buddhist images. In a report to government superiors, Hou agreed that the temples and Buddhist figures were "superstitious" yet argued that they were still important because they instilled fear in people and prevented them from doing "bad things." "This is something that complements laws and morals," he wrote.[1] In Republican China, the vast majority of inland residents in rural areas were poorly educated and local officials saw religion as a means to instill moral principles in their community. It was therefore understandable why officials like Hou were alarmed when Jingren students and faculty converted a local deity temple into their classroom, desecrated the images inside, and took down temple decorations. Hou lamented "superstitious" beliefs but nevertheless argued that the images had "aesthetic value," noting that "everyone in the county was very upset about this situation."[2]

Chinese history includes a long trajectory of civil service examination candidates and students engaging in political and social activism. During the Han dynasty, Imperial University students railed against the eunuchs' interference with court politics in a coup d'état against the regent Liang Ji (d. 159).[3] In the Song dynasty (960–1279), students at the Imperial Confucian College pushed the government not to compromise with the Mongols by conceding land. During the early seventeenth century of the Ming dynasty, Donglin Academy students rose up against the court eunuch, Wei Zhongxian, who persecuted their members and supporters. Examination candidates in the late Qing dynasty protested their government's cession of territories to the Japanese following China's loss in the First Sino-Japanese War (1894–1895).

2   Introduction

During the twentieth century, the first significant moment of youth mobilization occurred with the May 4th Movement of 1919, which began when five thousand students gathered at Peking University to protest the Treaty of Versailles and its provisions ceding control of German concessions in Shandong province to Japan.[4] The movement sparked a patriotic outburst among young, urban intellectuals, one aimed at their government's weakness, foreign imperialists, warlords, and Confucian traditions. In turn, many began to exalt Western ideas, particularly science and democracy.

The next manifestation of student power was the May 30th Movement of 1925, when demonstrators "were outraged by threats to China's national sovereignty and by police repression of the protestors."[5] Although those who boycotted Japanese goods were mainly workers, students and merchants organized and publicized the demonstration. In 1926, the Guomindang (GMD, or Chinese Nationalist Party) mobilized over one hundred thousand students to participate in the two-year Northern Expedition, meant to consolidate a nation fragmented by warlords. Soon after, students played a major role in shaping popular outrage when the Japanese invaded Manchuria in 1931, forming propaganda groups, printing leaflets, delivering impassioned speeches, and once again boycotting Japanese goods. In 1935, Japanese plans to put large parts of north China under puppet regimes triggered students to protest in the December 9th Movement.[6]

Although student political agitation helped extend Nationalist rule and shape resistance to the Japanese, the GMD nevertheless remained skeptical of "radical" youth and considered them a dangerous force in need of tight discipline and control. *Indoctrinating the Youth* thus focuses on the GMD's attempts to contain young people through youth organizations and military training during and after the critical period of the Second Sino-Japanese War and the Chinese Civil War (1946–1949), unlike the aforementioned historical movements, in which young students and examination candidates took the initiative to exercise their political power. In particular, the book concentrates on secondary school students, who have received far less attention from scholars of twentieth-century China and popular historical narratives.

On the mainland and Taiwan, secondary education was also known as "middle school," consisting of three years of lower middle school (equivalent to seventh, eighth, and ninth grades in the US) and three years of upper middle school (equivalent to tenth, eleventh, and twelfth grades in the US), with students between the ages of thirteen and eighteen. *Indoctrinating the Youth* focuses on "regular" middle school students rather than students who are training to be teachers or vocational school students. This demographic group is often neglected by standard histories; most scholarship on Chinese wartime education tends to emphasize higher education (which refers to post-twelfth grade, mainly university or college). Scholarly attention is devoted to university students, whose voices are more readily accessible in the historical record, yet the story of middle school pupils during this tumultuous generation is just as important. They represented a much larger proportion of the population than university students, outnumbering collegians by at least 10:1 in the 1930s.[7] According to the Ministry of Education (MOE), there were 627,000 secondary students in China on the eve of the Sino-Japanese War in 1937, compared to only forty thousand students enrolled in institutes of higher education out of a total population of more than four hundred million.[8]

Given the demographics of modern education, middle school and university graduates possessed relatively high levels of academic capital in Republican China. The scholarly literature on wartime higher education includes John Israel's *Lianda*, which explored universities' experiences, focusing on the most famous case: the long, courageous exodus of academics from three of China's leading universities (Peking University, Tsinghua University, and Nankai University) to Kunming, located in the remote and mountainous southwestern province of Yunnan.[9] Other studies include Hu Kuo-tai's "The Struggle between the Kuomintang and the Chinese Communist Party on Campus during the War of Resistance, 1937–1945," Jeffrey Wasserstrom's *Student Protests in Twentieth-Century China*, Helen Schneider's *Keeping the Nation's House*, and J. Megan Greene's "Looking toward the Future: State Standardization and Professionalization of Science in Wartime China."[10] Hu explored competition between the GMD and Chinese Communist Party (CCP) for the support of students and staff at colleges and universities, while Wasserstrom emphasized Shanghai's leading institutes of higher education during the war. Meanwhile, Schneider examined the development of the field of home economics as an academic discipline for women in Chinese colleges, while Greene argued that the GMD took advantage of its forced relocation to inland areas mainly to promote science and technology in universities, not only for the purpose of national defense but also in preparation for postwar industrialization and modernization. Only recently have scholars begun to turn more attention to secondary schools—such as Robert Culp's *Articulating Citizenship* and Keith Schoppa's *In a Sea of Bitterness*.[11] Contrary to the idea that a few students became politically active only after they reached university, Chinese secondary students at midcentury were just as active in student movements. Furthermore, in Taiwan the government actually mandated that all upper middle school students join the China Youth Corps (Jiuguotuan, CYC) and receive military training.

From the 1920s to the 1950s, the GMD struggled to prevent students from challenging government authorities and instead turn them into political assets. *Indoctrinating the Youth* examines these efforts to inculcate political loyalty in

4   Introduction

youth from the beginning of the Sino-Japanese War in 1937 until the end of the first eleven years of Nationalist rule on Taiwan (1949–1960). This was a crucial time in Chinese history, highlighted by the GMD's attempts to preserve control over mainland China and the party's subsequent 1949 transition to Taiwan. The late 1930s and 1940s were the final years in which the GMD maintained a foothold on the mainland, a significant period that provided the immediate backdrop to the Communist reforms of the early People's Republic of China (PRC). Following the GMD's exile to Taiwan, the 1950s were a vital decade that witnessed the party consolidate power on the island. Comparing the world of secondary education during these two periods provides an important analysis of how the Nationalists tried to mobilize youth in the two different settings, evaluating the continuities and changes in GMD policies on mainland China and Taiwan.

In particular, throughout this pivotal, chaotic period—during which China underwent profound changes, including a world war and a civil war that shaped its position in the modern world—the GMD ultimately failed to win the support of youth on the mainland but successfully controlled and monitored young people on Taiwan with the aid of mandatory military training in public schools, government-sanctioned youth organizations and teenage recreational activities, as well as GMD-sponsored civics curriculum. On the mainland, the GMD created the Three People's Principles Youth Corps (Sanmin zhuyi qingniantuan or the abbreviated Sanqingtuan, SQT), an organization not actually comprised solely of young people, and one which failed to meet their needs. However, on Taiwan the GMD established the China Youth Corps (Jiuguotuan, CYC), a radically different organization that catered specifically to teens and appealed to them primarily by sponsoring popular leisure activities. One of the reasons for the CYC's success was that the authoritarian GMD on Taiwan stifled dissent, making it much easier to indoctrinate and control youth through compulsory membership in the organization.

The SQT and CYC share some similarities with other countries' paramilitary youth organizations. Probably most well known was the Hitler Youth, which involved "premilitary training" including camping, hiking exercises, and preparatory drills, physical activities that CYC members participated in during summer camps.[12] Another correlation between the Hitler Youth and the CYC was the practice of having youth aid peasants on farms, as both organizations aimed to provide urban youth with farming experience, build their character, and keep them physically fit. The Hitler Youth differed, however, in that a core goal for German youth was to reeducate ethnic Germans "to the proper ways of the life and livelihood of their forefathers" in the countryside of conquered territories.[13]

Another prominent youth organization during the period was the Communist Youth League of China (originally named Socialist Youth League). Like the

GMD merging the SQT within the party in 1947, the CCP also cannibalized the Socialist Youth League.[14] At its July 1922 Second National Congress the CCP explicitly asserted that the Socialist Youth League should be under its control.[15] Similar to the SQT and CYC, Communist Youth League (CYL) members studied speeches by party leaders and took part in other ideological activities that molded the nation's youth into loyal patriots. Both the GMD and the CCP identified promising young organizers and leaders in the CYC and CYL who could later serve the party. The age range for membership in both organizations was similar, as well: fifteen to thirty for the CYC and fourteen to twenty-eight for the CYL

Many troubles plagued the GMD in the late 1930s and 1940s, including the Japanese invasion of China, Communist competition for the allegiance of the masses, intraparty factionalism, and a downward economic spiral caused by runaway inflation. Within this context of war, anxiety, and chaos, the GMD reacted to youth movements by issuing numerous disciplinary regulations, arresting and detaining secondary school students without warrants, doling out severe punishment for anti-government activities, and accusing all who disagreed with its policies of being "Communist-directed." However, the party simultaneously tried to forge a more positive approach to secondary school students. During the war, the MOE organized national schools that merged the various dislocated middle schools, aiding students in continuing their education. Nevertheless, in its attempts to control young people, the party formed the SQT in 1938. Its name derived from the political philosophy of Sun Yat-sen, the Father of Modern China, who believed that the country could be strengthened upon three principles: nationalism, democracy, and people's livelihood. In 1946, the SQT's membership peaked at 1.5 million people, just one year before it was quickly dismantled.[16] Although the GMD designed the organization for teenagers, a large fraction of older people filled the membership and, significantly, occupied leadership positions. Throughout the war years, young people often languished at the receiving end of directions and GMD ideological indoctrination, and many were profoundly confused about the SQT's fundamental purpose.

The political passions of some idealistic students led them not only to resent a tepid "youth" organization like the SQT but also prompted them to search for political leaders willing to fight the Japanese immediately, as the policy of GMD leader Generalissimo Chiang Kai-shek remained "unify first, then resist Japan" throughout the 1930s and even into the 1940s. Seeing unity and nationalism in the resistance to the Japanese, many students therefore gravitated towards communism, for the CCP emphasized anti-Japanese sentiment to build support, helping it appear more nationalistic and patriotic in the eyes of many. Yet another central difference between the CCP and GMD was the fundamentally different

6   Introduction

attitudes each party exhibited towards teenagers. The Nationalists believed in monitoring youth through tight control and discipline, while the Communists effectively co-opted and mobilized students into a broader Communist movement, allowing them to play a key role in the successful takeover of the mainland.

Following defeat at the hands of the Communists, Chiang Kai-shek and the Nationalist government retreated to Taiwan in 1949. The GMD had made many mistakes on the mainland, and some were soon rectified when it received another chance at governing on the island. However, the party remained dedicated to tightening its policies towards controlling young people. One method of control was via indoctrination, which meant inculcating youth with political ideas, discipline, and military training. As Nationalist leaders began to build a new modern state on Taiwan, they knew that youth would play a critical role. In 1952, the GMD founded another youth organization, the CYC, which set up activity centers for teens throughout the island. The generalissimo's son, Chiang Ching-kuo, led the corps for its first twenty years. The imminent threat of Communist invasion remained a grave concern in the 1950s, so the CYC led boys and girls through intensive military drills. Along with this patriotic and military education, the corps also organized sports, camping, and artistic activities. Soon, the CYC offered the best organized, government-sanctioned recreation available on the island, providing transportation and facilities to Taiwan's youth at almost no cost. These popular leisure activities truly set the CYC apart from the mundane indoctrination of the SQT, yet the differences between the two organizations also exemplified important shifts in GMD attitudes about the role of students and popular nationalism; on Taiwan, the party realized it had to establish an organization that reached out to students in an endeavor to defend the island against imminent Communist attack, attracting teenagers by offering fun recreational activities to enjoy.

It is impossible to analyze these youth organizations without examining the shifting context of secondary education itself, a topic often overlooked in the history of China during this period. Despite the loss of many middle schools in Japanese-occupied areas, the GMD's wartime management of secondary education remained fairly adequate. During the war, the MOE established thirty-four "national secondary schools" to merge middle schools that had been under the jurisdiction of city or provincial authorities. It supervised the registration of refugee students at these newly chartered schools and attempted to take care of the over five hundred thousand middle school students forced to relocate due to the fighting.[17] Surprisingly, when the war began there were 3,200 middle schools and 627,000 students in China. After it ended in 1945, there were 4,500 middle schools and 1,394,000 students, a substantial increase.[18] These figures not only reflected the GMD-controlled region but also Communist-controlled and formerly Japanese-occupied areas as well.

While it is important to explore GMD youth mobilization and secondary education, equally vital is understanding how both helped shape the party's internal politics. Chiang Kai-shek's goal of eradicating intraparty factionalism was another reason behind his establishment of the SQT. In doing so he ordered the dissolution of the organizations formed by the party's two main factions: the Whampoa Clique and CC Clique. Chiang had hoped to end the factionalism by bringing together both groups within the SQT. Although the Whampoa Clique and CC Clique officially disbanded their organizations, both factions remained powerful forces. Whampoa Clique members dominated the SQT and pitted themselves against the party machinery, which the CC Clique controlled. Thus, Chiang's purpose of eradicating intraparty factionalism was never achieved, as the cliques continued their bitter rivalry outside the SQT, eventually contributing to the demise of the corps. Moreover, examination of youth organizations during this period of nation-building also sheds light on the political rise of Chiang Kai-shek's son, Chiang Ching-kuo. On the mainland, the generalissimo entrusted Ching-kuo with the responsibilities of leading an SQT branch, as well as directing the Central Cadre School—an institution devoted to the intensive study of Sun Yat-sen and Chiang Kai-shek's writings. By the early 1950s on Taiwan, the elder Chiang had appointed his son as head of the secret police, director of the Ministry of National Defense's General Political Warfare Department, and leader of the China Youth Corps. With these strategic positions, Ching-kuo was able to draw on a powerful base of youth support, recruiting many loyal followers, particularly from the CYC. Along with the solid backing of the generalissimo, these factors eventually allowed Ching-kuo to beat out strong contenders, including the well-respected Chen Cheng and popular Sun Liren, and succeed his father as president.

Although the historiography of twentieth-century China often slights middle school students, scholars can uncover details of GMD secondary education policy in China and Taiwan, and the stories of individual teenagers, including the surviving records of youth organizations such as the SQT and CYC, in a wide range of sources. The Second Historical Archives (Zhongguo di'er lishi dang'anguan) in Nanjing is the primary depository for the records of the central government during the Republican period (1912–1949), and it houses the documents of the Executive Yuan, the executive branch of Nationalist China. These government files include GMD state reports on education in each province and major city, suggestions for educational reform, guidelines for the implementation of the Three People's Principles at all grade levels, and special investigations of refugee students who clashed with local residents during relocation.

In addition, the National Institute of Compilation and Translation (Guoli bianyiguan) in Taipei preserves the Ministry of Education's curricular standards,

8　Introduction

textbooks, teachers' manuals, and educational journals. These texts not only record how many hours were spent on each middle school subject and lay out the required curriculum, but they also reveal lessons in patriotism and civic duties in a modern society. Examining textbooks reveals the GMD's program of shaping students into citizens. Meanwhile, the National Institute of Educational Resources and Research (NIOERAR, Guoli jiaoyu ziliaoguan) has the complete collection of *Yearbooks of Chinese Education* (*Zhongguo jiaoyu nianjian*), which include statistics of secondary schools that relocated to the interior during the Second Sino-Japanese War. Also located in Taipei is the China Youth Corps headquarters, which provides commemorative volumes for each decade of its existence and a compilation of the corps' work reports. Moreover, memoirs of former CYC directors and administrators offer a personal glimpse of their experiences with young people from 1952 to 1960.

Likewise, the Hoover Institution Archives at Stanford University holds the Chiang Kai-shek diaries, which disclose the behind-the-scenes process of establishing the Three People's Principles Youth Corps, the generalissimo's anguish over student protests during the civil war, and his developing trust and confidence in his son, Chiang Ching-kuo. Stanford's East Asian Library also contains Republican-era educational materials and the complete series of *Free China* (*Ziyou Zhongguo*), a political magazine that criticized the CYC and military training. Finally, this study also makes use of several original oral interviews. Combined with documented sources, these help produce a history that is richer, more accurate, and more complete. Interviewees include former middle school students in 1950s Taiwan, as well as CYC staff, members, and participants. These vivid reminiscences reveal unique, personal experiences that enrich, extend, and (sometimes) even challenge the records found in official government documents.

A wealth of scholarship has strengthened our understanding of the relationship between the state and education in twentieth-century China. John Israel's *Lianda* describes how the MOE ordered three prestigious universities to move to the interior following Japan's 1937 attack on Beijing and Tianjin. This edict set in motion the process of relocation to the southwest for those at elite universities, but many other schools—including secondary schools—migrated as well. Ou Tsiun-chen also indicates that most educational institutions that evacuated from the war were universities, colleges, and technical institutes. Since there was such a large number of middle and elementary schools, the MOE could assist only a few. Some schools managed to survive in the Japanese-occupied zone, while others relocated to the hinterland.[19] Unfortunately, scholars have limited their focus to higher education and neglected the significant story of secondary education in Republican China.[20] Furthermore, they have written far less on wartime education in the late 1930s and early 1940s, concentrating instead on the late Qing, early Republican period, and Nanjing decade (1927–1937).[21] Examining this oversight is important—although the war disrupted education, many middle schools survived by relocating and setting up makeshift classrooms.

Chronicling the experiences of students aged thirteen to eighteen in secondary schools, and helping the historiography of modern China better reflect their unique stories, remains an important challenge in the face of so much scholarship driven by studies of higher education. In 1941, for instance, there were only thirteen Protestant colleges in China, compared to 255 Protestant middle schools.[22] In addition, middle school students comprised a more accurate representation of China's general population and more "typical" Chinese families. Cong Xiaoping estimates that over 50 percent of students in secondary schools were from rural areas.[23] In contrast, students in universities and colleges were mainly from urban, elite families. Three exceptions to the predominant body of work on higher education are Robert Culp's *Articulating Citizenship,* which examines middle schools' civic education in the early Republican decades and touches on the onset of the Sino-Japanese War; Peter Zarrow's *Educating China,* which shows how language, morality and civics, history, and geography textbooks published for the Chinese primary and secondary school system played a major role in shaping new social, cultural, and political trends from 1902 to 1937; and Cong Xiaoping's *Teachers' Schools and the Making of the Modern Chinese Nation, 1897–1937,* which explores the unique nature of teachers' schools for secondary education that possessed Western and Chinese ideals.[24] While *Articulating Citizenship* is an extremely valuable study, it nevertheless centers on secondary schools in the lower Yangzi region, revealing little about the massive migration of middle school students to the southwest during the war. Culp argues that students were able to shape their own conceptions of citizenship that they encountered in schools, engaging in different modes of civic action without much direction from the GMD.[25] For example, beginning in the early 1920s, middle school students throughout the lower Yangzi region commemorated the May 4th Movement by giving lectures and parading in the streets—"ritually replay[ing] the dynamics of mass mobilization that had been central to the initial protest movement."[26]

Given what Culp, Zarrow, and Cong have examined, an investigation of the subsequent years after 1937 reveals that during the war and following the retreat to Taiwan, the GMD tightened its control over youth activities by co-opting students into its organizations, often by force. This approach was very different from the party's policies before 1940, when students had more freedom in choosing the level of their political engagement. For example, beginning in 1953, the GMD mandated that all upper middle school students in Taiwan undergo military training,

10   Introduction

taking advantage of existing student activism for its own revolutionary project. Thus, *Indoctrinating the Youth* picks up the story of GMD secondary education where Culp and Zarrow finished, analyzing refugee students' wartime migration to the interior, the GMD's recruitment of students in the Three People's Principles Youth Corps in the late 1930s and 1940s on the mainland, the Nationalists' efforts to woo students in Taiwan's China Youth Corps, and GMD civics textbooks published from 1937 to 1960 in China and Taiwan.

In terms of government organizations targeting middle school students on mainland China, only three major works in English have examined the Three People's Principles Youth Corps in depth. Lloyd Eastman's *Seeds of Destruction* devotes a chapter to the corps, while Huang Jianli's *The Politics of Depoliticization in Republican China* sporadically explores the youth organization and Kristin Mulready-Stone's *Mobilizing Shanghai Youth* addresses the SQT's wartime activities in that city.[27] Huang examines GMD efforts to manage students through the SQT during the Sino-Japanese War, and maintains that the GMD did not form the corps specifically to deal with the problem of numerous refugee students trekking to Communist-occupied areas. Indeed, the organization was one of the many governmental and party agencies that dealt with this issue, but its involvement came much later. According to Huang, the GMD established the corps to curb students' anti-government activism and steer them towards GMD loyalty.

A different body of scholarship studies the more general growth of student activism in twentieth-century China. John Israel's pioneering *Student Nationalism in China, 1927–1937* demonstrates the increasing alienation between students and the GMD government and the burgeoning attraction of the CCP for many youth. Faced with serious threats from Japanese imperialism after 1931, students and the GMD disagreed bitterly over how to save their country from foreign aggression. Youth sought immediate and uncompromising solutions to national crises, rejecting the GMD government's adoption of gradual economic and social reforms to strengthen the country.[28] Israel's analysis provides the critical backdrop for this narrative, setting the context for the challenges over secondary education and student activism that confronted the GMD over the ensuing generation.

Both Jeffrey Wasserstrom's *Student Protests in Twentieth-Century China* and Suzanne Pepper's *Civil War in China* cover the anti-civil war movement, in which students protested China's all-out fight between the Communists and the GMD. This movement swept through universities and middle schools in most major cities in GMD-controlled areas.[29] While Wasserstrom focuses on university demonstrations in Shanghai, Pepper writes of similar occurrences in the southwestern cities of Kunming and Chongqing. Unfortunately, both generally explore university-level student participation in the anti-civil war movements, not the involvement of middle schoolers.

In addition, this study is framed to cross the "1949 divide," following the GMD's building of the modern state in Taiwan, and comparing youth education policies brought by the Nationalists from the mainland.[30] It seeks to analyze the way GMD government institutions and youth organizations configured middle school students, and how they tackled similar problems both on the mainland and on Taiwan. The Nationalist government was determined to exert control over youth to ensure stability in its modern state-building process. This book is thus the first to trace Guomindang policy on youth chronologically from the 1937 outbreak of the Sino-Japanese War to the consolidation of Nationalist power on Taiwan by 1960. While few historical studies have crossed the 1949 divide between the straits, one is J. Megan Greene's *The Origins of the Developmental State in Taiwan*. Greene examines the GMD's nation-building projects both in China and on Taiwan but does so through the lens of industrial science policy, as opposed to education.[31] Although not geographically crossing the straits, other important histories that cross the 1949 temporal line include Robert Culp's book on commercial publishing, Margaret Tillman's study of childhood welfare, Janet Chen's book on the urban poor, Susan Glosser's work on family reform, and Gail Herschatter's landmark study on prostitution.[32]

Another relevant body of scholarship examines the GMD's political indoctrination of students in Taiwan through the China Youth Corps and military training. In particular, Li Tai-han illuminates the inextricable connection between the two, including how the CYC oversaw the training of military instructors before they were dispatched to upper middle schools throughout the island.[33] Monte Bullard's *The Soldier and the Citizen* analyzes how military personnel, youth, and adult civilians underwent political socialization in 1950s and 1960s Taiwan. Like Li, Bullard relates how young people experienced this process through military training and CYC activities designed to instill patriotism and militarism.[34] Meanwhile, Thomas Brindley concentrates on the CYC's youth service mission and its relations with government organs and the GMD party, based on documentary and field research he completed from 1983 to 1994.[35]

Chapters 1 and 2 focus on the GMD's management of middle school students on the mainland, while chapters 3 and 4 analyze the Nationalists' regulation of young people on Taiwan. Although China scholars have studied the Communists' Long March in depth, most have generally overlooked the GMD's exodus to the southwest during the Sino-Japanese War. The story of its mass migration, especially in the realm of education, is important and warrants deeper examination.

12   Introduction

Chapter 1 follows these refugee students' journeys, outlining the arduous trek that middle schoolers, teachers, and principals embarked on starting in 1937. The subsequent eight years of intense war saw the GMD government strengthen its responsibility to middle school students while, as Rana Mitter and Helen Schneider note, "the state was disintegrating under the pressure of Japanese invasion as well as its own flaws and contradictions."[36] The Nationalist government became increasingly interested in managing and improving the quality of its students' lives. Amidst the onset of war, the GMD government established "national middle schools" by merging several schools together and relocating them to the interior. Middle schools came under the control of the Ministry of Education for the first time, whereas in the past they were under the jurisdiction of provinces and municipalities. During the war some students not only had to discontinue schooling but were also unemployed. Many did not have homes and the GMD feared that they would join the Communists. Provincial governments established bureaus to control these youth, and selected some for specialized job skills training. Meanwhile, Executive Yuan (the government's executive branch) records reveal many cases of middle school principals and refugee students who came into conflict with Buddhist monks, local "strongmen," farmers, and military training classes, all while traversing the unfamiliar terrain of the interior.

During the Sino-Japanese War, the GMD also sought to mobilize youth by recruiting them into the Three People's Principles Youth Corps. Chapter 2 analyzes the factors that influenced Chiang Kai-shek's orders for the GMD's Extraordinary National Congress to adopt a resolution to create the SQT in 1938, and what finally led to its dissolution nine years later. Besides providing a new instrument to integrate the diverse intraparty factions, Chiang formed the SQT to infuse "fresh blood into the party."[37] The SQT was also useful for recruiting and disciplining the waves of refugee students driven from the northern and coastal cities by the Japanese invasion—but this concern with student drifters did not come until after the corps' establishment. Once again, the GMD government sought to maintain control and the political loyalty of young people. Eventually, the SQT and GMD actually became rivals, especially over recruitment after the corps tried to enlist older members who possessed political status: the traditional recruitment grounds of the GMD party machinery. Soon, recruitment to the SQT became incompatible with GMD membership, as different factions held power over the two organizations—the Whampoa Clique controlling the SQT, the CC Clique (under the brothers Chen Lifu and Chen Guofu) dominating the party. This competition, along with existing intraparty conflicts, contributed to the SQT's failure and ultimately led to its demise in 1947.

Following defeat by the Communists in 1949, the Nationalist regime retreated to Taiwan, where it established its government and searched for ways to consolidate power over the island. Chapter 3 explores the GMD's formation of the China Youth Corps and its function as an anti-Communist, pro-GMD organization in its formative years. It began as an adjunct for an authoritarian state, meant to instill patriotism and "martial spirit" in youth. The CYC was a national, institutionalized structure of social control intentionally established by those at the top of the GMD hierarchy to prevent the development of student protests that threatened to undermine the legitimacy of the Nationalist government. The youth organization soon acquired official status, allowing it to gain financial support from the government and penetrate every secondary school, college, and university on the island. Recruitment subsequently became far easier. As opposed to the SQT, the CYC emphasized leisure activities for students to enjoy and only recruited youth in upper middle school and college—unlike the SQT, which enlisted older nonstudents as well. Nevertheless, despite the improvement from its predecessor, the CYC still received criticism, ranging from attacks on mandatory membership and excessive costs, to accusations of its resemblance to the Communist Youth League and Hitler Youth.

Chapter 4 explores the appointment of military personnel as military instructors (*jiaoguan*) or enforcers of proper moral behavior in upper middle schools, a key example of the direct imposition of the party state in 1950s secondary education on Taiwan. GMD leaders considered military instructors appropriate teachers of military training because the party exhibited a heavy military flavor, especially after the Nationalists' defeat on the mainland left Chiang Kai-shek lamenting how the GMD was not as tough as the Communists. The generalissimo "told his comrades that the Communists had proved themselves 'abler and more devoted' members of a revolutionary party" and even expressed admiration for their superior discipline and morality.[38] The chapter examines why and how Chiang first imposed compulsory military training in schools on Taiwan in the early 1950s. With the goal of counterattacking Communist China, he turned to upper middle school students as an important sector of society that the GMD could train to build a reserve army. He called upon military instructors, who themselves were trained in military schools and the Ministry of National Defense's General Political Warfare Department, to teach mandatory military courses. Government military instruction was quite gendered in 1950s Taiwan, and most schools were gender segregated, with female military instructors at all-girls upper middle schools, while all-boys upper middle schools had male military instructors. Female students underwent target practice and learned nursing skills, while males received basic skills training in infantry, martial law, and map reading. (Upon upper middle school graduation, all males were required to serve two years of mandatory military training.) The instructors indoctrinated males and females alike with GMD

14   Introduction

revolutionary and military history. Their duties also included ensuring that students did not criticize the government or president and overseeing CYC activities. Importantly, the military instructors' firm control prevented major student protests against the government in the early decades of GMD rule on Taiwan. Nevertheless, like the CYC, this implementation of military training also met vociferous opposition. Critics condemned it for its interference with academic studies and outdated techniques. However, in the 1950s outspoken critics of the state had to be extremely cautious under the governance of the authoritarian GMD regime in Taiwan, where they could be thrown in prison or sentenced to death.

Chapter 5 allows for an intriguing comparison of civics textbooks and curricular standards used in secondary schools on mainland China from 1937 to 1949 with those published on Taiwan from 1949 to 1960. By and large, the contents remained the same. However, post-1949 revisions reflected a new, national policy intent on pacifying the Communists and the urgent need to build a new nation on the island. Civics textbooks conveyed to students the political values and behavioral norms of "modern" Chinese citizens. They provided clearer definitions of "nation" and, eventually, emphasized the role students had to play in building one. They offered lessons in civic consciousness and Chinese nationalism, in which students learned about their relationships with family, community, nation, and world.

The history of secondary education during this period reveals connections between pre-1949 China and post-1949 Taiwan, as well as the lessons learned by the GMD from its mistakes on the mainland. These connections included the establishments of youth organizations on both the mainland and Taiwan and the imposition of military training in schools on both sides of the strait. Yet the softer appeal of the CYC's leisure activities was part of the GMD's success on Taiwan, whereas the SQT failed to offer such programs. During the 1950s, CYC members enjoyed participating in recreational activities as well as acquiring military skills. Many of the skills taught at CYC camps overlapped with military training in schools, except the corps' activities were more fun, hands on, and not supervised by strict, coercive military instructors. In particular, Chiang Ching-kuo was quite conscious of the fact that unqualified military instructors had haphazardly put students through useless drills on the mainland. Once he was in Taiwan, he ensured that military instructors underwent rigorous training before they were dispatched to all upper middle schools on the island. The GMD also exhibited tighter control and discipline over youth on Taiwan than it had on the mainland through military training. It was able to mobilize young people with greater success in a smaller environment, one where Taiwan had become a single-party state and the GMD no longer had to vie with the Communists for young people's allegiance.

CHAPTER ONE

The Relocation of Middle Schools during the Sino-Japanese War, 1937–1945

On July 7, 1937, Japanese and Chinese troops clashed near the Marco Polo Bridge (Lugouqiao), launching the full-scale hostilities of the Second Sino-Japanese War.[1] The Japanese military soon captured nearby Beijing and quickly advanced into northern and coastal China. In response, Chiang Kai-shek's Guomindang government moved its capital inland from Nanjing, first to Wuhan, then to Chongqing, deep in the mountains of southwest China's Sichuan province, which made the capital relatively safe from a Japanese land assault.

The devastation of this war directly affected countless people living in China, forcing civilians to migrate inland to escape the fighting. Up to one hundred million are thought to have fled from north to south and then east to west to escape the Japanese Army.[2] The GMD in particular made a serious effort to organize refugee relief and public health campaigns (often manned by students). Although woefully inadequate, the efforts laid the groundwork for postwar developments in these fields. Another transition was the growing control of government authority over the lives of refugees and other populations on both sides of the battlefront.[3] Major GMD efforts at nation-building (in terms of the penetration of the state, and even the modernization of public health, education, and gender roles) were underway at the grassroots level of unoccupied China.

The relocation of refugees required the state's deep involvement, for only the state had broad enough power to fulfill these plans. In newspapers and magazines, a visible and vocal critique of the absence of state investment in relief efforts attributed the failure of relief to the failure of the GMD government. Without an efficient state providing direction and coordination, the relief work managed by civic organizations had only minimum effect. The GMD needed to establish a national system of relief. The refugee crisis thus redefined the boundary between state and civil society by entrusting greater responsibilities for social welfare to the wartime state. The relief of mass refugees demanded the further involvement of the wartime state and centralization in the overall management of natural and human resources. It was under such public expectation that the GMD government set up a national infrastructure for refugee relief.[4]

16   Chapter 1

On April 23, 1938, the government formed the Development and Relief Commission (DRC), and from spring 1938 to the early 1940s, it gradually grew into a gigantic welfare complex. The DRC not only absorbed old voluntary organizations but also replaced them as the primary benefactor of refugees, with the former playing a still indispensable but reduced supporting role. The DRC also took charge of civilian evacuation, coordinating refugee transportation and mobilizing the masses. It divided war-affected regions into eight relief zones and mapped out a transit network through these zones, linking coastal China section by section to Free China (the region under GMD control). Masses of refugees depended on the network for directions, daily necessities, and monetary subsidies. During the peak of retreat in 1938 and 1939, the DRC maintained control over twenty-six of the thirty-four general stations.[5]

The Japanese invasion drove waves of refugee students out of occupied cities in northern China and the eastern seaboard, where officials either closed schools outright or relocated them away from occupied territories. The migration to the interior critically impacted the development of GMD education policy, especially concerning secondary education. Yet the GMD successfully regulated and managed middle schools, expanded the state's hand in secondary education, and provided a form of stability for students despite the war's disruption. This included implementation by the GMD Ministry of Education (MOE) of the Three People's Principles in schools, including those in the minority regions of Tibet and Mongolia, in order to assimilate non-Han peoples into a singular Chinese nation. At the same time, middle school students faced conflicts between local and national interests—as well as traditional and modern ways of life—when they encountered monks, farmers, and villagers in their trek to the interior. In addition, some refugee students became victims of corrupt education administrators, who exploited the chaos of war for themselves.

Understanding the overall organization of secondary education in China is key to analyzing how the system changed and survived the war. During the 1930s and 1940s, middle school students were generally between twelve and twenty years of age, but due to the disruptions of war and other factors they were occasionally even older.[6] Students traveled directly with their principals and teachers, leaving behind their families and homes. Faculty members struggled for physical survival, even as they developed curriculum and conducted lessons.

Danke Li writes that "Chongqing . . . became the national center for education . . . in China" during the eight years of war (1937–1945).[7] However, refugee students also went elsewhere, including Guizhou, Henan, Shaanxi, Shanxi, and Yunnan—which demonstrates that the GMD central government was able to extend its reach outside the nerve center of Chongqing and into other areas of the interior via an expanded state apparatus that managed education. During the Sino-Japanese War, the unoccupied western and central provinces of China under GMD control were referred to by the Western world as "Free China," and in China itself as "the interior" (*da houfang*). In addition, China was also divided between Japanese-occupied territories and the Chinese Communist Party's (CCP) base areas. What follows is the story of students and schools operating in "the interior" under Nationalist rule.

Analyzing relocated middle schools extends some of the themes explored by historians like Rana Mitter and Aaron William Moore, including studies on GMD state-building during the war and expanded notions of citizenship and social management that emerged during this period.[8] For example, Mitter notes that "the Nationalists quickly created an official portrait of a defiant retreat into the interior, and were quick to praise the patriotic actions of those who had come all the way to Sichuan."[9] The five hundred thousand displaced middle school students who migrated with their principals and teachers were key to this triumphant narrative, in which patriotic citizens heeded Chiang Kai-shek's call to "carry out the task of national survival and independent continuation, and to complete the great destiny of our war of resistance and national reconstruction (*kangzhan jianguo*)."[10]

War and displacement therefore played a major role in altering the educational landscape throughout all of China—including the once-thriving areas of northern and coastal China, as well as isolated minority regions like Mongolia and Tibet. In Japanese-occupied districts, 110 middle schools with more than 41,700 students were forced to relocate or shut down. Of the 3,264 middle schools in the country, 1,296 (40 percent) were located in these occupied areas. As a result of the war, 20,510 middle school teachers and staff (one-third of the country's total) suffered tremendously. Minister of Education Chen Lifu (1938–1944) wrote that one half of the nation's 571,800 middle school students were impacted directly.[11] It is not clear what Chen meant by "impacted directly" other than being displaced or discontinuing their education since his figure contrasts with Rana Mitter's number of five hundred thousand refugee middle school students.

At least three factors contributed to the GMD's success in handling the refugee students. First, despite the loss of territory and constant enemy air raids, the GMD was generally successful in handling the refugees and managed to advance Chinese education at all levels. For example, the number of middle school teachers, staff, and students actually increased dramatically. According to the MOE's 1948 *Second Yearbook of Chinese Education* (*Di'erci Zhongguo jiaoyu nianjian*), there were 3,200 middle schools and 627,000 students in China on the eve of the war. By 1945 there were 4,500 middle schools and 1,394,000 middle school

18   Chapter 1

students.[12] The *Yearbook* provides two sets of figures representing the first and last years of the war. According to these, the number of middle schools increased by 803 and the number of normal and vocational schools decreased by 252 and 70, respectively.[13] Ou Tsiun-chen credits this growth in secondary education during the war to an increase in the number of provincial and municipal schools operating in the nineteen provinces and municipalities under Chinese control, along with the GMD's establishment of thirty-four government-run national middle schools, twenty-eight normal schools, and fourteen vocational schools.[14] A second component of the GMD's success was its ability to remove so many refugee students out of harm's way and transfer them across such great distances. And the Nationalists' third major accomplishment was the sheer fact that the government was able to keep these schools functioning throughout the entire war—that students were educated at all.

According to Huang Jianli, students during the war migrated "from renowned educational institutions of comfortable coastal cities to makeshift campuses" in the interior, where living conditions were harsh and poor.[15] Before the conflict, most lived relatively secure and sheltered lives as children of the well-to-do, urban elite. Robert Culp indicates that the children who attended secondary schools during the Nanjing decade (1927–1937) came from "families whose income was in roughly the top 10 to 15 percent of the urban national average."[16] As Huang writes, the war meant that these privileged students were "cut off from their parents' wealth and . . . heavily dependent on meager government stipends, which massive hyperinflation regularly consumed throughout the duration of the war."[17] The arduous, eye-opening journey was a culture shock for these elite students forced to trek among the masses into poverty-stricken rural areas.

Yet aside from the life-altering changes experienced by uprooted teachers and students themselves, local residents in the interior were also profoundly changed by the numerous refugees who fled to their communities. In particular, teachers who retreated inland to places like Chongqing made significant (generally positive) impacts on local students there. Danke Li notes how some students in Chongqing received an excellent education through these highly qualified and politically progressive teachers from the coast, many of whom were vigorous about propagandizing the war since they had just lost their homes to the Japanese in major cities such as Beijing and Shanghai. Zhu Shuqin, who attended Baxian Girls' School in Chongqing, recalled how many of the teachers who fled to Sichuan were actually well-known professors (or famous scholars) who could only find jobs teaching in middle or elementary schools.[18] These teachers brought with them a "new pedagogy and extracurricular activities, such as public speaking class and teams and theatrical lessons and performances that enriched [Chongqing students'] education and lives as well as energize[d]" them to mobilize local support for China's war against Japan.[19]

Those who succeeded in leaving before enemy occupation encountered many hardships over the course of their migration. Along with fears of the invading army, some students and their principals immediately clashed with interior residents, including Buddhist temple leaders, local strongmen, and farmers. Displacement also prompted the GMD to explore and implement several important changes to its education policy and to exert stronger, more centralized control over some middle schools (which traditionally were run entirely by local officials). However, most students persevered despite the challenges and successfully pursued their education even amidst invasion, dislocation, and fighting.

The GMD's Establishment of National Middle Schools for Refugee Students

To understand the secondary education system during the Sino-Japanese War, one must become familiarized with its development during the early Republican period (1912–1937). In 1922, fifteen years before the Japanese invasion, the National Federation of Education Associations—a professional organization of educators—and the MOE jointly developed the New School System (Xin xuezhi). Throughout the 1920s and much of the 1930s, many upper middle schools became comprehensive, offering courses in specialized academic areas, teacher training, and various technical fields.[20] The New School System also consolidated normal schools and some higher-level vocational institutions into existing middle schools at varying rates across the region.[21] The result was a dramatic decrease in the number of students choosing the teacher-training track.[22] On the eve of the Sino-Japanese War in 1937, most middle school students focused on regular academic programs designed to help them advance to institutes of higher learning.[23] A large majority of these schools were "regular" (nonnormal and nonvocational) middle schools; during the 1930s, these served nearly 75 percent of all secondary students in China. Consequently, the Nationalists geared education policy from 1937 to 1949 with an eye towards primarily regular middle schools.

The GMD unit charged with serving refugee students was the Ministry of Education, which after 1937 presented students with only two, uncompromising options: either they could continue their studies or choose to have the MOE sponsor their enlistment in the Nationalist Army.[24] Very few accepted the latter offer; by the end of 1940, the MOE had officially referred only 480 students to the military.[25] Nor did the armed forces necessarily mind, for even in the midst of war there was no need for education and military service to compete for China's youth.

20   Chapter 1

The country's manpower was abundant: in 1937 there were only some 627,000 total students attending Chinese secondary schools, while the nation, according to wartime minister of education Chen Lifu, had thirty to forty million potential able bodies.[26] Along with middle school students there were only forty thousand students attending institutes of higher education. Thus, those enrolled in secondary and higher education altogether constituted an extremely tiny proportion of China's 1937 estimated population of five hundred million. Moreover, Chen believed that the nation's future depended on young, educated people; thus the vast majority remained exempt from conscription. However, Chen had a strong conviction "that the educational system, including curricula and institutions, should be revised to meet wartime needs and to come more firmly under state control."[27]

Along with discontinuing school, all students during the war (not just those who were displaced and had to relocate with schools) also faced a myriad of other serious problems, including the prospect of unemployment and homelessness. According to the archives of the Executive Yuan (the executive branch of the GMD government), homeless rates in occupied areas escalated, fueling GMD worries that poverty and displacement would drive radicalized youth into areas controlled by the CCP and embolden them to embrace communism. In response, the government decided to register youth in GMD-controlled areas, enrolling them in local bureaus that each provincial government was charged with establishing, in order to monitor the refugee students. The Minister of Education served as de facto head of each office; however, provincial governments first screened a select number of youth from among local students to participate. Since there were many training organizations and schools under the control of the central government, all selected youth had to be "filtered" first by the provincial government. Provincial governments were also responsible for running a number of programs for the selected displaced students, including training classes in "skills, thinking, physical well-being, and job placement."[28]

In another effort to tackle the problem of refugee students, the MOE expanded its central authority by taking direct control of specific schools, which before the war had fallen under the jurisdiction of provincial or municipal authorities. Beginning in November 1937, the Ministry established registration centers in key cities and began gathering displaced middle school students. The MOE formed the first of the "national middle schools" (*guoli zhongxue*) the next month. With the further displacement of schools and students following the advance of Japan's invading forces, the MOE continued to establish national middle schools, sometimes converting them directly from former city or provincial schools, at other times building brand-new campuses. Many national colleges and universities had associated middle schools that featured experimental classrooms for teacher training before the war, and the MOE also converted these into national schools as well. By the end of the war, the Ministry had chartered forty-eight national middle schools in total.[29] As of 1945, there were also an additional two national female middle schools and three national overseas middle schools, which were comprised of students of Chinese descent who had fled to China from foreign countries under Japanese occupation. In addition to its efforts to monitor, register, and (in some cases) provide training for refugee students, the central government also directly funded these national middle schools established by the MOE during the war.

The Ministry had actually created China's first national middle school three years prior to the full-scale outbreak of war in 1937. The Japanese had invaded Manchuria (the northeast) in 1931 and renamed it Manchukuo.[30] That occupation subsequently prompted many civilians, including students, to flee the region. Some middle school students moved four times, trekking several hundred miles progressively southwest in order to continue their studies: from their hometowns in the northeast to Beijing, Nanjing, Hunan province, and finally Sichuan province. On March 26, 1934, the MOE established National Northeast Zhongshan Middle School—the first national middle school—in Beijing.[31] Initially, the school only accepted refugee students from the northeast, yet there were still more than six hundred enrolled. All students attended for free (including room and board) and received stipends at the end of each month. In the spring and fall, the school distributed clothing to the students.[32] Li Meilin, a former pupil, recalled that lower middle school students wore scouting uniforms, while upper middle school students wore military uniforms.[33] In October 1936, the government built a new campus for National Northeast Zhongshan in the town of Banqiao, near Nanjing, and that December a majority of the students migrated south from Beijing. The Japanese captured Shanghai in November 1937 (one month before the Nanjing Massacre) and the school moved once again—this time southwest to the city of Xiangxiang in Hunan province, where classes did not resume until the Beijing branch shut down in 1938. In the spring, the Japanese attacked northern Hunan, prompting the school to pick up once again and travel west to Weiyuan county in Sichuan, utilizing Jingning Temple as their refugee campus.[34] Remarkably, some of these particular students did not make it back to the northeast until the fall of 1946, a full fifteen years after first fleeing the Japanese. When the school finally returned, it remained a national middle school and did not fall under the aegis of Liaoning province. Even more amazing than National Northeast Zhongshan's epic journey was its ability to grow significantly despite the turmoil. It had 530 students in 1937—by the end of the war in 1945 there were 838.[35] These figures and the school's ability to survive for fifteen years attest to the GMD's success in helping it relocate multiple times and keep it in operation.

22   Chapter 1

Students and staff at the first national middle school formed after the outbreak of full-scale war began their journey in December 1937, when the MOE established Henan Temporary Middle School to accommodate refugee students and teachers from secondary schools in Hebei province, Inner Mongolia, Beijing, and Tianjin.[36] One month before, the Ministry had sent delegates to the cities of Kaifeng and Xuchang in central China's Henan province. There they recorded each refugee student and teacher, and prepared them to relocate farther inland. Students and teachers traveled together to Xichuan county, located deep in the remote, mountainous region of southwest Henan, where it was certain the Japanese would not attack. Henan Temporary Middle School functioned as a lower middle, upper middle, normal school, and *jianshiban*.[37] (*Jianshiban* required fewer years of training than regular normal schools.) The lower middle and normal schools settled in Shangji, while the upper middle school stayed in Yongquanguan and the *jianshiban* was established in Xiaji.

Perhaps in an effort to boost morale while anticipating a long war, the MOE soon dropped the word "temporary" (*linshi*) from the names of displaced schools in January 1938. Henan Temporary Middle School thus became National Henan Middle School, and in April 1939 it changed its name once again to National Number One Middle School. Besides having its main campus in Xichuan, the school also had branches in Xixiakou and Yongquanguan. National Number One had 1,143 students in 1937. In January 1944, it received additional refugee students and teachers from Shandong, Jiangsu, Henan, and Anhui provinces, and over the course of the war this school also relocated multiple times. As the Japanese Army approached in April 1944, National Number One moved further west of Henan to Chenggu in Shaanxi province, where it remained until the war's end. By then the number of students had dropped to 1,032.[38] Overall, however, enrollment remained relatively consistent for the duration of the conflict, another testament to the GMD's success in sustaining student education in at least some of its national middle schools.

The story of National Number Two Middle School also began in December 1937, when the GMD arranged for refugee students from Nanjing and the southeastern provinces of Jiangsu, Zhejiang, and Anhui to gather in central China's Hankou, Hubei province, to register for another government relocation school: National Sichuan Temporary Middle School.[39] In January 1938 it became National Number Two Middle School, established in Hechuan near Chongqing. The school immediately accepted teachers from Hankou, Yichang (also a major city in Hubei), and Chongqing. Altogether, 1,800 students and 200 teachers joined National Number Two, meeting at a main campus converted from an old hospital in Beibei (a suburban county of Chongqing). While the normal school also met at the main campus, National Number Two's lower middle students met in Hechuan's civil, or Confucian, temple, while upper middle grades utilized Puyan Temple just outside the city.[40] Eventually, when the Japanese surrendered in August 1945 National Number Two moved northeast to Jiangsu province, where the majority of its students originated. Those who were not from Jiangsu returned to their home provinces.[41]

Relocation impacted secondary school students not only in China but also throughout the Chinese diaspora in Asia. When the Japanese occupied Thailand and expelled overseas Chinese, the Thai government collaborated with them and specifically shut down schools, forcing Chinese students to flee to China, and prompting the GMD to respond to the emergency. In Baoshan, a remote area in western Yunnan province near the border with Burma, the MOE established the National Overseas Chinese Middle School particularly for these international refugees—the majority of them from Thailand. Instruction began on May 15, 1940, while at the same time the National Overseas Chinese Middle School absorbed a private school called Education Overseas Middle School. That first year consisted of thirteen classes in total: seven upper middle and six lower middle.[42] In February 1942 the school added "first" to its name as the GMD government formed more schools tailored to international Chinese refugees. Later in August the Japanese bombed Baoshan and struck the school, prompting a move east to Qingzhen in Guizhou province. In August 1944, it was dismantled and merged with National Second Overseas Chinese Middle School.

Tensions between Middle Schools and the GMD Military

Despite contributing to GMD patriotic morale, embodying national reconstruction, and helping the growth of centralized power, these wartime schools nevertheless clashed at times with GMD authorities and even the Nationalist Army itself. On November 30, 1942, one incident involving the death of a National Number Two Middle School student exposed tensions between displaced schools, central authorities, and the GMD's major youth organization: the Three People's Principles Youth Corps (Sanmin zhuyi qingniantuan; SQT). According to a military police report submitted the following month, an SQT branch in Hechuan county consisting of special military training class freshmen organized a drama troupe to perform a play. The group had seven members in its council, including two students from National Number Two. Nevertheless, the SQT borrowed a facility from the military training class for the performance and did not invite students from the school to attend. In response, more than a hundred National

24   Chapter 1

Number Two students arrived demanding tickets for the sold-out performance, prompting an argument that soon escalated into violence. Someone from the military training class fired his gun "to stop the fight," instantly killing fifteen-year-old National Number Two student Zheng Xuepu.[43]

In the aftermath of Zheng's death, the central government clashed with school officials over different versions of the incident and the culpability of military personnel. According to a report from the Secretariat of the Administration, the MOE believed that three National Number Two students should have been allowed to attend the play: Zhang Yanling, an SQT member who was part of the drama group; Lu Shengkui, a band member in the performance; and Zhu Yongkang, who possessed a ticket for the show. The MOE also learned that the military trainees had dragged Zhang Yanling away during the scuffle. Unarmed students demanded that Zhang be released, and the teachers had tried to stop the situation from "getting out of hand" until the gun was fired.[44] The Secretariat condemned the shooting, noting that the weapon had not been fired towards the sky, but horizontally towards the crowd. The MOE therefore called for the military to hold the gunman responsible for Zheng's death, along with the punishment of Fang Caiqin, chairman of the SQT branch of the Special Military Training Class and branch leader of the Political Department of the Central Special Military Training Class. The report also demanded punishment of several others, including the director of the drama group council and the National Number Two students who "disturbed the peace."[45]

Meanwhile, the middle school students and their principal, Yan Liyang, were outraged. According to Yan, the three students were quite "reasonable" in assuming they could attend the performance and had the right to be at the military facility. When the fight broke out, military officers exacerbated and inflated the confrontation, injuring Zhang Yanling and dragging him away. This prompted the other two students to return to school and seek help. A crowd came back to the scene with Yan in tow, demanding the officers release their friend. Instead, the military personnel opened fire, injuring two and killing Zheng Xuepu. The principal and students also indicated that the gunshot wound was located on Zheng's back, insisting he had been shot from behind while defenseless and running away.[46]

In an angry report to Minister of Education Chen Lifu, Yan echoed the frustration of many refugee teachers and students with military personnel, calling the military men "thugs" and emphasizing that public order officers had "abused" his three students, who simply wanted to attend the performance.[47] According to the principal, when he arrived at the scene the lead officer changed his story and accused the three students of "stirring up trouble."[48] A third report was produced when the central government sent its own representative to investigate the incident, once again concluding that National Number Two held "some responsibility" because the three uninvited students had crashed the performance.[49] It also blamed the public order officers for allowing one of the students who had a ticket to attend but not the other two. The final report also included a doctor's confirmation that Zheng had indeed been shot in the back while fleeing the officers. In the end, a judge sentenced two special military training leaders, Yang Tongchen and Lei Yangmin, to three years in prison. Two others, Zhao Lunchuang and Chen Guang, were held "directly responsible" for killing Zheng and received six years.[50]

The entire episode could have been avoided if this national school had relocated to the remote countryside like other middle schools instead of remaining in such close proximity to Chongqing, where the military conducted training. However, the feud that led to the shooting—along with the disagreement over the response and charges of misinformation—all revealed the level of distrust between National Number Two students, school administrators, GMD authorities, and the military. On the one hand, displaced institutions and their students felt protected by Nationalist troops and welcomed the relative security of regions free from Japanese occupation. Moreover, they were part of the GMD's patriotic narrative of a "defiant retreat." However, at the same time many resented the associated hardships and the exertion of stronger outside control over previously independent schools.

The Plight of Provincial, County, and Private Schools

While the national middle schools relocated to escape the Japanese Army during the war, many provincial schools continued to come in close contact with the enemy. (Education officials categorized secondary schools as "national," "provincial," "county," or "private.") Keith Schoppa's *In a Sea of Bitterness* illuminates the wartime experience in one particular province—Zhejiang—on the southeastern Chinese coast, examining what he dubs "guerrilla education" in five middle schools. Schoppa doubts that the education displaced students received along the way was very effective, considering how often schools had to move from one location to the next, which "must have consumed huge amounts of time that was theoretically available for studying."[51] His analysis is logical—constant relocation disrupted students' education. In dangerous, life-threatening environments they were more concerned about survival and did not have the luxury of continuous study.

Nonetheless, GMD publications sought to trumpet the wartime schools and emphasized the success they had in educating students despite hardship. According to the GMD-published *Documents on Revolution (Geming wenxian)* series on

26   Chapter 1

secondary education during the war, the subject of Schoppa's study, Zhejiang province, published a journal, *Zhejiang Education* (*Zhejiang jiaoyu*), which recorded an account of several Zhejiang middle schools' experiences during the early stages of the conflict. In late 1937 the Japanese Army conducted a ten-day campaign affecting many of the province's schools, beginning in November after Hangzhou (the capital) surrendered amidst retreating GMD forces.[52] The Japanese Army bombed and destroyed many campuses, mainly those located in cities and towns. In addition, it captured approximately five hundred students from various schools, taking over their institutions and forbidding students from voicing "anti-Japanese sentiments."[53]

Some students managed to escape and fled to GMD-controlled areas, where they continued their studies. Although the Japanese Army occupied many towns in western Zhejiang (near Anhui province's border), some rural areas still remained under GMD rule. Of western Zhejiang's eight provincial middle schools that fled, the largest was Yuqian's Number One Temporary Middle School, with eight hundred to nine hundred students.[54] On October 9, 1939, the principal and other administrators decided it was time for the school to flee. Since there were too many students, they split them into two groups that took different routes. Led by the principal, the first group featured younger students and briefly settled in Xiaofengzhang village until the Japanese occupied it. At that point the principal instructed the students to return home.[55] Before they dispersed, the teachers divided them into small groups and had all of them provide their addresses in order to contact them once the Japanese departed.

The other group of Yuqian's Number One Temporary Middle School students consisted of older students in higher grades. They fled to Changqiao Hongjia, where a place had been prepared for their arrival.[56] Japanese air raid strikes began on the morning of October 10 while they were traveling. Remarkably, every student carried a gun while marching amidst enemy bombs that constantly dropped around them. *Zhejiang Education* likened it to a cross between a "regular middle school" and "guerrilla warfare"—students escaped when the enemy occupied an area but returned once the Japanese left.[57] Each student even helped the army by carrying extra central military rifles to deliver to the provincial government. While fleeing, some opted to leave behind their bedding (which they moved faster without) rather than abandon the guns. This act exemplified the sacrifice and heroism some students displayed while involved in the war effort. Once they delivered the rifles, the provincial administration expressed its gratitude by giving the students a few pigs to slaughter for food. GMD's *Zhejiang Education* proclaimed that the students' "brave, patriotic spirit is worthy of admiration."[58]

Relocation of Middle Schools   27

While the Japanese continued bombing Yuqian, another school in the same city, Number One Regional United Normal Middle School, moved into the wilderness on October 9, 1939.[59] The students stopped in Changhua county's Lulingpu that night and continued to move each subsequent day. Teachers held seminars with small groups of students—the war itself was an obvious topic of class discussion—and they educated students about Japanese violence towards the Chinese. Whereas before they had taught four full classes a day, sections were slimmed down to small seminars, always allowing the students to keep moving, while "classrooms" became nothing more than small village huts converted for a short period. Teachers even conducted classes outdoors when they were particularly deep in the wilderness.

Zhejiang Education celebrated these (and other) schools that successfully escaped the enemy under the headline "How to React to Sudden Change" (implying Japanese attacks).[60] Still, as Schoppa notes, there is much doubt that "guerrilla education" was actually effective for students who were trying to study while escaping the Japanese invasion. But it was important at that time for the GMD to draw from these courageous stories (perhaps exaggerated) in order to boost wartime morale and advance the Nationalist cause. In this way, GMD literature portrayed displaced middle school students as active participants in the resistance to the Japanese and central to the nation's subsequent political future.

Conflicts with Local Residents

In addition to the evolving GMD curriculum and the trauma of refugee relocation, displaced schools also encountered varying receptions from local residents in the interior—ranging from sympathetic welcomes to outright hostility. Schoppa provides examples of locals who generously assisted students. Aside from allowing Shaoxing Middle School youth to borrow their pots to cook rice, local residents of Zhejiang province's Dongyang county also slaughtered and prepared a large hog for them.[61] Initially, local communities were understandably alarmed by the sudden influx of students who needed food and other essentials. But when some schools offered immediate help in organizing and contributing services for the local community, tensions between students and residents eased. Thus, Schoppa maintains that the Zhejiang province "guerrilla schools" had positive impacts on the many locations to which they fled.[62]

Yet countless examples of hostile encounters indicate that such relations were not always smooth. Sometimes students themselves caused a souring of relations with villagers. On other occasions, principals and teachers joined students in clashing with Buddhist monks, especially when the refugees attempted to convert

28   Chapter 1

local temples into temporary schools. By no means were these novel occurrences: as far back as the Ming dynasty (1368–1644), officials had attempted to turn heterodox temples into schools.[63] During the last years of the Qing dynasty, particularly prompted by the 1898 reform movement, the modernizing government had called on educators to convert Buddhist and Daoist temples into schools. And Rebecca Nedostup notes how the state launched an "anti-superstition" campaign during the Nanjing decade (1927–1937), when the GMD seized temples and "openly encouraged educators to convert civil temples to night schools and other features of mass education."[64]

Wartime displacement only exacerbated such long-standing tensions between schools and temples, and there were many such cases reported to the government from 1938 to 1944. In Sichuan, Jiangji County Vocational Middle School students destroyed Guangshou Temple's Buddhist images and occupied the site after their principal encouraged them to convert the temple into their new school building. In response, Chongqing's Office of the Secretary insisted that the school compensate the temple. In another peculiar episode, a Tibetan monk, Qimiao, rented out a temple to Hunan Provincial Temporary High School, which served both lower middle and upper middle grades (only the latter used the temple). Initially, he believed that "education was very important."[65] However, a letter to Chiang Kaishek purportedly written by the monk reported that relations soon became acrimonious after the school refused to pay rent. In addition, the letter accused the students of pouring liquid soap into the temple's pond, poisoning three hundred fish. (Some Buddhists adopted the practice of *fangsheng*—"rescuing" live fish and other animals from slaughter by buying them to place in temple ponds or release into the wild, because of their prohibition on taking life.) According to the letter, students also ate the monks' food and stole their personal belongings and property, including furniture. As director of the temple, Qimiao asked Chiang Kai-shek to have the school compensate him 600 yuan.[66]

However, the Hunan Provincial Government soon conducted an investigation and discovered that "a local scoundrel" had completely fabricated the accusations. In fact, someone had used the monk's name to concoct the entire story. When government officials approached Qimiao, he maintained he never wrote the letter and had cordial relations with the school and its students.[67] Examples such as these indicated that when students and faculty relocated to new areas, conflicts were likely to result with local residents. In this incident, an imposter had tried to sabotage the relationship between the school and temple. The fact that nonlocal students were now turning temples into schools made the situation more explosive than in earlier eras.

Relocation of Middle Schools   29

More conflicts between refugee students and Buddhist monks flared as the war dragged on. In one case, a Boy Scout group from Pingliang Middle School in Gansu province destroyed a Buddhist statue in Nantai Temple.[68] According to the monks, while students stayed at the temple they disrupted those who were reading sutras aloud by leaping on stage and proclaiming, "the government should preside over the rights of Nantai Temple, not the monks!" The monks reported the incident to the local court, which concluded that Pingliang Middle School's principal wanted to convert the temple into a school, thus encouraging his students to do "bad things" while they stayed there. In response, the Gansu Provincial Government submitted an unfavorable report of the monks, accusing them of lying and blaming them for the entire ordeal. It deemed the monks "too traditional for believing everyone should be Buddhist" and criticized their opposition to "modernization, including students' education."[69] On one occasion, the monks were performing a ceremony of burning incense and collecting money at the same time and place where the Boy Scouts were camping. The monks claimed students beat a seventy-three-year-old monk named Qing Lian, yet when officials visited the temple to inspect the alleged victim, they did not find any wounds on his body. Consequently, the Gansu Provincial Government concluded that the monks "meddled too much" in local affairs by "thinking everyone should be Buddhist" and "collecting money during the war."[70] In essence, the monks interfered with the provincial government's wartime effort, and Wang Zizhi, the principal of Pingliang Middle School, along with his students, were right to persuade others to oppose the monks and shun Buddhism. However, provincial government officials did assert that the principal should have kept his students under control and prevented them from acting so impulsively.[71] Still, accusations of lying monks carried significant weight and helped contribute to talk of unsavory Buddhist "superstitions."

Meanwhile, from the perspective of some interior residents the arrival of displaced, relatively wealthy, and educated students from the northeast and coastal areas was an assault on their way of life, including both traditional agrarian values and Buddhist beliefs. Temples were not the only sites forced to house relocated schools, often with little compensation. In Jianshi county, Hubei province, Wei Cigang complained that the principal of a relocated lower middle school, Yi Yandao, and his students vandalized Wei's farmland and barn. Principal Yi forced Wei to turn over his farm to the school and sign a contract stipulating that the school could rent his land. The school staff depleted the ripened wheat on Wei's farm that his family depended on for sustenance. Wei also argued that his farm was a dangerous place for students, reasoning that "a school located on open land

30   Chapter 1

would be an easy target for bombing." He suggested that the school move to the mountains for the safety of the students, though he clearly had personal motives in doing so.[72]

In other places, locals responded with far more ferocity than farmers like Wei. In a report written to the National Executive Yuan (Guomin xingzhengyuan), Lu Minhun, the principal of Capital Minorities School, complained about a problem with a "local strongman" after the school relocated to Caijia village's Longche Temple in Chongqing's Ba county. Chinese custom held that when people moved to a new area they were supposed to contact village heads and bestow gifts upon them. Unfortunately, Capital Minorities School did not adhere to this custom and instead personally offended the local strongman, Wu Anyi, by neglecting to pay its respects. Wu then threatened to murder someone at the school and set it on fire after claiming that faculty, staff, and students had destroyed the temple's images. Wu gathered a number of Buddhists and demanded the school pay for the damages. In response, Principal Lu argued that Sun Yat-sen himself had called on his countrymen to "break down feudal superstitions and refrain from idol worship," thus the school was only following the late president's decrees. The principal also wrote that Wu was creating difficulties because of rural resistance to modern and formal education, not for the sake of Buddhism or the temple. Lu noted that the nearby City God Temple had been converted into a market selling Chinese products; another temple, Haitang Temple, had become part of a park; and a third, Wenquan Temple, had turned into the local office for the MOE. According to the principal, nobody objected to the conversion of these, but Wu and his accomplices opposed the school and were thus "destroying education."[73]

After the Executive Yuan received Principal Lu's report, it replied that the Sichuan Provincial Government should handle the case. Provincial officials investigated the Capital Minorities School and discovered it was actually private and illegal, and therefore ordered it shut down. Lu subsequently penned a letter directly to Chiang Kai-shek, in which he explained that the school had been registered in Nanjing but had to relocate to Sichuan when the Japanese invaded the city. According to him, once the school settled in Sichuan the provincial government wanted to shut it down because it could not provide any financial support for education. The principal argued that education was "very important for the nation"—if his school did not receive funding, nobody would be willing to work for it in the future.[74] Furthermore, he asserted that if the provincial government closed down his school, it too would be "destroying education."[75] Unfortunately, Executive Yuan documents do not reveal how (or if) the issue was ever resolved.

Corruption Cases in Displaced Schools

Wartime relocation not only exposed tension between schools and locals, it also provided opportunities for corrupt administrators to benefit from the misery of others. In one case, the Shanxi Province Association reported to the MOE that Principal Shen Disheng of National Number Five Middle School failed to distribute government stipends to his students. When the students rallied to demand that he provide the funds, he instead sent henchmen to beat the youths, putting some in the hospital. Most of the injured hailed from Shanxi province, having relocated to Chongqing.[76] Principal Shen only served the school for four months before the Ministry sent a replacement in August 1939.[77]

Such examples of financial corruption were the most common complaints. In another episode, an education supervisor reported in March 1940 that Principal Ge Weifen of National Number Six Middle School was guilty of malfeasance, embezzling the school's funds by increasing his own salary while reducing students' "tea-drinking money." When Ge purchased school supplies, he also pocketed some of the items. Moreover, he went so far as to fabricate the identities of nonexistent teachers, padding the faculty roster and stealing the extra government salaries. In addition, when sick students did not come to school to claim their stipends, Ge kept the money for himself instead. Along with theft and embezzlement, more dramatic forms of corruption emerged in this particular relocated school, another testament to the disruption of the war. According to the education supervisor, under Principal Ge's leadership "nobody enforced order" at National Number Six and the school descended into chaos. The supervisor described how "student dormitories were filthy," resulting in "illnesses and even death."[78] Besides suffering from physical deterioration, the school also exhibited scandalous behavior, including teachers and students involved in illicit affairs. The supervisor also raised alarms over the fact that many of National Number Six's students were dating.[79] The education supervisor reported that some girls had even become prostitutes while others openly cohabitated with male students.[80] In yet another incident, Yi Maoqin, the principal of Girls' Middle School in Sichuan province's Guang'an county, was accused of evicting students from some classrooms and instead moving his family in to live. When they criticized him, Yi expelled a number of students. In the same county a fire that destroyed Guang'an County Middle School was blamed on the principal's mismanagement, prompting students to demand his termination.[81]

Besides unscrupulous principals or teachers, students were also vulnerable to victimization from security personnel and local police, the very people who were

32   Chapter 1

supposed to protect them. For example, when Yixun Girls' Middle School relocated to Chongqing from Wuhan, its principal did not establish ties with the local powers and the school remained insular, perhaps because relocation was particularly dangerous for a girls' school. As a result, thieves constantly robbed the dormitories, prompting the school to hire a local policeman to patrol the campus. However, the policeman not only was unable to stop the intruding thieves, he also stole many possessions from the school himself. Not until a Green Gang chief's daughter transferred to the school did the robberies end.[82] (Evidently, the Green Gang was more powerful and intimidating than local law enforcement.)

In essence, the central government had the power and ability to establish and relocate national middle schools, but it could not supervise their day-to-day business. When displaced students became victims of corrupt principals or teachers, the GMD exercised little ability to ameliorate the problems or prevent such unsavory situations from occurring in the first place. Also, students' tense encounters with farmers, villagers, and Buddhist monks in the interior differed from the more immediate distress caused by immoral principals and teachers. Students could leave a local area that bore hostile residents, but they could not easily separate themselves from unscrupulous principals or teachers, whom they depended on for guidance and sustenance while so far away from home. Often students were trapped in unfortunate situations they could not escape. Furthermore, in such incidents students were not heard directly but represented by others on their behalf. In the above examples, the complaints were not reported by students themselves but rather by the Shanxi Province Association or the education supervisor. Nor do the archives always reveal how or if the government addressed or resolved these problems (with the exception of National Number Five Middle School, where the MOE replaced its crooked principal). Unfortunately, most likely the GMD did little: the government had an overwhelming number of wartime concerns that took priority over reportedly corrupt administrators or faculty. While the war allowed for greater centralized control over secondary education curriculum and provided the GMD a strong hand in actively relocating schools, the state had limited control over the actual behavior of students and faculty.

～

The Sino-Japanese War was a dangerous and chaotic time that brought tremendous challenges for China's civilians. However, the GMD managed to successfully aid the majority of the displaced population's middle school students by lifting them out of places of harm, establishing national middle schools, registering refugee students, and offering a degree of stability in an environment full of instability. Many of these students found refuge in the interior, where they were able

Relocation of Middle Schools   33

to continue their education despite having their studies interrupted by Japanese air raids and the necessity to flee. Jessie Lutz notes that the migration of students during the war "announced to the world that China would survive as a sovereign nation."[83] The GMD also proudly viewed the students' retreat to the interior as an act of defiance to the Japanese enemy and a display of patriotism symbolizing China's national reconstruction. Not only did middle schools endure and function throughout the eight-year conflict, the number of schools and students increased remarkably. All of this was no small feat for the GMD.

The war also provided opportunity for the state to expand its powers by chartering national middle schools. Before the conflict, all secondary education was under local (provincial, county, or municipal) authorities. However, even after the war these middle schools remained "national" and did not revert back to provincial or municipal control. Similarly, many specific GMD education policies and curriculum changes introduced during the conflict also remained in effect after hostilities ended, including the Nationalists' heavy emphasis on party indoctrination (such as the Three People's Principles) in secondary education. That trend would continue after the Nationalists fled mainland China following their defeat by the Communists in 1949, as party indoctrination grew even more intense in Taiwan's schools and the GMD exerted stronger influence over curriculum in the 1950s. Another clear manifestation of this growing centralized power during the war was the GMD's formation of a new youth organization, the Three People's Principles Youth Corps (SQT). Meant to be an organization that would indoctrinate youth in party ideology and suppress those engaged in anti-government activities, its origins and demise are explored in the following chapter.

Despite the GMD's overall success in relocating middle schools, it could not prevent some of the challenges refugee students faced as they trekked deep into the interior. This included antagonistic farmers, villagers, local strongmen, and Buddhist monks, who acted in such a manner because they rightfully felt that the sudden influx of refugees into their communities disrupted their lives. Students often incited such hostility by insisting local residents change their traditional and religious ways (which the students viewed as "backwards") and become more "modern." This conflict between tradition and modernity was a constant source of contention in many cases, prompting some communities to regard refugee students as ungrateful and pushy guests who imposed and overstayed their welcome. Besides these tensions with local residents, students also occasionally encountered an even more serious problem in the form of corrupt principals and teachers, whom they had a much more difficult time confronting. Ironically, while the GMD proved it could go to remarkable lengths to rescue students from the Japanese, it was usually unable to save them from their own dangerous or unscrupulous teachers, principals, administrators, or aggressive Nationalist officers. Yet despite these challenges, for most middle school students the story of mass relocation was ultimately one of remarkable tenacity, an extreme commitment to education, and triumph—for the majority of youth were able to continue their studies amidst the destruction of war and an invasion that severely disrupted their lives.

CHAPTER TWO

The Three People's Principles Youth Corps on the Mainland, 1938–1947

When the GMD controlled the Chinese mainland in the 1930s and 1940s, two of its factions, the Whampoa Clique and the Central Club (CC) Clique, competed for support on upper middle school and college campuses. Each was intent on creating a core group of pro-GMD youth sympathizers that would pledge loyalty to the party and promote factional goals. Some scholars and Chiang Kai-shek's contemporaries claim that the generalissimo secretly encouraged such factionalism to remain the indisputable and supreme head of the party.[1] Nevertheless, in 1938 Chiang came out publicly against the crippling infighting caused by the two camps. He ordered the dissolution of their subsidiary organizations and formed the Three People's Principles Youth Corps (Sanmin zhuyi qingniantuan, Sanqingtuan for short, and hereafter SQT).

An analysis of the SQT's founding and evolution in the late 1930s and 1940s sheds light on a number of important issues related to the history of the Chinese Nationalists on mainland China and Taiwan. In particular, this chapter explores the SQT while minimizing the connection between European fascism and youth organizations in China that many contemporaries at the time drew—and some scholars continue to espouse. It also emphasizes Chiang Kai-shek's use of the SQT to eliminate factionalism within the GMD, even as it eventually contributed directly to that very dissension. The way in which the organization sought to distance itself from an increasingly unpopular party, while still managing to recruit fresh members to the GMD, reveals the irony and uncertainty that lay behind this first generation of Nationalist youth organizing. Finally, the chapter also explores how the SQT became fixated on wartime refugee students, analyzing the reasons behind its successes and failures during the Second Sino-Japanese War and Chinese Civil War, and its role in establishing Chiang Ching-kuo as a national leader.

36   Chapter 2

Factional Rivalry within the GMD and the "Fascist" Question

In 1925, GMD leader Sun Yat-sen's death left the party without a clear successor. Competing personalities, including Chiang Kai-shek, Wang Jingwei, and Hu Hanmin, each claimed a group of loyal followers.[2] Over the next seven years, Chiang's faction grew stronger, especially after the success of the Northern Expedition (1926–1928). By 1932, his supporters constituted the party's most powerful group.[3] However, according to Huang Jianli, "Chiang's camp was far from homogeneous," and was itself subdivided into two major groups that competed for positions and influence in government: the Whampoa Clique and the CC Clique.[4] Military officers "who had earlier been taught by, or had associated with, Chiang [during his tenure] as commandant of the Whampoa Military Academy" (1924–1926) headed the Whampoa Clique.[5] Huang maintains that "the strength of its membership lay in its control of the military and police forces."[6] Meanwhile, party organization leaders, most notably brothers Chen Guofu and Chen Lifu, led the CC Clique. According to Lloyd Eastman, the term "CC" was "thought to represent either 'Central Club' or the 'two Chen's.'"[7] As Huang notes, through its control of the GMD's Central Organization Department, the CC Clique grew "to exert a strong influence over civilian party members and in areas such as provincial and city administrations, as well as banking, education, and journalism."[8] Besides serving as the head of the Central Organization Department, Chen Lifu was also minister of education from January 1938 to December 1944.[9] After 1933 the Whampoa Clique leaders began to exert "a great deal of activity toward supplanting the Chen brothers' influence, especially in newspaper publishing and educational circles."[10]

The Whampoa Clique went by various names, including the Blue Shirts (Lanyishe), Vigorously-Carry-Out Society (Lixingshe), the Revolutionary Youth Comrades Association (Geming qingnian tongzhi hui, RYCA), and the Revival (or Renaissance) Society (Fuxingshe).[11] Leaders of the faction organized into satellite organizations, front groups, and a hierarchy of three levels: from top to bottom, the Vigorously-Carry-Out Society, the RYCA, and the Revival Society.[12] Scholars and contemporaries often refer to the group as the Blue Shirts.[13] However, Huang prefers the term "Whampoa Clique," since most of its leaders were either graduates of the Whampoa Military Academy or closely associated with the school. Moreover, he argues that "[the term] 'clique' best expresses the factional dimension."[14]

The Whampoa Clique was certainly not fascist. In fact, the GMD wished to disassociate itself from organizations that were known to be fascist, especially since the emergence of Chiang Kai-shek's loyalists occurred simultaneously with the rise of the Nazis.[15] Frederic Wakeman argues that Chiang himself never used the term "fascism" and maintains that his regime was an authoritarian military dictatorship rather than fascist.[16] Furthermore, Wakeman argues that the GMD's most striking difference from European fascism was "its inability or unwillingness to create a true mass movement, which in turn reflected the regime's persistent distrust of social mobilization and political participation."[17] In his 1979 memoir, Gan Guoxun, one of the Lixingshe founders, was infuriated by allegations that the Blue Shirts were fascists.[18] Moreover, a 1936 Blue Shirts training manual insisted that the view that the Blue Shirts' ideology was fascist was "misguided."

However, Chiang did admire the Hitler and Mussolini regimes for a number of reasons, including their overall efficiency, the way in which the dictators emphasized patriotism and demanded loyalty to both a personal leader and political party, and the military strength of Europe's fascist armies. Chiang even spoke privately to his followers of the need to "Nazify" (*nacuihua*) China.[19] Moreover, government records indicate that many in the Whampoa Clique were "sent to Germany and Italy for military training" and, according to Wakeman, they returned to China "full of admiration for fascism and convinced of its value under present conditions in China."[20] Most admirers of fascism agreed that it was a useful method of control: "control of the nation as a whole (for the Blue Shirts) [and] of party organization and national culture (for Chen Lifu)."[21]

Whether there was a fascist tint to the GMD in the decade before the outbreak of war with Japan in 1937 has long been a subject of debate among scholars. Frederic Wakeman and William Kirby argue most convincingly that it was not fascist, while Maggie Clinton contends that, in fact, it was.[22] Kirby explains how A. James Gregor defines fascism as a step towards modernization, viewing it in its original Italian context as "an industrializing and modernizing movement in both performance and intention."[23] Gregor characterizes fascism as a "developmental dictatorship appropriate to partially developed or underdeveloped national communities" and considers as following the "fascist persuasion" a wide variety of national movements, whose differences he recognizes while arguing that they all share a "pragmatic fascism."[24] He defines "pragmatic fascism" as "the intention of creating a totalitarian political system, an integrated social order in which all men, all classes, and all productive categories would be marshaled to the nationalistic and developmental 'ideal purposes' of the authoritarian state under the aegis of the charismatic Leader."[25] Kirby identifies two problems in applying this approach to 1930s China. First, if fascism is defined in this manner, then Nazism itself—with its anti-modern bias—was not fascism, while regimes as different as Franco's Spain and Castro's Cuba may be called "fascist." That National Socialism

38   Chapter 2

was not, in fact, fascism would have come as quite a shock to Chinese of the 1930s. Second, Gregor's definition assumes a desire for mass mobilization and participation that was quite absent among GMD admirers of fascism.

Kirby maintains that no Chinese enamored by European fascism was seriously willing to make the efforts of mass mobilization or countenance the social upheaval that occurred in places like Nazi Germany. The GMD's different segments addressed each other, not their masses. If Chiang Kai-shek tried to create a basis of mass support through the New Life Movement that began in 1934, it was to be a carefully orchestrated, controlled affair. Furthermore, even the Blue Shirts—who most openly espoused the fascist model—at most shared "ideological traits" with European fascism, their activities were limited by their own secret organization, and they never achieved predominance even within the GMD. Kirby argues that there exists no coherent scholarly approach to fascism that can accommodate its various admirers in China, with their divisions, rivalries, and different interpretations of the term. There was no fascist movement in China but rather a prevailing style that coincided with the emergence of a close Sino-German relationship in the 1930s.[26]

Maggie Clinton explains that she uses the term "fascism" to describe the CC Clique and Blue Shirts' politics because they were not conservative, predemocratic, or merely authoritarian. In addition, she maintains that the term "allows us to grasp the simultaneously revolutionary and counterrevolutionary dynamics of the political solutions that the [two cliques'] militants offered, and hence an opportunity to better understand the historical conditions under which fascism emerges and coalesces."[27] Clinton argues that the CC Clique and Blue Shirts shared a common worldview that was indeed fascist. Each group considered itself a revolutionary vanguard locked in a struggle against liberals, communists, and foreign imperialist powers to save the Chinese nation. She presents Chinese fascism as drawn from global currents yet a manifestly localized phenomenon.

Earlier important contributions to this question of the GMD's relationship with fascism are Eastman's pioneering research and Maria Hsia-Chang's critique of Eastman's work.[28] Eastman and Hsia-Chang have debated whether the Whampoa Clique, the GMD faction most sympathetic to European modes of authoritarianism, deserved the label "fascist." Eastman, who adopted a broader definition of the term, argues that the group fit the criteria because its method and ideas were similar to those found in Hitler's Germany and Mussolini's Italy. Members admired and emulated European fascist movements, and some even embarked on a conscious attempt to create a Chinese version of fascism. Hsia-Chang prefers a stricter definition of fascism and claims that Whampoa Clique leaders were not referring to the ideology when they spoke of a "fascism" that might save China.

Instead, they were only alluding to "the mobilizing and control capabilities of fascism" as they attempted to create a non-fascist, mass-mobilizing dictatorship under Chiang Kai-shek.[29] Whampoa Clique leaders insisted that one must not conceive of fascism as "a type of ideology, but rather as a method . . . for pacifying the interior and driving out the foreign enemy."[30] Thus, when Chiang himself studied the Nazis, he was not concerned with information about their ideology, but rather with how Hitler had achieved strict discipline and obedience among followers.[31]

The key question is not whether Eastman misused the "fascist" label but whether the Whampoa Clique engaged in the sort of extensive mobilization associated with fascism. Huang's study indicates that, although leaders of the group were "aware of and interested in the European fascist method of mobilizing mass support, it did not take any concrete action as far as students were concerned."[32] When the GMD decided to depoliticize the student population in 1930, it maintained this policy for the next nineteen years and the Whampoa Clique and other factions within the party never seriously opposed it.[33]

Moreover, the two men who actually drafted the GMD's policies restricting student activism in the 1930s were perhaps the most unlikely "fascists" in the Nationalist regime—one was among the leading liberal educators in early twentieth-century China. Rather than a conscious emulation of European fascism on the part of Chiang, Dai Jitao and Cai Yuanpei provided an ideological basis for the GMD to begin depoliticizing youth organizations. Of the two, Dai, an important party theorist and personal secretary to Sun Yat-sen, was most responsible for nudging the party in this new direction of limiting student activism.[34] After Sun's death in 1925, Dai became one of the most authoritative interpreters of the Three People's Principles and a major polemicist of the GMD in power. Moreover, Dai was also a member of the Standing Committee, the supreme decision-making body of the GMD.[35] His initiatives later received significant support from an even more unlikely source, Cai Yuanpei, China's leading liberal educator and former chancellor of Peking University (1917–1926) and minister of education (1911–1912). Educated in Germany, Cai was also a founding member and first president of Academia Sinica (1928–1940), Republican China's preeminent research institute.[36] The May 4th Movement of 1919 occurred during Cai's tenure as chancellor, when a wave of nationalist and anti-imperialist protests swept through Chinese campuses, with Peking University as its organizational center. The students called upon the Chinese government to reject the Treaty of Versailles and dismiss pro-Japanese officials. (The police arrested and assaulted the students after they burned down the residence of one.) Cai sought to convince students that they should attend to their studies, preparing themselves for a future as political reformers; he

40   Chapter 2

preferred that they avoid involving the university in overt political activities, as this threatened his vision of a university independent of political disputes. However, although Cai was opposed to violence, he was sympathetic to their cause and widely celebrated by many. Another testament to Cai's liberalism was his emphasis on the need for academic freedom in China, a constant theme in his educational writings, which also called for the independence of education from state and religious control. In opposition to the propagandistic education promoted by the state and religion, he advocated an open-minded education. It is important to distinguish between Dai's authoritarian approach and Cai's liberal position when they both appealed to students to return to their studies. Both agreed on efforts to institute party control over students without agreeing on philosophical assumptions—and both were clearly not influenced by fascism.

Together, Dai and Cai produced four basic policy documents the GMD eventually endorsed. The first established principles for the future organization of student unions: according to Huang, "they were to be renamed student self-governing associations (SSGAs) (*xuesheng zizhihui*), confined to individual schools, barred from interfering with school administration and charged with the twin objectives of inculcating the Three People's Principles as the basic spirit of student self-government and promoting the development of intellectual, moral, physical, and social education."[37] The second and third documents featured organizational charts for the proposed SSGAs at institutes of higher education and secondary schools. These documents barred the proposed SSGAs from organizing student political gatherings and limited them to promoting activities solely related to education and student welfare. The fourth document articulated rules regarding "the frequency of meetings, elections and the composition of congresses and executive committee meetings."[38] The GMD instructed all SSGAs to adhere to the fourth document when drafting their constitutions, which had to be submitted to party authorities for approval.[39] In January 1930, the Standing Committee of the Central Executive Committee endorsed all four documents, formally adopting Dai and Cai's policies as an official GMD platform discouraging student political activism.

While Dai and Cai helped provide stronger limits on student political freedoms, the Whampoa Clique continued to recruit young people into their front organizations, before and after the GMD established the SQT in 1938. However, the scale of student involvement was limited. Even after the GMD launched the SQT, clique personnel dominated its leadership and operation. According to Huang, the corps "did not become a channel of political mobilization, but developed instead into an instrument for depoliticizing the students and making them

Three People's Principles   41

focus their minds on education and moral discipline."[40] Before and after the founding of the SQT, the Whampoa Clique also attempted to use schools, the military, and the workforce to instill their ideas. In particular, they expanded their influence among students through university military training programs provided in regular school curriculum and at middle school summer camps, foreshadowing the China Youth Corps' military training of students on Taiwan during the 1950s.[41] From 1932 to 1937, both the Whampoa Clique and the CC Clique attempted to cultivate pro-GMD student cadres.[42] However, these activists formed only a small fraction of the two GMD camps, and they constituted an even smaller proportion when measured against the total student population. Thus, according to Huang, "their recruitment was not an exercise in large-scale political mobilization but the cultivation of a small vanguard unit."[43] Their job was to reinforce the GMD's politico-educational effort to monitor schools closely and check the influence and activities of anti-GMD student radicals.[44]

The Founding of the Three People's Principles Youth Corps

In March 1938, the GMD publicly announced its intention to form the Three People's Principles Youth Corps.[45] The following month, at Chiang Kai-shek's order, the GMD's Extraordinary National Congress adopted a resolution creating the organization.[46] Chiang officially launched the SQT on July 9, 1938, with considerable fanfare, yet the initial conception and the planning stages must have started months before the first public announcement in March.[47] The SQT's official published history from 1946, *The First Draft of Volume One of Historical Materials on the Three People's Principles Youth Corps* (*Sanmin zhuyi qingniantuan tuanshi ziliao diyi chugao*), briefly notes that the GMD leadership considered the idea as early as May 1937, two months before the outbreak of war.[48] Eastman accepts this claim, yet several contemporary accounts place the founding of the organization sometime after the war began.[49] In an early wartime speech, acting SQT secretary-general Zhu Jiahua suggested that the idea originated in the fall of 1937, while Kang Ze, a prominent SQT leader from 1938 to 1944, recalled that GMD leaders began discussing the matter that September.[50] Kang was a former leading member of the officially disbanded Revival Society, a front group of the Whampoa Clique, and he later ran the SQT as director of its organization department. As for Chiang Kai-shek, the generalissimo mentioned the youth corps in his diary for the first time on November 3, 1937, in which he placed the SQT, which he referred to as *qingniantuan*, first on a list of things "to pay attention to."[51] Thus,

42   Chapter 2

Huang is correct when he surmises that GMD leaders likely conceived of the organization within two months of the first military clash between Chinese and Japanese forces at the Marco Polo Bridge in July 1937.[52]

Contrary to scholars who insist that Chiang secretly encouraged conflict among competing GMD cliques, when the generalissimo announced the formation of the SQT he specifically saw it as an attempt to put an end to party factionalism once and for all. On February 4, 1938, Chiang's sixth item on his "to-do" list read: "Give a speech to the main officers of the Vigorously-Carry-Out Society. These people give me different reports. They are engaged in a power struggle. The local officials are immature and supervision is not strict enough."[53] Chiang then wrote sarcastically that "they want to become leaders."[54] Sure enough, the following day he "thoroughly scolded the Vigorously-Carry-Out Society officers," and on April 3 he broadened his crackdown and ordered the complete dissolution of the CC and Whampoa Cliques.[55] That same month, Chen Lifu, Chen Guofu, and other major CC Clique leaders called together a meeting of approximately 450 followers in Wuhan, the temporary wartime capital, where they announced the dissolution of their subsidiary organizations.[56] Two months later, Whampoa Clique members also assembled in a Wuchang secondary school and decided to dismantle their faction's front groups.[57] Still, although the CC Clique and Whampoa Clique officially disbanded their satellite organizations, both factions remained powerful.[58]

On July 25, 1939, Chiang himself supervised an SQT membership ceremony and administered the oath of allegiance. All SQT members stood and listened as Chiang read the preface of the party's rules and main points (the GMD rules were the exact same as the SQT's). He even proclaimed that the purpose of the SQT was to establish "revolutionary character," the foundation for all GMD regulations. In total there were twelve creeds in the GMD party's rules: bravery, filial piety, love, trust, peace, courtesy, obedience, thriftiness, cleanliness, helpfulness, knowledge, and persistence. All SQT members recited the twelve creeds after Chiang.[59]

The SQT devoted its first year of existence to planning and preparation. Chiang himself assumed the organization's directorship and appointed General Chen Cheng his secretary-general. Although Chen formally held this post, his many other duties prevented him from assuming full-time leadership of the corps.[60] By mid-1938, he was already serving as commander of the Ninth Military Area, dean of the Army's Central Training Corps, and governor of Hubei province.[61] His nominal appointment to the SQT simply signaled that he was on course for high political office.[62] Consequently, Zhu Jiahua served as acting secretary-general, and in 1940 Zhang Zhizhong took over the position. However, regardless of the secretary-general, effective leadership of the corps usually fell to lesser subordi-

Three People's Principles   43

nates. Both Chen and Zhang were former instructors at the Whampoa Military Academy, but the person who essentially ran the SQT (as director of its organization department) was Kang Ze, a former Whampoa student. Kang ranked lower than Chen and Zhang in terms of seniority, but he was the dominant personality in the corps until 1944, whereupon Chiang Ching-kuo took a leading role.[63]

Kang's eventual removal from SQT leadership proved, once again, that Chiang aggressively rebuked those who promoted factionalism between the old "cliques." By May 1945, Chiang was infuriated with Kang for pitting the SQT against the party.[64] On one occasion, during the Sixth National Party Congress on May 18, 1945, Kang and his followers feuded directly with Chen Lifu and Chen Guofu over a proposal to increase GMD party representatives from 360 to 480, knowing well that added members would benefit the CC Clique.[65] The situation turned so bitter that Chiang himself was forced to host the meeting because he feared the controversy would prevent the election from taking place (different groups usually took turns hosting the Congress meetings). Chiang agreed to a compromise by decreasing the number of representatives to 460, a proposal that passed by a majority ruling.[66] Nevertheless, the generalissimo was terribly upset with Kang, calling him a "scum" or "renegade" (bailei) in his diary.[67] Chiang thought that Kang had intentionally used the SQT in the fight against the CC Clique. As its primary leader, Kang was prohibiting the organization from cooperating with the party, and Chiang identified him as the main culprit for the division between the two GMD units. On May 26, 1945, Chiang made a note to himself "to pay attention to what Kang Ze says and does," and expressed how he was "frustrated thinking about the Kang Ze problem."[68] By this time, he had grown extremely distrustful of Kang.

The Purpose of the Three People's Principles Youth Corps

The SQT's founding rules mimicked those of the Nationalist Party, yet within a few years its leader was feuding with the Chen brothers and the organization was refusing to "cooperate" with the party. What exactly then was the SQT's purpose? On June 16, 1938, Chiang delivered a speech addressed to all of China's youth on the occasion of the SQT's launch. In it, he stated three main reasons for establishing the corps: to "complete the task of Resistance and Reconstruction," "secure a concentration of fresh strength for the National Revolution," and "give concrete expression to the Three Principles of the People."[69] On the other hand, Chen Lifu, who controlled the party, maintained in his memoir that the GMD created the SQT because it wanted to abolish the party's probationary membership system—

"probationary members participated in small group meetings to learn about the party, but the party never held a formal basic training program for new members."[70] When the GMD elected Chen to draft the SQT's rules, he proposed that "all probationary party members first had to join the Youth Corps."[71] After turning twenty-five, they would automatically become regular party members.[72] Chen frowned on having the SQT become a separate entity from the party, and believed instead its only purpose was to train the party's young people, thus preventing disputes between the SQT and party members.[73] However, in 1938 Chiang Ching-kuo proposed that SQT members be made equal in status to full-time party members.[74] Adding to Chen's chagrin, Kang Ze was unwilling to even allow corps members to become party members when they reached twenty-five, and as SQT's head of organization division, Kang was permitted by Chiang Kai-shek to sign a directive in 1938 allowing members to remain in the SQT after turning twenty-five and not requiring them to join the GMD.[75]

This ruling led to considerable friction between the SQT and the GMD. Chen felt that Chiang had made a grave mistake, and later wrote that when he initially drafted the SQT rules he explained to Chiang how "an independent unit must not be created outside the party."[76] According to Chen, the SQT represented "new blood," while the party grew "old and weak."[77] These two autonomous entities became greater adversaries, with the Whampoa Clique supporting the SQT and the CC Clique, led by Chen Lifu and his brother Chen Guofu, controlling the party. In particular, Chen blamed the ambitions of two major Whampoa Clique figures, Chen Cheng and Kang Ze, for coveting the SQT leadership in hopes of taking over the party someday.[78] From the start in 1938, almost all SQT members belonged to the Whampoa Clique and the youth organization became independent from the party. In response, the party resisted the SQT's nature as a separate entity by attempting to exert control over the corps. What began as a cooperative effort to build a strong student organization sympathetic to the GMD in 1938 had quickly devolved into a bitter political rivalry by 1945.

In addition to Chiang and Chen's explanation of the SQT's founding mission, Huang offers another reason for the SQT's establishment. He argues that the GMD formed the corps to assist with political rejuvenation in two major ways: "first, by providing a new instrument to integrate the diverse intra-party factions and, second, through the infusion of fresh blood into the party."[79] By 1937, as many as 90 percent of the party's two million members were reportedly "inactive," meaning there were no documented examples of their participation in party work.[80] GMD leaders were concerned with the situation, and at the opening session of the Extraordinary Congress on March 29, 1938, Chiang Kai-shek warned that the GMD had "become virtually an empty shell, without any real substance; the form of the party persists, but the spirit of the party has almost completely died out."[81] Similarly, Chiang made it clear in his later speeches and writings that he had organized the SQT to "give a new life to the GMD," and even likened the GMD to the nation's main artery, with members of the SQT fresh corpuscles within that artery.[82]

Concurrent with the SQT's establishment, the GMD's deputy leader, Wang Jingwei, cosponsored a resolution prohibiting the establishment of suborganizations within the party.[83] Together with Chiang, Wang pushed through a resolution that laid out six basic principles for the structure of the SQT, one of which prevented the organization from becoming a tool for behind-the-scenes, factional politics. The corps' constitution prohibited members from participating in other political parties and factions (with the obvious exception of the GMD). Despite the SQT's subsequent role in fomenting GMD infighting, it is clear from these measures that Wang and the other supporters of the resolution initially conceived of the SQT just as Chiang had noted in his diary—as an organization that would integrate intra-party factions or, at the very least, stand apart from them.[84] Thus, Huang is correct in noting that the GMD's original objective in 1938 was to use the SQT to reform the parent party, both "by providing a platform in which diverse factions could work together and by acting as a medium through which fresh talent could be inducted."[85]

Furthermore, GMD leaders deliberately de-emphasized the relationship between the party and the SQT when the youth organization was formed. According to Huang, when General Chen Cheng and other leaders toured battle zones during the early part of the war, they encountered disparaging remarks such as "the GMD has no sacrificial spirit and is no longer revolutionary," or soldiers and civilians insisting that "the CCP and not the GMD is leading the battle against the Japanese"—a reflection of the party's poor image that continued to circulate and contribute to the leadership's decision to reform.[86]

Thus, the GMD made deliberate efforts to enhance the SQT's appeal among young people by publicly distancing it from the party. Despite its connection to the GMD, the official title of the SQT intentionally remained the "Three People's Principles Youth Corps." Some proposed to prefix it with the name "Guomindang," but this idea was deliberately suppressed—officially because omitting the name of the party would broaden the appeal of the SQT to those not necessarily committed to the GMD.[87] Yet certainly underlying this decision was the concern that the party's poor image would put off potential SQT recruits.[88] A number of party members even attempted to do away with the prefix "Three People's Principles," the official ideology of the GMD. But others managed to ward off these endeavors by arguing that even the CCP had publicly declared its dedication to the Three People's Principles as the "highest guiding principle in the war of resistance against

46   Chapter 2

Japan."[89] Interestingly, Chiang's diaries note that Zhou Enlai quickly refused the invitation to have CCP members join the SQT.[90]

Analyzing the SQT's founding mission reveals much about GMD leadership and factionalism in the late 1930s, but it is equally important to understand how and why the organization's purpose shifted and evolved within a few short years. A vital purpose of the SQT was to recruit and discipline the waves of refugee students driven from northern and coastal cities by the Japanese invasion, but this concern with student drifters did not come until after the corps was established. According to Huang, many of the displaced students held "strong patriotic reactions to the Japanese invasion," which were "seen by the GMD as something of a problem, if not potentially dangerous."[91] In spite of the need to mobilize support for the war effort, the GMD remained apprehensive about mass participation in politics. For instance, on February 6, 1938, acting on a personal order from Chiang Kai-shek, the Ministry of Education secretly ordered all schools to prohibit political speeches or discussions without first subjecting participants to careful scrutiny, regardless of their credentials.[92] Similarly, when the Student Federation for the Salvation of China (Zhongguo xuesheng jiuguo lianhehui) sought the MOE's permission and sponsorship of its second congress on March 20, 1938, to debate the issue of "saving-the-nation-through-studies," it was rejected.[93] The MOE replied that such an event was unnecessary, and that wartime students had only two options: continue their studies or join the military and paramilitary services.[94]

Huang also discusses how the GMD attempted to constrain student activism through direct political measures, such as "indoctrinating students with GMD values, cultivating a small group of pro-GMD student activists, and expanding the [SQT] in schools."[95] The GMD tried to indoctrinate its values mainly through political education in the classroom, including compulsory lessons on the ideology of the Three People's Principles, other teachings of Sun Yat-sen, and party policies adopted at its various plenary meetings. The GMD aimed to make students understand and appreciate the party's ideology and policies, yet despite the political overtones of these measures, Huang argues that "they [did] not constitute a signal for students to indulge in political activism."[96] Instead, the GMD wanted them as tools to check student radicalism and become politico-educational instruments in molding "a new generation of students who shared the GMD's political outlook, including its wish for students to shun activism and concentrate on academic pursuits and self-cultivation."[97]

Reports of young people migrating to the CCP stronghold in northwestern China heightened GMD worries over this problem of placating wartime students. The SQT was one of the many government and party agencies which addressed the dilemma of refugee students drifting to Communist-occupied areas, but it was not the organization's main goal and its involvement came much later. Significantly, there was no reference to any links with drifter students on the occasion of the SQT's launching.[98] According to Huang, it was not until four months after its inauguration that the corps became involved, "when it began to establish a network of youth reception centers (*qingnian zhaodaisuo*) aimed at providing free accommodation for refugee students, recommending them for jobs, and enlisting them for social and wartime services."[99]

The Composition of the Three People's Principles Youth Corps

By definition, youth included young women, and the SQT actively sought to recruit females. However, the membership remained overwhelmingly male; women who did join were generally students.[100] Also, even though the SQT was officially the youth group of the GMD, actual "youth" occupied a small percentage of the organization's composition in its early years. Initially, it barred people from even joining until they turned eighteen. In July 1939 the minimum age was dropped, but only to sixteen. "Youth" usually refers to young people in their teens or early to mid-twenties—given these restrictions and the average age of its membership, the SQT in its formative years looked more like an organization for the middle aged.[101]

Under the SQT's first constitution, people up to age thirty-eight were eligible for ordinary membership.[102] It is unclear who determined that rule, or why, especially considering that the GMD never enforced an age limit in its entire history. If establishing such a limit distinguished the SQT from the GMD, the fact that it was so high (thirty-eight) also set it apart from other prominent youth organizations around the world, another indication that the Chinese were not following Western models. The SQT's maximum age was twenty years more than that imposed on Germany's Hitler Youth. Eighteen was also the age limit for Boy Scouts of America in the 1930s and 1940s, as it has always been from the organization's founding in 1910.[103] However, the SQT's age limit only applied to ordinary membership, and a constitutional clause allowed cadres and special categories (such as educators and those who had "contributed to the cause of revolution under the GMD leadership") to be exempted from the age restriction.[104] Therefore, it was technically possible (although not common) for SQT members to be over forty or fifty years old.[105]

Comprehensive figures on the age composition of SQT members in its first two years are unavailable, but later data allow for inferences. In July 1939, the

48   Chapter 2

organization revised its constitution to reduce the maximum age limit from thirty-eight to twenty-five years.[106] Taking this change into account, Huang estimates that possibly more than half of all SQT members in its first two years exceeded twenty-six years of age.[107] In September 1947, when the SQT merged with the party, 20 percent of the corps members were over the age of thirty years—a large proportion considering the organization was meant for younger people.[108]

Adapted from Huang, Table 2.1 displays the occupations of SQT members. Apart from the 1947 figures, which are only available to April, the rest indicate data at the end of the calendar year. Slight variations appear in other sources, but this particular set is the most comprehensive and likely most reliable.

Trainees of political and military courses comprised the largest number of SQT members before 1941: more than a third in 1939 and about a quarter in 1940. During the war, these trainees taught short-term courses aimed at effectively implementing wartime policy objectives. The GMD drew most of the trainees from the existing pool of civil servants, party political organizers, military and police personnel, and a tiny number of refugee students who had decided to abandon their studies. In Chiang Kai-shek's inaugural speech to China's youth on June 16, 1938, he proclaimed that the SQT "aims to bring together the best youths of the whole nation, whether soldiers, laborers, farmers, merchants, or students," thus

Table 2.1. Occupational Composition (%) of Three People's Principles Youth Corps Members

	1939	1940	1941	1942	1943	1944	1945	1946	1947
Students	8.1	13.7	31.61	36.99	40.28	44.87	46.6	46.21	46.59
Trainees of political and military courses	37.1	25.7	15.98	12.67	11.51	9.29	8.27	7.31	6.79
Government and party administrators	15.3	18.2	14.78	14.07	13.53	13.1	13.06	13.01	12.83
Military and police personnel	17.2	19.6	14.41	12.21	11.31	9.82	9.09	9.9	9.76
Educators	9.9	11	9.87	9.01	8.58	8.34	8.29	8.25	8.43
Workers, peasants, and merchants	3.3	4.5	6.75	7.25	7.28	7.65	7.91	8.49	7.84
Self-employed and others	9.1	10	6.79	7.81	7.51	6.98	6.78	6.8	6.76

Source: Adapted from Sanmin zhuyi qingniantuan zhongyang tuanbu [Central Executive Committee of the Three People's Principles Youth Corps], *Sanmin zhuyi qingniantuan dierjie zhongyang ganshihui gongzuo baogao* [Work report of the Second Central Executive Committee of the Three People's Principles Youth Corps] (n.p., August 1947), 90–92, cited in Huang Jianli, *Politics of Depoliticization in Republican China: Guomindang Policy towards Student Political Activism, 1927–1949* (Bern: Peter Lang, 1996), 125.

categories for military personnel, workers, peasants, and merchants are also found in Table 2.1.[109] However, students from secondary schools and universities, who were probably the most suitable representatives of traditional "youth," were actually quite neglected in early recruitment drives. By December 1939, one and a half years after the SQT's launching, only 8.1 percent of its members were students.

This imbalance in the organization's composition, with public servants and trainees of various sorts making up more than 70 percent of the membership, immediately raised alarm among some SQT leaders, who warned that this was "not only erroneous, but a serious danger because such a development will drive a wedge between us and the mass of young people."[110] But the SQT did not seriously begin a massive recruitment of students until early 1941. The reason for the slow pace of student recruitment partly lay in the debate of the SQT's Standing Committee over whether members should recruit in schools. In October 1938, the committee passed a set of guidelines to establish SQT branches and subbranches in colleges and universities, which was later approved by Chiang Kai-shek.[111] However, official statistics released in 1945 reveal that not a single SQT branch was established in a higher education institute in 1938.[112] The lack of action was due to the GMD's decision to abandon the temporary wartime capital of Wuhan in late October 1938 in the face of fierce Japanese attacks. Like almost everyone else in Wuhan, once the evacuation order was issued, the majority of personnel based at the SQT headquarters also started retreating to Chongqing. Due to geographical obstacles and a congested transport network, the SQT headquarters' move turned out to be a difficult three-month journey, arriving in Chongqing in Sichuan province on January 9, 1939.[113] The entire SQT organization more or less ground to a halt while its command center was relocating. Moreover, many schools and their students were also busy packing and retreating towards the safety of the Sichuan basin and the surrounding southwestern corner of China. It was only after conditions had become more settled in early 1939 that SQT branches appeared at higher education institutes.

The SQT also attempted to expand its organization into upper middle schools. Students in primary and lower middle schools participated in scouting. Reverend Yan Jialin founded the first Chinese Boy Scouts group at Wuchang Wenhua Academy on February 25, 1912, shortly after the 1911 Revolution.[114] The first Chinese Girl Scouts was established in 1919, nine years after Girl Guides of the UK was formed.[115] Under GMD rule, scouting quickly expanded in schools in southeast and central China. Robert Culp argues that Chinese educators and GMD leaders advocated scouting because it provided students with lessons on "etiquette and hygiene rooted in Euro-American culture with skills training and the promotion of civil service . . . [which] encouraged forms of cultural citizenship."[116] In

50   Chapter 2

1934, the MOE even made scouting a required class in all lower middle schools.[117] Meanwhile, the SQT targeted upper middle school students who were usually between the ages of sixteen and eighteen years. It was not until July 1939, when the SQT constitutional restriction prohibiting recruitment below eighteen years of age was formally amended to sixteen years, that the corps could even recruit secondary school students. Notably, SQT units in upper middle schools were placed under the charge of local SQT branches, while higher education institutes were directly affiliated with the headquarters, an indication of the lesser importance placed on secondary education students.[118]

As a leader in the SQT organization of small neighborhood groups in the wartime capital, Te Fang Chou Ch'ien later recalled her youth in Chongqing during the Japanese bombings from 1937 to 1939. She led several marches, military drills, and mock warfare practices, similar to the activities that future China Youth Corps members participated in during the 1950s in Taiwan. Ch'ien was a leader of the women's corps in her middle school. As part of the curriculum, young male students pursued military training while young women received nurse's training and rifle practice.[119] This type of training would also continue in the upper middle schools of the Republic of China on Taiwan.

Besides their focus on attracting upper middle school and college students, SQT leaders also began seeking young people outside the formal education system. In September 1939, the SQT Standing Committee met three times and affirmed its interest in recruiting "social youth" (*shehui qingnian*), the term used to describe young people who were not enrolled in school.[120] Thus, the SQT's emphasis on students did not come until the end of 1939. Ironically, the SQT's reorganized mission and growing attempt to recruit younger members directly contributed to the GMD factionalism it was meant to stop. Zhu Jiahua, who was intermittently acting secretary-general of the SQT on behalf of Chen Cheng, had himself sounded the alarm about "some comrades . . . who either talked of the SQT as a different entity from the party or said that the SQT was meant to replace the party."[121] The extent of this situation was serious enough to prompt Chiang Kai-shek to issue a stern warning that "no one should feel . . . that the SQT is intended as a replacement for the party," and that this attitude was "absolutely an erroneous view."[122] But this reassurance was insufficient to curb the party rank and file's resentment towards the SQT. After all, it was Chiang himself who had absolved SQT members from the requirement to leave the organization at twenty-five years old and join the GMD.

In its initial two and a half years of operation, the SQT preferred to recruit from more mature sectors of the population and, as a result, more than two-thirds of its early members came from the civil service, as well as the military, police, and political training academies. For instance, in 1940 the SQT tried to recruit more mature members who possessed political status. In fact, these were the traditional recruitment grounds of the GMD.[123] The party accused the SQT of engaging in unethical encroachment, bringing their rivalry to a boiling point. However, the party itself was also guilty of poaching, for it too had expanded aggressively into schools during the war to recruit young students as members. Both the GMD party headquarters' Central Social Department and the Central Organization Department, which were led by Chen Lifu, spearheaded party expansion to confront subversive Communist activities in schools. As a gesture of Chinese unity against the Japanese invaders, the GMD and CCP had formalized a united front at the beginning of the war and both sides tried to avoid confrontations by attempting to maintain a congenial relationship. But these feeble attempts at cooperation were further weakened once the GMD completed its retreat inland and resettled in the wartime capital of Chongqing. By January 1939, there were already signs that the GMD had begun to renew its open hostility towards the CCP.[124]

Table 2.2, adapted from Wang Liangqing's *A Study of the Relationship between San-min Chu-I Youth Corps and the Kuomintang 1938–1949*, provides a look at the demographic relationship between the GMD and SQT. The total number of party members listed does not include those living overseas or in the military. Yet the SQT data are drawn from the actual recruitment numbers. The number of GMD party members in 1942 is unknown, while the number for 1947 is based on figures gathered in November. During that time, the SQT was dissolved and its members joined the GMD (although there were many who were already members of both organizations), thus the 1947 data are inaccurate. The number of party members decreased from 1938 to 1939 because the GMD required all party members to reregister in 1939. Since some people did not, the figures went down.

To achieve this rising number of recruits in subsequent years, the SQT not only expanded its activities in the schools and lowered its age limit, but Chiang Kai-shek himself also offered guidance and strategies on how to attract potential members. On July 17, 1940, Chiang delivered a speech to the Central Executive Committee on recruitment. According to him, the GMD's goal was to save the country during the Second Sino-Japanese War, while the Communists were not concerned with the nation. The speech was full of GMD propaganda. For example, Chiang exhorted SQT members:

> Whether or not the Communists have many people and strategies, they cannot defeat us. We have to prevent the Communist movement and their use of young people . . . Those who have been numbed by the Communists,

Table 2.2. Number of GMD Party Members and SQT Members and Their Ratio (1938–1947)

	1938	1939	1940	1941	1942	1943	1944	1945	1946	1947
Number of GMD Party members	633,402	471,227	1,139,928	1,745,697	—	2,144,147	2,777,972	3,114,638	3,563,063	3,800,773
Number of SQT members	9,207	89,664	259,147	421,161	537,706	620,461	887,865	1,245,001	1,545,944	1,340,255
Party members vs. SQT members ratio	68.8:1	5.3:1	4.4:1	4.1:1	—	3.5:1	3.1:1	2.5:1	2.3:1	2.8:1

Sources: Statistics for GMD Party Members in 1938–1939: Zhongguo Guomindang dangyuan shinian lai de fazhan qushi [Ten-year developmental trend of China's Guomindang Party members]; Statistics for GMD Party Members in 1940: Zhongyang zuzhibu tongjishi (zhi) [Central Organization Department Statistics], Zhongguo Guomindang diwujie diqi zhong quanhui hou dangbu zuzhi ji dangyuan tongji tiyao [Fifth plenum of the Seventh Central Executive Committee Party Organization and party members statistical abstract of the Guomindang]; Statistics for GMD Party Members in 1941: Zhongguo Guomindang dashidian [Collection of Guomindang's major events], 591; Statistics for GMD Party Members in 1945: Diliujie zhongyang zhixing weiyuanhui dierci quanti huiyi zhongyang zuzhibu dangwu tongji baogao [Report from the Sixth Plenum of the Third Central Executive Committee of the Guomindang]; Data for 1943–1944 are determined by the number of recruitments in 1945 and the number added in previous years. Statistics for GMD Party Members in 1946: Diliujie zhongyang zhixing weiyuanhui disanci quanti huiyi zhongyang zuzhibu dangwu tongji baogao [Report from the Sixth Plenum of the Third Central Executive Committee of the Guomindang]; Statistics for GMD Party Members in 1947 are difficult to determine because the Party and SQT had been combined; Statistics for SQT members (1938–1946): Sanmin zhuyi qingniantuan dierjie zhongyang ganshihui gongzuo baogao [Second Plenum of the Central Executive Committee of the Three Principles of the People Work Report], 89–90. All sources cited in Wang Liangqing, *A Study of the Relationship between the San-min Chu-I Youth Corps and the Kuomintang 1938–1949* (Taipei: Kuomintang History Library No. 4, Historical Commission, Central Committee of the Kuomintang, Modern China Publishers, 1998), 116–117.

no matter where they go, they always mention international issues and do not speak about nationalism. We can easily ask them, "Are you Chinese?" The Communist party tried to allure young people to be spies in underground conspiracies against the GMD. All these kind of actions are neither fair nor just. For those who were deceived, we can ask them, "Do you feel disgraced?" . . . In terms of recruiting new members, we need to be cautious in order to avoid opposite results. We rather have few good people than many bad people. The SQT members who teach at schools should follow the New Life Movement in routine activities. We need to be positive, serious, clean, and disciplined so ordinary teachers will respect us and ordinary students will be influenced by our spiritual mood and be willing to accept our leadership. We should not compete with the Communists based on numbers. Especially on how to serve society, we must be the frontrunners and take responsibilities . . . We need to be different from the Communists so others will follow us.[125]

Chiang even accused Communists of being unpatriotic because "they were preoccupied with international affairs," namely those of the Soviet Union, instead of focusing their attention on China. In addition, he continually repeated that SQT members should cultivate their own character in order to influence others to change. Thus, he urged teachers who belonged to the SQT to carry out "New Life Movement" practices in school to influence other teachers and students to follow the GMD. This referred to a movement that emerged from a February 19, 1934, speech at Nanchang, in which Chiang had called for a "movement to achieve a new life" for China. The New Life Movement's program of moral reform was based on traditional Chinese virtues and on similar Christian values, such as frugality and simplicity. Its purpose was to curb the spread of Communism by revitalizing the spirit of the Chinese people, thus enabling China to achieve true national unity. Although in 1934 the movement made some progress towards achieving its aims, it lost momentum thereafter.[126] Still, Chiang saw the New Life Movement as a model for building and maintaining SQT membership.

After Zhu Jiahua took over as head of the Central Organization Department in December 1939, the GMD quickened its expansion into schools. Zhu differed from most of the other party bureaucrats in that he had exceptionally strong ties with the education system.[127] He taught at Peking University, served as president of Sun Yat-sen University and Central University, held the position as minister of education twice from 1932 to 1933 and 1944 to 1948, and later headed Academia Sinica from 1940 to 1957. Zhu was particularly keen on expanding party influence further into the schools, and by the end of 1941 the Central Organization

54   Chapter 2

Department boasted thirteen area party branches (*qudangbu*) and 434 area sub-branches (*qufenbu*) in schools, claiming a total active membership of 12,417.[128]

Therefore, both the party and SQT expanded their respective organizations rapidly during the initial years of the war. In their simultaneous efforts, they became enmeshed in a fierce competition for the same pool of potential recruits. Along with this rivalry, the loose talk about the SQT replacing the GMD and the ongoing CC Clique and Whampoa Clique factional struggle all contributed to a growing, bitter relationship between the party and the corps. This crisis eventually forced the SQT to focus its energy almost exclusively on the student community.

Measures to lessen the conflict between the party and SQT, and turn the corps' focus on students, emerged in July 1939 at the fourth plenum of the Preparatory Youth Corps Central Executive Committee. The first step came in the form of an amendment to the SQT's constitution: the original age limit of eighteen to thirty-eight years was changed to sixteen to twenty-five years old. The official draft history of the SQT stated plainly that this was aimed at "making the ages of Youth Corps members more compatible with entry requirements of the GMD, and thus defining more clearly the relations between the SQT and party."[129] However, following the SQT's establishment, entry requirements for the GMD no longer included any regulations: there had never even been any maximum age limits in the party's history. With regard to minimum age requirements, the amended GMD constitution in March 1929 permitted those above the age of twenty years to join as full members after one year of probationary training. These minimum age limits and the probationary system were abolished altogether following the formation of the SQT in 1938.[130] The real significance of this constitutional amendment lay in changing the maximum age limit from thirty-eight to twenty-five years and its intended effects on improving relations between the SQT and the party.

To provide two examples of the different ages and occupations of SQT members, Figure 2.1 shows the front covers of two SQT membership cards, while Figure 2.2 exhibits the inside. Liu Tianshen (membership card on the left in Figure 2.1 and top in Figure 2.2) was a sixteen-year-old high school student when he joined the SQT on January 1, 1940. By the time the membership card was issued to him on June 30, 1947, he was a Xiamen University student. Liu Yumin (membership card on the right in Figure 2.1 and bottom in Figure 2.2) was a twenty-nine-year-old Nationalist Army soldier fighting in the Sino-Japanese War when he joined the SQT on June 10, 1938, in Wuchang. The card was issued to him on September 1, 1947, when he was a thirty-eight-year-old Nationalist Army general fighting in the civil war. It is interesting to note that both cards were issued in 1947, the year the SQT was dismantled on September 12. Thus, the inside grids of both cards, intended to document regular membership fees and payments, are blank.

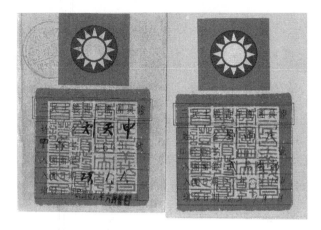

Figure 2.1. The front covers of Liu Tianshen (left) and Liu Yumin's (right) SQT membership cards. When they joined the organization, Liu Tianshen was a sixteen-year-old high school student in 1940 and Liu Yumin a twenty-nine-year-old Nationalist Army soldier in 1938. (Author's collection)

Figure 2.2. The inside of the cards featured a photo of the participant. The grids were to catalog monthly fees and biannual payments. These cards were issued in 1947 shortly before the SQT dismantled, so they are blank. (Author's collection)

56   Chapter 2

It is significant that the Socialist Youth League (SYL) of China set age limits on its members as well. The May 1924 Central Executive Committee abolished the joint SYL and CCP sessions, instructing CCP cells to take over their functions. Until the meeting, the SYL and CCP were not clearly separated. However, a May 1924 resolution separated the two, setting twenty-five years as the maximum age limit for SYL members. It also stated that the SYL's task was to create a youth movement among workers, peasants, and students.[131] At the Third National Congress in January 1925, the SYL was renamed the Communist Youth League (CYL). In a May 14, 1925, announcement regarding exchanging members, the CYL's Central Bureau indicated that CYL members should be introduced to the CCP when they turn twenty-five years old. Those who were under twenty-five years and already CCP members were to simultaneously become CYL members.[132]

The rivalry between the SQT and the GMD was most intense in their competition for new recruits. Taking advantage of when the upper age limit was thirty-eight years, the SQT recruited aggressively from the civil service as well as the military, police, and political training academies—all the usual grounds for party recruitment. However, the new maximum age limit of twenty-five years was closer to the common definition of "youth," reducing the area of overlapping recruitment and lessening the degree of rivalry. In return, the party reciprocated by agreeing not to recruit members unless they were over twenty-five years old.

In November 1940, three other related developments revealed that the SQT headquarters had decisively reoriented itself towards the student population. First, the Central Executive Committee issued a program of activities for the corps, covering topics including organization, training, propaganda, and social services. Under organization, the program called for a recruitment emphasis on "youths at schools."[133] The second development was the Standing Committee's passing of a set of combined instructions on the promotion of SQT activities in upper middle schools and institutions of higher education on November 21, 1940.[134] These instructions systematically laid out the order of establishing subunits or branches in schools and the proper lines of authority governing them. Finally, four days later the Standing Committee of the GMD Central Executive Committee passed a new set of guidelines aimed at resolving the conflict between the party and its youth wing. Three out of the seven points in the guidelines called for a warmer relationship between the two, and the document asked the SQT to submit itself to the party's leadership and requested the party's assistance in the corps' development. According to the guidelines, the SQT was supposed to concern itself primarily with education and focus its activities on students, leaving politics and general society (including working youth) to the party.[135]

Three People's Principles 57

This almost exclusive emphasis on students represented a turning point in the SQT's short history, and the organization's recruitment of students became systematic and widespread after 1940. The tension between the party and the corps was responsible for forcing the SQT to shift its attention to students, while the ruling that the SQT should concern itself primarily with education—leaving politics to the party—also signaled that the corps was not to serve as a channel for student political activism even after its recruitment reorientation.

The GMD instead decided that the SQT would operate as a wartime instrument to constrain student political involvement. The corps' role in depoliticizing students began with limiting student representation in leadership positions and the range of activities provided for student members. At the highest level, where officials formulated policies and supervised operations, students were virtually unrepresented. Young members under the age of thirty had little voice in either the SQT Central Executive Committee or the Central Supervising Committees, while at the national level only 8 percent of the representatives to the First National Congress of the corps held in March 1943 were students.[136] At the lower level of SQT branches in upper middle schools and universities, student cadres held positions (no more than 5.26 percent), revealing how excluded youth were from deciding their own activities, even within local chapters.[137] This rejection of student leadership at every level demonstrated how GMD leaders intended the corps to play more of an educational role rather than serve as a channel for student consciousness.

SQT Activities

Such an emphasis was also reflected in the range of activities provided for SQT members, for most centered on the theme of political education. At group meetings, student members read and discussed compulsory works, mostly on GMD ideology and policy. The SQT instructed schools affiliated with the corps' branches to set up "Chiang Kai-shek libraries" (*zhongzhengshi*) as part of the propaganda effort, designed to encourage students (especially SQT members) to study Sun Yat-sen's teachings and Chiang Kai-shek's speeches in greater depth. The range of publications stored in such mini-libraries was limited to works of this nature.[138] The SQT also encouraged essay and oratorical contests, but topics were usually limited to Sun and Chiang's teachings, government policies on resistance and reconstruction, and defense science.[139] Similarly, on Taiwan, the future China Youth Corps also held oratorical contests on Sun Yat-sen's Three People's Principles in the 1950s. The SQT also permitted youth drama groups and choirs, but

58   Chapter 2

prohibited scripts and songs that were "ideologically incorrect" or threatened to endanger morals and manners.[140]

In addition, SQT activities included summer and winter camps. Chiang Kai-shek first suggested youth camps in a personal order dated May 30, 1939.[141] The SQT organized two camps that year, with a total of eight hundred students, and within three years there were seven camps hosting 5,408 students. By 1943, 7,072 students visited twelve camps.[142] At camp students participated in five main kinds of activities: "spiritual training" (*jingshen xunlian*), technical skills, medical and rural services, recreation, and military tasks.[143] Of these, the bulk of the program was allotted to "spiritual training," which included a heavy dose of political lectures and small-group discussions.[144] The "Record of Training Events at the 1942 Guan County Summer Youth Training Camp of the Three People's Principles Youth Corps" declared that the youth camps' objective was "to cultivate disciplined life," "increase political understanding," "improve physical and mental health," and "stimulate an attitude of good service."[145] According to the SQT's own published history, these camps were well designed to "complement the effectiveness of formal education" by changing "the romantic life of university and secondary school students" and "correcting their confused thinking."[146] Figure 2.3 is Liu Tianshen's certificate showing his completion of five weeks of training at an SQT summer camp in August 1943. It identifies him as a twenty-year-old student. The certificate also lists Chiang Kai-shek as the director and Zhang Zhizhong as the secretary-general. In Figure 2.4, a large group of girls is seen attending the first Three People's Principles Youth Corps summer camp on August 1, 1939; while Figure 2.5 show a large group of boys marching at the 1941 SQT summer camp in Chongqing.

Although the common perception of the SQT was that of a dysfunctional and divided organization, Kristin Mulready-Stone argues that the Shanghai branch was an exception because it was deeply dedicated to the GMD cause and effectively resisted the Japanese from August 1939 through December 1941. It strove to function as much as possible as a normal branch, setting up chapters in schools in the International Settlement and providing detailed intelligence to the wartime capital of Chongqing on the activities of collaborators and Communists. Following orders, its members and cadres traveled across war zones to attend training sessions and meetings in Chongqing while daily risking their lives by remaining loyal to the GMD in occupied Shanghai. Mulready-Stone maintains that the Shanghai branch's "vibrancy contradicts the conventional wisdom on the SQT as a petulant, factionalized and counter-productive organization which served, in Lloyd Eastman's words, as one of the seeds of the GMD's destruction."[147] In Shanghai, without the GMD trying to control their every move, the SQT branch was proactive and successful while the organization was a burden to the GMD elsewhere in the country. Mulready-Stone insists that it was not having close contact with Chongqing that was so advantageous to the Shanghai branch, freeing them to work in the service of national aims in forms that excited them like "underground propaganda and intelligence work, struggling not only against the Japanese, but also their fellow countrymen who had betrayed the motherland through collaboration."[148] However, after the war ended and the GMD could exert its control over a branch like the one in Shanghai, the central government smothered its enthusiasm and turned it into just another largely ineffective SQT branch. The Shanghai branch illustrates how it was largely the GMD's obsessive need to micromanage and control that ultimately doomed the SQT.

The most controversial and political SQT activity was the student members' surveillance and suppression of Communist and other anti-GMD suspects in schools.[149] SQT student cadres monitored Communist and dissident influences

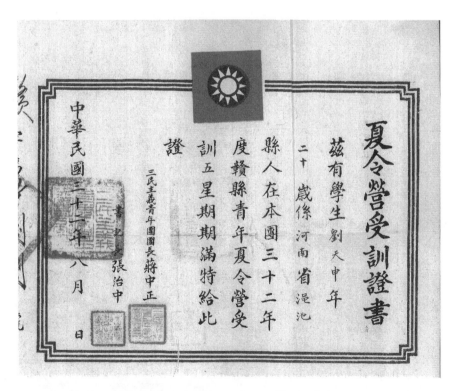

Figure 2.3. Liu Tianshen's certificate for the completion of five weeks' training at an SQT summer camp in August 1943. He is listed as a twenty-year-old student. (Author's collection)

Figure 2.4. Girls attending the first Three People's Principles Youth Corps summer camp on August 1, 1939, after Chiang Kai-shek suggested youth camps in a personal order dated May 30, 1939. Courtesy of the Central News Agency (Taiwan).

Figure 2.5. Three People's Principles Youth Corps summer camp participants parade in Chongqing on July 30, 1941. The original caption noted that Chiang Kai-shek observed the marchers. Courtesy of the Central News Agency (Taiwan).

Three People's Principles   61

in schools throughout the war. However, at the same time the GMD leadership tried to dampen the SQT's political operations. Chiang Kai-shek explicitly opposed the growth of such spying activities and spoke out against them repeatedly. At a dinner party hosted for the SQT plenary meeting on July 19, 1939, he emphasized, "We should not even ask corps members to perform surveillance and investigative tasks . . . As for special tasks such as investigation, if there is a need for them, we would train a [separate] group of people to handle this."[150] Four years later, on April 15, 1943, Chiang reacted to reports of increased political strife in schools by issuing a special order on the "future direction of the student movement." He criticized SQT leaders and cadres for engaging in "unnecessary conflicts" and insisted that the "management of reactionaries" should be the responsibility of school principals and party branches, with the corps merely assisting. "Henceforth," Chiang instructed, "our corps should neither indulge in sporadic fights nor duplicate the work of party branches." To "replace the past manner of contest [against the CCP] by force, surveillance, and spying," Chiang ordered the SQT to focus on two main activities: (1) improving the welfare of students through the promotion of labor services and cooperatives, as well as through physical health and self-governing activities, and (2) preparing students for future roles in the reconstruction of China, such as engineers and pilots.[151] Consequently, the discouragement of political activities badly affected the morale of many SQT branches in schools, ultimately leading to an identity crisis where most members became confused about the purpose and nature of their mission.[152] Despite corps leaders' early detection, this crisis was never satisfactorily resolved during the SQT's lifespan.[153] A 1945 official publication reviewing the SQT's performance over the previous seven years honestly confessed:

> What is the nature of the corps? What is its position? Hitherto these [issues] remained unconfirmed and unclear . . . Regarding the nature of the corps, some people consider the corps as a social organization and hence believe it ought to have social services as its central activities. Some others deem the corps to be an educational organization and hence believe it ought to have the training of youth as its sole function. There are others who think that the corps is a political organization and therefore advocate participation in political activities. There are even those who regard the corps as a spy organization and hence adopt the attitude of "keeping a respectful distance."[154]

Although the problem remained unresolved as late as 1945, many GMD institutions and leaders explained to SQT members and the general public that the corps'

62   Chapter 2

political content ought to be limited and emphasized its educational role. For example, the MOE was clear that its endorsement of the organization's expansion into upper middle schools and institutions of higher education was "to improve the atmosphere in schools," a term frequently used by GMD authorities to describe the restraint of political restlessness in schools, and to properly guide students in their "thought, conduct, studies, as well as physical and mental health."[155] In the ministry's view, the SQT was the national youth organization most suitable for the task of moral education in schools.[156]

The Merger

In 1945, amidst the closing stages of the war with Japan and as part of the GMD effort to implement major constitutional changes in China, Chiang Kai-shek again reviewed the SQT's functions and studied the party's organization plan.[157] According to the generalissimo's diaries, he contemplated "immediately merging the SQT with the party and establishing the SQT under all levels of the party: central, provincial, and county."[158] One of the factors was the need to resolve the persistent rivalry between the SQT, dominated by the Whampoa Clique, and the party, controlled by the CC Clique. The agreement reached by late 1940 pushed the SQT to concentrate on student recruitment and turn its direction towards socioeducational activities. While the number of students increased significantly to constitute the core of the organization's membership, they were by no means the only members. Even by 1945, more than half of the SQT members were not students.[159] Indeed, the SQT did not always abide by the age limits agreed upon in 1940. Both the organization and the party continued to breach each other's domain to poach members.[160]

There were even reports of murders between SQT members and party cadres. For instance, in mid-1947 both the SQT and party created branches in the western region of Hunan province, an area notorious for its lawlessness.[161] After the arrival of the SQT and party, organized crime increased in the region. On May 7, 1947, violence broke out between the two rivals.[162] On January 28, 1948, party members killed a county magistrate, Huang Yingchuan, in Dayong, western Hunan. Huang had sided with the SQT. For three days, both sides fired shots at each other.[163]

Another situation that involved SQT and party violence occurred on Taiwan in 1947. During the 2-28 Incident, party members accused some SQT members of being left-wing insurgents.[164] Chiang sent an army division to the island on March 8, 1947. The soldiers killed many SQT leaders and members charged with having leftist leanings. Since the party and SQT were already locked in a bitter struggle, the youth organization sided with the insurgents against the provincial government in Taiwan. GMD officials also took advantage of the 2-28 Incident to crush the SQT on the island. In a cable to Chiang Kai-shek on March 29, the director of the Central Investigation Bureau, Zhang Zhen, accused Taiwan's former SQT regional director Li Youbang of being a Communist and a covert 2-28 conspirator.[165] According to Zhang, the SQT, which had branches operating in Kaohsiung and Taipei, led this insurgency. Zhang sent Li Youbang to Nanjing to be tried; Li was acquitted, but the trial ruined his political and military career.[166] This fierce, sometimes violent, rivalry between the SQT and GMD party in western Hunan and Taiwan particularly alarmed Chiang Kai-shek, and by 1945 virtually every provincial GMD headquarters and local SQT branch were in conflict with one another. Chiang ultimately decided to dissolve the SQT and merge it with the party in 1947.[167]

At the Sixth Plenum of the Third Central Executive Committee, Peng Guojun and seven people, mostly CC Clique members, proposed two solutions: first, dissolve the SQT, convert all its members into party members, establish a youth department in the party, and form youth groups in every province and city. The second solution was to completely separate the SQT from the party.[168] Zhang Jiong, the party leader of the Hunan branch, also suggested that the SQT merge with the party or become subordinate to the party.[169]

Apart from the need for unity, financial limitations constituted another major reason for the SQT–GMD merger. While party spending, especially on the military, contributed to the severe problem of runaway inflation, it was at the same time a victim of the vicious cycle of rising prices and diminishing monetary value. In 1945, the GMD's move towards constitutionalism compounded the problem of inadequate funding for party activities. It forced the GMD to make a clearer distinction between its party organs and government agencies.[170] The state treasury refused to finance expenditures for party affairs and thus called for the GMD to reduce its party organization expenses and become self-financed. As part of the cutback, the GMD leadership considered it necessary for the SQT to merge with the party because the national education budget included the corps.[171]

On May 14, 1947, Chen Cheng, Chen Lifu, Sun Ke, Dai Jitao, and seven other senior GMD officials met with Chiang Kai-shek to suggest that the SQT should amalgamate with the party.[172] On June 8, Chiang met with Ching-kuo to discuss the SQT.[173] Ching-kuo contributed a report with suggestions on how to reform the SQT, which the elder Chiang noted in his diaries as "very good" and "detailed."[174] At this point, Ching-kuo was his father's most trusted aide.[175]

Three months before the merger, Chiang Kai-shek wrote that "the root of the revolutionary crisis lay in the GMD's corruption and people's distrust."[176] He

64   Chapter 2

lamented how "the party officers were corrupt and had lost [the people's] trust, and were undisciplined [*fuhua yu shixin sanman*]."[177] Moreover, he deemed the SQT "ineffective [*shixiao*]" and considered a thorough reform.[178] On June 27, he summoned Chen Lifu, head of the GMD Central Organization Department, and Chen Cheng, secretary-general of the SQT, and decided that the SQT should merge with the party. Chen Cheng agreed, and the following day he gathered his high-ranking officers and told them that the two entities would combine.[179] The following night, he invited the Central Executive Committee members to dinner and instructed them with key points on how to change the SQT and the party.[180] On June 30, Chiang ordered the SQT to be integrated into the party. However, the civil war delayed the merger.[181]

The merger finally took place on September 12 when a motion was carried at the fourth plenary session of the Sixth Congress of the Central Executive Committee.[182] Chiang expressed how pleased he was with the smooth passing of the bill. It boosted his confidence that nation-building would be successful because it was accomplished "for our party, our SQT, our officers, and our country to save our party and ourselves. It is not for my own gain in status but all for the interest of revolution, sacrifice, and spirit."[183] Chiang continued the lofty praise of the swift passing of the bill by stating that it "comforts the souls of the President [*zongli*] and the martyrs in heaven" (referring to the late President Sun Yat-sen).[184] The Chen brothers and other factions were pleased with the merger. The SQT's separate executive committee was eliminated and its status as a supposedly independent organization ended.

Rather than seeing the SQT's disbandment as a moment of failure—recognizing how the organization's founding had been compromised from the start—Chiang instead had high expectations for the merger. Urging his followers not to dwell on the potentially divisive issue of "personnel allocation" and instead to focus on "formulating concrete revolutionary plans," he hoped that the merger would turn out to be an act of political revolution and not merely a technical or routine restructuring.[185] Unfortunately, his wish was not fulfilled. By the time documents finalizing the merger were drafted in September 1947, two major CCP forces had already breached GMD defense lines and crossed the Yellow River.[186]

Later, after the defeat and exile of the GMD from the mainland, Chiang remained adamant in 1950 that the Nationalists' demise was not because the CCP was strong, but rather because his own party suffered from disintegration in organization, breakdown in discipline, and collapse in morale.[187] He specifically lamented that the September 1947 merger between the SQT and the party had turned out to be a merely superficial, technical reorganization. Although the merger brought an end to the SQT's existence as a formally autonomous organization, Chiang called it an "absolute failure" because intraparty factional rivalry continued unabated and became hopelessly irreversible.[188]

With the merger, SQT leaders as well as the rank and file merely transferred their membership over to the party without any changes in duties and policies. Leaders at the levels of corps headquarters and branches were simply absorbed into the enlarged executive and supervisory committees at the respective levels of the party, keeping essentially their original duty of overlooking youth affairs because most were placed with a newly created "Central Youth Department" at the party headquarters and freshly established "youth movement committees" at the provincial, county, city, and local branch levels.[189] Party leaders did not issue any new instructions on student political activism and the newly formed youth department carried on activities very much as before. Prior to the merger, the SQT served as an instrument to depoliticize students; now the party's Central Youth Department and its youth movement committees took over this role.

SQT Suppression of Student Protests during the Civil War (1945–1949)

There was not a single major student protest during the eight years of war against Japan (1937–1945). However, this was not a sign of the success of GMD student policy but a reflection of the circumstances created by the war.[190] The decision to fight Japan was an enormously popular one among the public, including most young people. It was a unifying force in China and offered the GMD relief from student demonstrations that had occurred before the war began.[191] The wartime removal of students from renowned educational institutions in comfortable coastal cities to makeshift, inland campuses also contributed to diminishing activism. Although this period was a relatively quiet time for student activism, it prepared many to become anti-civil war protesters during the late 1940s. When the GMD decided to wage war against the Chinese Communists immediately following the eight-year Sino-Japanese War, student activism quickly erupted across the country.[192]

Right as the Japanese surrendered and just before student protests exploded across China, Minister of Education Zhu Jiahua (1944–1948) wrote to Chiang Kaishek insisting that the existing student self-governing associations' (SSGAs) regulations were adequate. Zhu had faith that the regulations prevented students from interfering with school administrators and participating in off-campus organizations or activities.[193] However, wave after wave of anti-GMD student movements soon dispelled this belief. Despite the vehemence of these protests, the GMD never considered abandoning the SSGA regulations, and decided instead

66   Chapter 2

to tighten them even more. In December 1947, Zhu's Ministry of Education unveiled a modified set of SSGA regulations that imposed a greater degree of control.[194] The spirit of these new rules remained the same as those issued in January 1930; once again, the main goal was to ensure that SSGAs concentrated on channeling student energy towards the promotion of scholarly accomplishments, not active political participation.[195] As in the 1930 version, the 1947 regulations included explicit clauses confining student organizations' activities to individual schools, prohibiting them from forging interschool connections and participating in outside activities.[196] The most notable difference between these 1947 and 1930 regulations was the addition of numerous clauses that allowed school authorities overwhelming direct control over the SSGAs.[197] The GMD appointed school teachers to sit in and supervise all SSGA meetings and other activities to ensure that they operated within the defined parameters. Unfortunately for the GMD, its use of the SQT to promote its policies in schools and to attempt to exert control over SSGAs actually turned many of the country's young intellectuals against the party.

During the civil war, the GMD subscribed to the misconceived notion that campuses would automatically quiet down if they could root out Communist agitators among the students. It refused to acknowledge the legitimacy of the protesters' opposition to the civil war by deeming their activism an underground Communist plot. Unfortunately, this misconception and suppression led the public to blame the GMD rather than the Communists for the civil war.[198]

Chiang Kai-shek's personal writings throughout the civil war revealed his frustration with the waves of student protests and his desire to "clean up Communists in schools."[199] GMD authorities planted informants and secret agents in schools where students were most active.[200] Besides these, Suzanne Pepper notes that pro-GMD students, including SQT members, also were charged with "organiz[ing] and lead[ing] student activities as loyal Nationalist supporters."[201] However, she writes that "it was common knowledge that the brightest and more energetic student leaders in the country's best schools were all critical of the government and its war policy."[202] From 1947 to 1949, A. Doak Barnett traveled in China as a Fellow of the Institute of Current World Affairs and correspondent of the *Chicago Daily News* foreign service. When Barnett attended a March 1948 luncheon with a group of professors from several leading Beijing universities, they agreed that "the most brilliant students are Leftist, and they are the most popular ones also."[203]

That popularity frequently translated into large-scale gatherings and public events. On the evening of November 25, 1945, six thousand students in Kunming, Yunnan province—which had a large concentration of schools during the war—

attempted to hold a forum on Lianda campus to protest the civil war.[204] GMD troops and policemen disrupted the meeting by firing guns over the heads of demonstrators, throwing hand grenades, and cutting off the microphone. Infuriated, Lianda's SSGA, which was an underground Communist organization run by the Communist Party's Labor Committee in Yunnan (Zhonggong Yunnan sheng gongwei), organized over thirty thousand students from thirty-one universities, high schools, and technical institutes to boycott classes from November 26 to November 28.[205] During the strike, the SSGA called for all workers, farmers, businessmen, and students to unite against the civil war and "fight for peace, democracy, and unity." It implored the GMD to abolish its ban prohibiting the freedom of speech and assembly. Students put up posters and bills with slogans against the civil war on the walls of Lianda, Yunnan University, and other colleges. They sent an appeal to students all over China, asking for support. On December 1, Zhou Shen, the SQT secretary of Yunnan province and chief of propaganda, along with over a hundred GMD military officers went to the campuses, beating students with wooden sticks and destroying their posters.[206] GMD authorities tossed hand grenades and fired into student crowds, wounding many and killing three students and one teacher. The victims were Pan Yen and Li Lulian of Teacher's College, seventeen-year-old Zhang Huachang of Kunhua Industrial Institute, and Yu Zai, a music teacher from Nanjing Middle School.[207]

In yet another incident, on February 22, 1946, seven thousand university and high school SQT members in Chongqing participated in an anti-Soviet, anti-Communist protest demanding that the Soviet Union withdraw from Manchuria. When the students marched on Minsheng Road, they destroyed the offices of *Xinhua News,* the official Communist newspaper. The SQT purposely chose February 23 to launch the Shanghai Student Protect the Country's Sovereignty Movement. When the Shanghai Consulate General held a reception in honor of the twenty-eighth anniversary of the Russian Red Army's establishment, around 1,500 SQT students surrounded the Consulate General and chanted "Immediately withdraw the Manchurian Red Army, protect Manchuria's sovereignty! Down with any treacherous parties! Down with the Soviet Union!" and "Down with Stalin!"[208]

According to Huang, a variety of law enforcement personnel drawn from the police and the army (including members of the military police and the demobilized youth army) assisted the pro-GMD students, who produced posters and publications depicting the party in a glowing light and denigrating the CCP and its Marxist policies.[209] A favorite topic of their propaganda attack was the CCP's land confiscation program in rural China.[210] In his study of student protests in Shanghai, Jeffrey Wasserstrom reveals how SQT members on the city's campuses

68   Chapter 2

"stag[ed] loyalist rallies, disrupt[ed] radical gatherings, organiz[ed] anti-radical student associations, [and ran] for election to school councils . . . to protect [Chiang Kai-shek's] prestige and gain converts to their cause."[211]

Meanwhile, Pepper notes that GMD "decision makers remained constricted by their belief that if only the very few 'real' Communist agitators among the students could be eliminated, their movement could be controlled."[212] Yet Chen Lifu explained the difficulty of rooting out actual Communists: "The problem is to uncover and deal with real Communists without making mistakes about people who are not . . . It is a great problem in student groups."[213] Leaders of the student activists, particularly SSGA officials, were "the chief targets of beatings, arrests, and abduction by an assortment of law enforcement personnel." Informants tipped off law enforcers who drew up "blacklists of activists and suspected underground Communists." At times, "these students, if not caught off campus, might be apprehended in night raids on school dormitories." They would often be tortured, executed, or they simply "disappeared."[214]

The involvement of some GMD students with law enforcement agencies in anti-Communist repression sometimes caused more harm than good. They succeeded in eliminating some actual Communist agitators, but certainly not all. Student anti-war protests continued, and the harsh methods employed to subdue the protests further alienated many students and fostered wider resentment.[215] The government's attempts to restrain protests only intensified students' opposition to the GMD and their refusal to support the war against the CCP. The student protests began as a movement to demand a peaceful solution to the GMD–CCP conflict, but they developed into one that challenged GMD authority. As Pepper notes, since the GMD government was China's legitimate ruler at the time, the general public believed that it "alone had the power to reform itself and end the war."[216] Thus, anti-war protesters blamed the GMD more than the CCP for the responsibility of the war, directing their efforts against it in hopes of compelling it to act.

Ultimately, the GMD regime failed to win support from both intellectuals and students. The Communists had gained significant ground in military battle, occupied territory before Chiang Kai-shek's army struck back, and had moved swiftly among the peasants. At the same time, the CCP infiltrated universities and colleges, particularly in Beijing. There, cadres and individuals encouraged students to oppose the policies of the GMD government, and as early as 1946 student protests began to merge with the dissent and disgust that intellectuals directed towards GMD rule. According to Jessie Lutz, "[The] student movement of 1945 to 1949 contributed to the acceptance of the Chinese Communists as the only alternative to the Nationalists. The students moved from specific protests addressed to the [Guomindang] as legitimate authority to confrontation politics de-

Three People's Principles   69

signed to embarrass and destroy the regime."[217] In this way, the Communists were much more successful in wooing large numbers to their cause, thus effectively counteracting GMD efforts to capture youth allegiance to the Nationalist government. In response, GMD leaders vowed never again to make the same mistake on Taiwan.

Chiang Ching-kuo's Political Career on the Mainland: Dean of the SQT's Cadre Training School in Gannan and the Central Cadre School in Chongqing

The SQT was not only central to shaping the GMD and Nationalist youth during the late 1930s and 1940s, it also became important to the developing relationship between Chiang Kai-shek and his son, Chiang Ching-kuo, who would use his management of student organizations to win his father's respect and, ultimately, achieve leadership of the party on Taiwan. In the spring of 1938, the elder Chiang appointed twenty-eight-year-old Ching-kuo deputy director of the Provincial Peace Preservation Corps in Nanchang, largely at the suggestion of Xiong Shihui, governor of Jiangxi.[218] When the SQT was launched in July 1938, Ching-kuo became a member of its central committee and director of its Jiangxi branch.[219] However, Ching-kuo's principal responsibility in Jiangxi was the government position that Xiong had created especially for him. The governor also opened a political training institute in Nanchang and reassigned Ching-kuo as commander of military education and deputy director of the Education and Training Department, as well as to the position of director of training for new draftees in the Peace Preservation command. In this new position, Ching-kuo soon found himself approving the execution of a deserter, the first time he had taken responsibility for a person's death.[220] Later, as head of the secret police (1950–1965) in Taiwan he would order thousands of people to prison and execution.

The elder Chiang strategically sent his son to Gannan, the southern region of Jiangxi province, because it had been Mao Zedong's Soviet base (1931–1934). Determined to eliminate the Communists, the generalissimo had them surrounded by October 1934, prompting the Long March from Jiangxi in the southeast to Shaanxi in China's northwest. As Jay Taylor notes, in order to administer his territory and carry out his reforms in Gannan, Ching-kuo "needed trustworthy subordinates, specifically a corps of incorruptible inspectors to assure that the local officials [implemented] his programs."[221] He felt the best way to obtain such followers was to open his own cadre school. The elder Chiang agreed, and in March 1939 he appointed Ching-kuo director of the Cadre Training School of the SQT's Gannan branch to train local party cadres.[222] The Central Military Academy

70   Chapter 2

selected seventy-two of the one thousand graduates of the political training classes of that year to attend the school that Ching-kuo opened in Chizhuling, a mountainous village.[223] Another seventy-two students enrolled in the school through an examination. Ching-kuo regularly spoke at the site, where some classes met in caves. Occasionally, he even slept in the barracks with the students, rising at dawn and leading them in their oaths of allegiance to the Republic of China (ROC) and his father.

In late May 1939, Ching-kuo received a telegram from his father ordering him to come to the wartime capital of Chongqing.[224] During this trip, Ching-kuo formally became a GMD party member.[225] At this time, he was frustrated with the SQT's failure to become a dynamic force capable of mobilizing youth. With his experience as the director of the cadre school in Gannan, he believed that the key to the success of the SQT was to develop a large group of honest and dedicated young cadres. In 1943 Ching-kuo attended the First National Conference of the SQT in Chongqing, where he proposed that the corps expand its Youth Cadre Training Class (Sanqingtuan de qingnian ganbu xunlianban) into a large Youth Cadre School in Chongqing that would produce thousands of youth leaders. Since his father approved the idea, the conference endorsed it. In 1944 Chiang Kai-shek summoned Ching-kuo back from Jiangxi and appointed him to be the school's dean of education (*jiaoyu zhang*), with the elder Chiang himself serving as president.[226] With this appointment, Ching-kuo immediately went from regional to national leader. The Youth Cadre Training Class grew to become the Central Cadre School (Zhongyang ganxiao, CCS).[227] The SQT had played a crucial role in elevating Ching-kuo's status in the GMD, and his involvement with youth organizations would continue to shape both his standing with his father, as well as his popularity and acceptance within the party.

On May 5, 1943, the CCS formally opened its doors, with 256 students in its first class training to be future teachers.[228] Local SQT chapters recommended 297 students to receive one-year training in Chongqing.[229] The CCS was a one-year cadet training ground, somewhat resembling Sun Yat-sen University, a Comintern school in Moscow that trained Chinese revolutionaries from both the GMD and Communist parties.[230] In 1925, Ching-kuo had traveled to Moscow on his own and spent five years studying communism at the university; although Chiang Kai-shek initially opposed his son's plan, he later agreed.[231] At the time, the GMD and the CCP were allied in the First United Front in preparation for the Northern Expedition. Chiang needed Soviet support—according to Taylor, "sending his son to Moscow served his political and professional interests and was quite consistent with his ideological bent at that time."[232] Sun Yat-sen University educated students on the basic theories of Marxism and Leninism. It also taught them methods of mobilization and propaganda, as well as theoretical and practical military instruction. In all, Ching-kuo spent twelve years in the Soviet Union before he returned to China with his Belarusian wife, Faina, or Fang-liang.

As dean of the CCS, Ching-kuo was responsible for building a curriculum from scratch. He determined that the courses would focus on intensive study of Sun Yat-sen and Chiang Kai-shek's thoughts.[233] Concerned with the fate of the country, the CCS tried to implement Sun's Three People's Principles doctrine as its guiding educational philosophy, cultivating revolutionary spirit and skills. Ching-kuo also invited prominent professors from Central University to give lectures on philosophy, history, mathematics, English, and Chinese classics.[234] He introduced the disciplinary style that he had experienced in Russia.[235] Ching-kuo also tried to combine Leninist revolutionary methods and Neo-Confucian traditional ethics to cultivate a group of followers loyal to his father and committed to GMD ideology, encouraging each student to adopt a good attitude and social skills, and not to practice nepotism or favoritism towards friends and family when choosing future leaders.[236] The latter teaching was particularly ironic, considering Ching-kuo himself had secured each of his appointments through his own father. CCS students later became Ching-kuo's loyalists, his most powerful supporters for the remainder of his subsequent political career. As head of the school, he had the chance to recruit followers to form his own personal group for the first time.[237] Many alumni, including Lee Huan, who later served as director of the China Youth Corps (1973–1977) and premier of Taiwan (1989–1990), stayed loyal to Ching-kuo even after they graduated from the CCS.[238] Another faithful alumnus, Pan Zhenqiu, later held the position of Taiwan's commissioner of Provincial Department of Education (jiaoyu tingzhang) (1964–1972), as well as director of the China Youth Corps (February 13, 1979, to March 16, 1987).[239] Throughout his life, Ching-kuo recruited many to work for him, yet CCS graduates remained his most trusted followers.[240]

Unfortunately, Ching-kuo did not have the opportunity to conduct the Central Cadre School training program for a second year. When the Japanese surrendered in 1945, his father dispatched him to the Soviet Union to negotiate a new Sino-Russian Treaty with Stalin and regain control of Manchuria.[241] Stalin demanded that the Nationalists force the immediate pullout of all US soldiers from China before he was willing to seek a Soviet deal in Manchuria.[242] According to Taylor, when Ching-kuo reported this proposal to his father, the generalissimo "was not about to swap still generous American assistance for vague promises from Stalin."[243]

It is thus important to understand the two subsequent youth organizations that Ching-kuo directed on Taiwan—the Anti-Communist and Anti-Russia League of the Chinese Youth and the China Youth Corps—and the role they played in his ascendancy to political power on the island. In particular, the CYC has survived much longer, and was more successful, than both the short-lived League and the SQT. Unlike its predecessors, the rise of the CYC also marked a dramatic new relationship between Nationalist youth organizations and the GMD, for the CYC completely focused on becoming a traditional "youth" organization. By 1945, the SQT still drew more than half its members from other sectors of society, even after the push to concentrate on student recruitment in 1940. The CYC would prove to be a watershed in the relationship between Nationalist politics and Chinese youth, drawing its largest support from students, devoting itself to providing recreational, service, and social activities for teenagers, and benefiting from the higher percentage of young people attending secondary school in 1950s Taiwan, compared to the mainland. While the SQT was enmeshed in an intense rivalry with the party throughout the late 1930s and 1940s, the CYC would become a cheerleader for its parent party, mobilizing mass support for the regime in times of crisis, inculcating political loyalty in a new generation of Chinese students, and ushering Ching-kuo's rise to power.

CHAPTER THREE

The China Youth Corps in Taiwan, 1952–1960

This patriotic youth organization was established in accordance with the glorious public declaration by our president of a "great anti-Communist patriotic youth union," under the guidance of the loftiest precepts of the Three Principles of the People. The Youth Corps will make great efforts to strengthen faith in revolution, increase revolutionary knowledge, master military skills, and train strong young physiques. Its purposes are to overthrow Soviet imperialism and thoroughly eliminate the bandit gang of Zhu De and Mao Zedong; to strive for our country's independence, freedom, and national survival, and development; and to establish a wealthy, strong, healthy, and joyful new China under the Three Principles of the People.

—*Excerpt from the China Youth Corps' Statement of Purpose, 1952*

The Three People's Principles Youth Corps ultimately failed because of its rivalry with the GMD party. However, when the regime retreated to Taiwan in December 1949 it had an opportunity to rectify its past mistakes. According to political scientist Monte Bullard, as party leaders began to consolidate their rule on the island in 1950, they knew that Taiwanese youth would play a critical role. "After all," wrote Bullard, "many . . . had been among the students of the May Fourth Movement, the Northern Expedition, and the student movements of the 1930s."[1]

Since the GMD recognized how much the Communists had emphasized their Youth League on the mainland, it was quick to recruit students in youth organizations. For over twenty-nine years, the GMD struggled with the Communists for the allegiance of young people, a battle it ultimately lost.[2] The Communist Youth League, originally called the Socialist Youth League, was founded in October 1920, even before the Chinese Communist Party formed in July 1921. By April 1949, the Youth League had a membership of two hundred thousand—a large number, but relatively small for a country of China's size.[3] Neither party was

73

74   Chapter 3

particularly successful in recruiting youth during the 1930s and 1940s, but the CCP still maintained a clear advantage over the GMD. By the end of 1950, Youth League membership had grown "to 3 million" then "to 9 million in 1953, 20 million in 1956, [and] 25 million in 1959."[4]

On Taiwan, the GMD established the China Youth Anti-Communist Save (Our) Country Corps, also known as the China Youth Anti-Communist National Salvation Corps (Zhongguo qingnian fangong jiuguotuan) in 1952 to combat the Communists and indoctrinate Taiwan's youth through extracurricular education and training. Most citizens referred to it simply as "Save (Our) Country Corps" (Jiuguotuan) or China Youth Corps in English.[5] In the US, the *New York Times* announced that the CYC succeeded the Three People's Principles Youth Corps (SQT).[6] In addition to the CYC, the GMD also founded a short-lived predecessor in 1950—the Anti-Communist and Anti-Russia League of the Chinese Youth, or "the League" (Zhongguo qingnian fangong kang-e lianhehui).

Several scholars have touched on both groups as part of larger projects, yet it is especially important to analyze them together because the CYC successfully wooed Taiwan's youth in its formative years by avoiding the mistakes of the League and antecedents such as the SQT on the mainland. In addition, an examination of the organization's leadership and political implications reveals how the CYC played a major role in helping the ascendancy of Chiang Kai-shek's son, Ching-kuo, in the GMD government. The organization's growth gave crucial political power to Ching-kuo during an important period in which he struggled for national leadership, before he eventually gained total control of the GMD regime on Taiwan. Finally, in addition to government sources and political speeches, evidence ranging from underground publications and personal interviews, to popular CYC pamphlets and music, all reveal several other important points: how students themselves utilized the CYC for their own purposes; the organization's impact on gender and teen culture in Taiwan's conservative postwar society; CYC attempts to instill a sense of unity and "Chineseness" on an ethnically diverse island; the organization's role in helping a generation of young people explore Taiwan's geography and recognize its natural beauty; and, finally, how 1950s GMD critics, opponents of the two Chiangs, and prodemocracy activists all recognized the centrality of the CYC in shaping the island's future.

The League (1950–1952)

Scholars have addressed the China Youth Corps in English and Chinese, yet very few English-language works have paid attention to its direct predecessor, the Anti-Communist and Anti-Russia League of the Chinese Youth. In particular, historian Li Tai-han and political scientist Wu Nai-teh have written on the subject.[7] It is important to examine the League, which was the first youth organization formed on Taiwan after the GMD retreated to the island in 1949, because it gives insight on the subsequent establishment of the CYC. On April 9, 1950, a meeting was held in Sun Yat-sen Hall (Zhongshan tang) in Taipei to prepare the establishment of the League—among the attendants were officials from National Taiwan University, Taiwan Teachers College (later renamed National Taiwan Normal University), National Chengchi University, and Taipei Industrial College.[8] Two days later, the new organization invited several important figures to serve as guiding members, including Chiang Ching-kuo and Fu Sinian. Fu was one of the leaders of the May 4th Movement. As a heralded educator and linguist, he was serving as president of National Taiwan University at the time.[9]

The League officially formed on April 27, 1950. Initially, college students (most from the mainland and recent National Taiwan University alumni) constituted the majority of the organization's workforce; specifically, National Taiwan University students and graduates were the largest group of staff members. The youth delegates first convened on October 31, 1950, Chiang Kai-shek's birthday. During the opening ceremony, Chiang himself was present, proclaiming that the new organization's task was more important than the goals of other youth groups in the past. Afterwards, he met and shook hands with each young delegate. Chiang's actions at the League's founding communicated to students the value he placed on the new organization.[10]

The League also adopted a slogan to uplift young people's spirits: "If China is ancient Greece, then Taiwan is Sparta. If China is Germany, then Taiwan is Prussia."[11] With allusions to classical Greece's most militarized state, the slogan clearly demonstrated the League's emphasis on the military. By referencing Prussia, the core kingdom of the German empire and the key to political unification in Germany, it also highlighted Taiwan's importance to political reunification with the mainland under the Republic of China (ROC). Furthermore, 1950s students on Taiwan held popular notions that Prussians were authoritarian, militaristic, and extremely orderly—stereotypes characterized by their army's unswerving obedience. It was, of course, slightly ironic that the League voluntarily compared Taiwan to Prussia in the immediate aftermath of World War II. Rather than play down such overt militarism, the League's slogans indicated that the GMD government was unafraid to embrace the image of an authoritarian German regime during the martial law period (1949–1987).[12]

Financial support for the League came from the General Political Warfare Department (GPWD, Zhengzhi ganbu xunlian ban) of the Ministry of National Defense (MND, Guofangbu), which Chiang Ching-kuo directed, and Taiwan

76   Chapter 3

Provincial Government's Department of Education (Jiaoyuting).[13] According to Li Tai-han, in late July 1951, the League sent 2,500 youth representatives to military camps operated by the army, navy, and air force.[14] By summer 1952, the numbers had increased to 4,650 youth in 155 teams.[15] At the army camps, League members sang, performed plays, delivered anti-Communist lectures and current news reports, and read books and newspapers to illiterate soldiers.[16] For example, in September 1952 a team of thirty-seven students from Taichung First Provincial High School, accompanied by a leader and two reporters, stayed at an army camp in the central city of Nantou for twenty-one days.[17] According to an army newsletter, county officials and local military officers welcomed the League team—it was a special occasion that drew much attention and fanfare in the region. The League emphasized military volunteerism and encouraged civilian youth to interact with soldiers, which ultimately became a hallmark of the CYC in the later 1950s.

In addition to mobilizing students to serve among soldiers, the League also organized teams of young men to guard restaurants and movie theaters in Taipei, constantly advising passers-by not to indulge in luxuries. If League members spotted women riding in vehicles to the market or children sent to school in cars, they would reprimand them for overindulging and wasting fuel. Most could not afford to own private cars during this period, therefore high-ranking officials borrowed vehicles from the government.[18] Some League students even recorded the license plate numbers of vehicles they considered to be "whirling around" too much, condemning the drivers in public and publishing the plate numbers in local newspapers.[19] In some ways, these actions echoed the tactics of youth groups that persuaded people to boycott foreign goods in China during the 1920s and 1930s, when supporters stamped "traitor" on the clothes of Chinese caught riding Japanese ships.[20] As Karl Gerth notes, Chinese boycotters harassed merchants who sold foreign products by "picketing stores, confiscating goods, sending intimidating anonymous letters and postcards, disrupting distribution channels, pasting posters on storefronts, and forcing shopkeepers to place advertisements in local newspapers in which they vowed not to sell imports."[21] By the 1950s, young people on Taiwan were conducting similar campaigns to reduce conspicuous consumption as a way to foster nationalism.

Chiang Ching-kuo's Rise to Power through Youth Organizations

The League and China Youth Corps played important roles in Chiang Ching-kuo's political ascendancy. According to Wu, the League was a powerful tool for Ching-kuo, who otherwise held little power before the GMD retreat to Taiwan in 1949.[22]

His leadership of the League foreshadowed how he would later use the CYC to advance his political ambitions. Compared with Chiang Kai-shek's colleagues, who had served longer in the GMD party and fought various battles alongside the elder Chiang, Ching-kuo's status in the regime was relatively low. During the Nanjing decade (1927–1937), when other ambitious party members were gaining political experience and building their networks, Ching-kuo was living in the Soviet Union (1925–1937). His relationship to his father was sufficiently complicated that he could not count on Chiang's full support. While in Russia, Ching-kuo even denounced his father as an "enemy" and "counter-revolutionary" after Chiang's bloody April 1927 purge of Communists in Shanghai.[23]

Wu argues that "the most important political dimension of the CYC in the political arena may be the role it played in [Chiang Ching-kuo's] struggle for national leadership."[24] He maintains that the CYC is inextricably tied to the story of how Ching-kuo defeated other competitors for national leadership and gained control of the regime. While the GMD was still on the mainland in 1940, Chiang Kai-shek appointed Ching-kuo as director of the Cadre Training School at the Three People's Principles Youth Corps' branch in Gannan, the southern region of Jiangxi province, which had been a Communist stronghold. Four years later, the generalissimo assigned his son the greater task of directing the SQT's Central Cadre School in the wartime capital of Chongqing: this new position allowed him a leadership role on a national scale, whereas his previous duty was confined to the regional level. From the ranks of Central Cadre School graduates he personally trained, Ching-kuo recruited his "most trusted" and loyal followers.[25]

Meanwhile, outside of the military the China Youth Corps was the only source of power in Ching-kuo's hands, and he subsequently used the group's success to continue his own political career. In 1950, Chiang appointed Ching-kuo director of the General Political Warfare Department of the Ministry of National Defense, intentionally setting up the position for his son to bolster his military power. Wu asserts that the CYC was placed under the GPWD, "even though its function had nothing to do with national defense," yet the move was certainly more coordinated.[26] According to Bullard, Ching-kuo designated the GPWD as the agency responsible for the political socialization of youth because the military was "one of the most disciplined organizations at the time" and "had the experience and knowledge to integrate youth activities into the national defense effort." The army also had "the necessary equipment (trucks, weapons, first-aid equipment, etc.) and physical facilities (camping areas)" to accommodate thousands of potential youth participants in summer and winter camps.[27] As head of the GPWD, Ching-kuo was charged with a secret police corps aimed at strengthening counterintelligence,

78   Chapter 3

purging Communist influence in the military, and exerting more GMD influence within the armed forces.[28] Placing the CYC under the auspices of the MND was therefore a useful tool in this process.[29]

When Ching-kuo directed the League, he specifically targeted youth. The League established regional branches all across the island, trying to woo local political elites into Ching-kuo's support base.[30] At its zenith, it was active in fifteen geographic locations—besides the main island of Taiwan, the organization also created branches on the smaller islands of Penghu, Jinmen, and Mazu.[31] The League was even active in the Dachen Islands, an archipelago located off the coast of Zhejiang province, where GMD and Communist forces continued fighting in the mid-1950s (including the Battle of Dachen Archipelago in January and February 1955). After the Communists took the islands, 14,500 civilians evacuated to Taiwan.

Despite the League's establishment throughout Taiwan and its offshore islands, several factors hindered its overall ability to mobilize young people. It was ineffective in garnering legal or governmental status and obtaining financial aid from the state. More importantly, according to Wu "it also lacked an ideology to mobilize and organize the students and the young."[32] He goes on to note that it was only a few years after the February 28 Incident, and tensions between the GMD regime and the Taiwanese were still high—especially among the educated. Secondary school students needed stronger incentives to enroll in GMD-sponsored organizations.

The Founding of the China Youth Corps

When the GMD established the CYC two years later, the atmosphere was less tense between the government and students. According to a 1963 CYC publication celebrating its tenth anniversary, the League automatically merged with the CYC when the latter was formed on October 29, 1952.[33] Unlike the League, the CYC acquired official status, allowing it to gain financial support from the government and "penetrate every school, college, and university" on the island. Recruitment subsequently became far easier. Another distinguishing feature of the CYC, as opposed to the League and earlier youth organizations on the mainland, was its emphasis on leisure activities. According to Wu, recreation made "the ideological indoctrination (patriotism and leader worship)" more appealing to the youth.[34] In addition, the CYC also incorporated cadres of the League directly into its organization, such as Lee Huan and Zhang Yusheng—both longtime followers of Ching-kuo appointed to be high-ranking officials in the CYC.[35] After Ching-kuo served as the CYC's first director for twenty-one years (1952–1973), Lee subsequently held the post (1973–1977) and later served as the premier of Taiwan (1989–1990).[36]

Throughout the 1950s, the China Youth Corps played a central role in the political socialization of many young Taiwanese. On March 29, 1952, Chiang Kai-shek first issued a directive to establish the new organization, one that he hoped would unite the country's youth better than the League and would stimulate support for the Nationalist government. According to the CYC's published history:

> On Youth Day, March 29, 1952, the late President Chiang Kai-shek . . . delivered a summons to establish an institution called the China Youth Corps, and encourage all the Chinese youth to continue the glorious tradition bequeathed by the young patriots who fought in the Northern Expedition and the victorious War of Resistance against Japan. Under the banner of anti-communism and restoration of national order, the Chinese youth, at home and abroad, gave immediate response. On May 31 the same year, the Executive Yuan of the Republic of China ratified the organizing principles of the China Youth Corps. On October 31, 1952, the China Youth Corps was officially founded in Taipei.[37]

Chiang Kai-shek wore a military uniform and delivered his speech at the Three Armed Forces Basketball Arena (Sanjunqiuchang) in Taipei.[38] Figure 3.1 shows CYC members gathered at the arena on October 31, 1956, to celebrate Chiang's birthday and the fourth anniversary of the CYC's establishment. On the same day, Figure 3.2 depicts youth representatives standing in front of the Presidential Palace. Figure 3.3 displays how on March 29, 1958, which is Youth Day, a female youth representative spoke at the arena where Chiang Kai-shek also delivered a fifteen-minute speech. According to Bullard, the importance of the China Youth Corps was reflected in the fact that Chiang took a personal interest in it and recommended its establishment with an address on China Youth Day, which commemorated the 1911 martyrdom of seventy-two young people in Huanghuagang, Guangdong province, during the revolution against the Qing dynasty.[39]

The generalissimo also emphasized the CYC's importance by establishing the organization on his birthday, October 31, 1952, as he had with the League's opening ceremony in 1950. Vice President Chen Cheng hosted the event, which was held in the Sun Yat-sen Hall (Zhongshan tang) in Taipei. Within the large hall, an ROC flag hung above a portrait of Sun Yat-sen on the wall, with six CYC flags on each side of the stage.[40] Along with Chen Cheng, Chiang also delivered a speech at the inauguration ceremony. "On the mainland, millions of young men and women are still locked in darkness behind an iron curtain," he began. "Our country has five

Figure 3.1. On October 31, 1956, China Youth Corps members gathered at the Three Armed Forces Basketball Arena in Taipei to celebrate Chiang Kai-shek's birthday and the fourth anniversary of the establishment of the China Youth Corps. Courtesy of the Central News Agency (Taiwan).

thousand years of cultural history and now we are suffering unprecedented disaster."[41] Chiang's mention of the "iron curtain" fit with the Cold War rhetoric. The term, popularized by Winston Churchill in a 1946 speech, is understood to describe the political boundary dividing Europe between the areas under control of the Soviet Union and its satellite states, and the North Atlantic Treaty Organization members or nominally neutral countries from the end of World War II until 1990. In 1952, Chiang borrowed it as a metaphor for the strict separation between Communist China and "free" China (Taiwan). The iron curtain was the symbol of the division between Communist China and Taiwan's competing ideologies and systems. Chiang went on to exhort the island's youth and encourage students to see themselves as central players in an important historical moment. "My young brethren of free China, using all of your efforts voluntarily and spontaneously to fit the revolution's demands, answer the country's call," he implored. "Let us have another revolution to revive the military, accept the unity of the leadership, channel a strong organization, and utilize our biggest strength to join in the work of the anticommunist, anti-soviet war. It really causes me to feel unparalleled gratification."[42] Chiang called on the CYC youth to join the revolution against the Communists.

Figure 3.2. Taiwan's 27,674 youth representatives stood in front of the Presidential Palace in Taipei on October 31, 1956, to celebrate Chiang Kai-shek's birthday and the fourth anniversary of the establishment of the China Youth Corps. During the occasion, the youth proclaimed that they would "protect the nation." Courtesy of the Central News Agency (Taiwan).

In addition to his personal appearance at the CYC's inauguration, Chiang also appointed his son to be the organization's first director. Both men were interested in publicizing themselves with youth and appearing at subsequent CYC events.[43] This was especially true of Ching-kuo, who was photographed with young people in many CYC publications. One image featured a smiling Ching-kuo being hoisted over the shoulders of boys belonging to a mountain-climbing group.[44] In another, he appeared chatting with a young cyclist participating in a long-distance bicycling tour during the 1953 CYC summer camp.[45] A third photograph depicted Ching-kuo with a group of youth at a CYC oath-swearing ceremony on January 5, 1953, at Taipei's Three Armed Forces Basketball Arena.[46] These photos were part of the GMD propaganda and party-controlled news. Ching-kuo and his father presented very different personas in their interactions with youth. The younger

Figure 3.3. On March 29, 1958, a female youth representative spoke on Youth Day with the China Youth Corps flag displayed behind her at the Three Armed Forces Basketball Arena in Taipei. Chiang Kai-shek delivered a fifteen-minute speech at the same occasion. Courtesy of the Central News Agency (Taiwan).

Chiang was casual and down-to-earth, while Chiang Kai-shek continued his formal and stern observations of students during his routine visits to high schools on Taiwan, consistent with his public style and countenance during the war years on the mainland.

Once the GMD established the China Youth Corps on Taiwan, the party clearly articulated the group's mission to the island's newly organized ROC government, which soon embraced the organization. The GMD and the CYC planned to channel Taiwanese youth towards constructive goals before any anti-government student organizations or movements could coalesce, and before dissenters could organize any strikes. According to American educator Thomas Brindley, who had studied the organization, "the early CYC on Taiwan was conceived not as an enlarged formalized structure to imitate a student movement of its own but to incorporate a wider approach to youth concerns and take on many more activities for youth than just political ones."[47] Compared to the party's past youth organizations, such as the Three People's Principles Youth Corps, the CYC took a broader approach to student concerns and focused more on youth activities beyond the realm of politics. This goal was a huge departure from the GMD's policy towards the SQT. Whereas less than half of the SQT's members were actually young people, the CYC from the start ensured that its members were between the ages of fifteen and thirty years old. Thus, it was far more successful because it addressed youth's interests from its inception, while the SQT neglected students' needs partly because the majority of its members were older.

The China Youth Corps' Mission

One of the reasons why Chiang Kai-shek established the China Youth Corps was to prevent student protest movements from forming against the government. His purpose was to utilize the organization as a channel to inculcate political loyalty in youth and ensure their support of him.[48] In this way (and similar to Ching-kuo's use of the Anti-Communist and Anti-Russia League of the Chinese Youth), Chiang Kai-shek also relied on the CYC to implement his political and ideological agendas.[49] Within the context of PRC threats, the government encouraged the island's youth to demonstrate patriotism and loyalty, and joining the CYC was an important way for students to do just that. Through the CYC, secondary school students were showing their allegiance both to Chiang Kai-shek and to the GMD government.

A memorial plaque located in the organization's headquarters in Taipei reflects this tense atmosphere during the early years of retrocession, and explains the CYC's formative mission:

> When the Central Government of the Republic of China moved to Taiwan in 1949, the Chinese youth, facing the precariousness of the nation's situation became unanimous in their conviction that only by dedicating themselves unrelentingly to the struggle against the Chinese Communists could they switch the nation's destiny to the course of peace, prosperity, and happiness. Therefore, the China Youth Corps intends to help youths with their intellectual and physical development. It offers programs of vocational training, community service, and wartime service for the youths, and cultivates their sense of comradeship for the final victory over the Chinese Communists and the restoration of national order ... In sum, the mission of the China Youth Corps is "to unite patriotic ... youths for the accomplishment of national renewal."[50]

As the CYC's first director in 1952, Chiang Ching-kuo expanded on the organization's raison d'être. He believed that the country needed to be protected by the strength of young people. According to one CYC publication, *Lüqi piaoyang*

84   Chapter 3

sanshinian (The green flag waves for thirty years), Ching-kuo urged the youth to use their military skills to fight the Chinese Communists and Soviet Russians because it was their duty to battle mainland youth who had succumbed to the lies of Communist "bandits," recover China, and rebuild national identity.[51] Thus, recreational activities offered during summer camp—such as target practice, horseback riding, paragliding, and sailing—were not solely for fun but also important ways to acquire military skills.

Newspapers reported that to qualify for CYC membership, youth had to abide by "belief in Sun Yat-sen's Three People's Principles, determined opposition against the Chinese Communists and the Soviet Union, and willingness to undergo youth corps training."[52] During the 1950s, the *New York Times* reported that the CYC's objectives also included "the strengthening of revolutionary conviction, the emulation of combat skills and the strengthening of physique to eliminate the Chu–Mao clique and strive for independence and freedom."[53] ("Chu–Mao clique" referred to Zhu De, commander-in-chief of the Communist People's Liberation Army, and Communist leader Mao Zedong.) In its formative years, the CYC's key purpose was to mobilize a strong army of youth to counterattack this Communist threat and regain the mainland under GMD control.

The China Youth Corps' Organization and CYC-Sponsored Youth Campaigns

Initially, all youth socialization programs, extracurricular activities, and military training were managed by the CYC—and each of these in turn was administered by the General Political Warfare Department under the Ministry of National Defense.[54] Beginning on August 1, 1952, the CYC was headquartered in a borrowed building it shared with the Political Warfare Staff College in Fuhsingkang.[55] (The GPWD was the predecessor to today's Fuhsingkang College (Zhengzhi zhanzheng xuexiao), which was founded on January 6, 1952, when Chiang Kai-shek presided over a formal ceremony inaugurating the school.[56]) Since Ching-kuo had experience working with the SQT on the mainland, and since he served as director general of the GPWD from 1950 to 1954, he entrusted both the military and the GPWD with the mission of politically socializing youth, designating the GPWD as the responsible agency.[57] From 1952 to 1960, the MND provided the budget for the CYC and military training programs in schools, with the GPWD actively managing most of the money.[58] In 1960, the budget and responsibility for military training in schools were transferred to the Ministry of Education (probably because the government's fear of Communist China's imminent attacks on the island gradually subsided).[59] However, it was not until September 26, 1977, that the MOE assumed all salaries. Before that, and from the beginning of the organization, individual schools paid the military instructors. Since some private schools could not afford to, the CYC lent them money.[60]

Despite having Ching-kuo as its director, the CYC's operations still depended largely on the support of Chiang Kai-shek. According to Wu, the elder Chiang had to legitimize the organization's formation, which he ultimately did. Yet even with his backing the CYC's first budget in its preparatory stage was a meager ten thousand Taiwan dollars (about $250 USD).[61] Chiang Ching-kuo had asked Provincial Governor (*sheng zhuxi*) Wu Guozhen for a larger sum, but his request was rejected, and Wu emerged as an outspoken opponent of the organization after he resigned in 1953.[62] However, the CYC was able to obtain more funds for its second budget—one hundred thousand Taiwan dollars ($2,500 USD).[63] Still, although the group started out with little manpower and funds, it managed to develop into a large organization under Ching-kuo's deft leadership.[64] According to Wu Naiteh, "Although Chiang [Ching-kuo] had not yet appeared to be the unquestionable would-be leader, his family background must have induced many people to give the organization a helping hand."[65] Wu goes on to note that Ching-kuo persuaded local governments to provide branches of the CYC with financial support for facilities such as community youth centers, youth hostels, and student dormitories.[66] The CYC also asked other government agencies, besides the Ministry of National Defense headed by Ching-kuo, to sponsor and finance programs.[67] As director of the General Political Warfare Department, Ching-kuo was able to work seamlessly with the military, especially when it came to organizing summer and winter camps. Fu Zheng, a contemporary CYC critic, later charged that by 1956 the organization's annual budget was three hundred million New Taiwan dollars. But the specifics for the huge budget (where the money came from and what it was spent on) remained highly confidential.[68] From its humble financial beginnings in 1952, the CYC grew to provide scholarships to thousands of Taiwanese students within a decade and continues to do so today. According to Bullard, "being a Youth Corps member meant a young person could travel and stay at official hostels for almost no cost. The only price that had to be paid, over time, was to accept the political socialization efforts of the system."[69]

From the late 1940s into the 1960s, at least two major contenders vied to succeed Chiang Kai-shek as leader of Nationalist China—Chiang Ching-kuo and Chen Cheng. The latter was a longtime trusted associate of the generalissimo. In 1924, he met the elder Chiang for the first time at Whampoa Military Academy. Consequently, he joined the National Revolutionary Army and fought alongside

86   Chapter 3

Chiang in the Northern Expedition (1926–1928), the Second Sino-Japanese War, and the civil war against the Communists. In 1949, Chiang appointed Chen as governor of Taiwan with plans for the island to become one of the GMD's strongholds. After the GMD retreated to Taiwan, Chen went on to hold key civilian government positions such as vice-executive of the GMD, vice president, and premier of the ROC. In the regime's early years on Taiwan, Chen was second only to Chiang Kai-shek, and the generalissimo's followers identified him as the most likely successor.

Meanwhile, Chiang Ching-kuo's status in the regime was relatively low compared to his father's colleagues, including men like Chen Cheng. They had been members of the GMD party for far longer than he had, and they had fought various battles right alongside his father. The only power Ching-kuo wielded in the 1950s was his role as head of the secret police, leader of the General Political Warfare Department in the Ministry of National Defense, head of the Anti-Communist and Anti-Russia League of the Chinese Youth (the League), and, eventually his position as director of the nascent China Youth Corps. Chiang Kai-shek appointed his son director for all four units, and Ching-kuo, who placed emphasis on politics and ideology, often came into direct conflict with Chen, who favored military power. Along with other issues, both leaders disagreed over education and management of the military.[70] Ultimately, on December 15, 1963, in the face of a substantial buildup of political power on the part of Ching-kuo, Chen resigned the premiership of the government and died of liver cancer two years later.[71]

When the party established the CYC, its main goal was to rally young students in the "fight" against communism, inculcating patriotism in their hearts, minds, and actions. Some of its early slogans, which emphasized the importance of military training and sacrifice for the country, were "One Must Endure Self-Imposed Hardships in Order to Succeed" and "When You Study in School, Do Not Forget to Save Your Country."[72] In the 1950s, Chiang Kai-shek and other GMD leaders still held out hope for returning to the mainland and reestablishing their regime. They viewed the CYC as a critical organization to prepare youth for potential combat in wartime. Most of the activities involved military or self-defense skills that would provide a foundation in warfare, such as marksmanship or first aid. At the time, GMD leaders and the island's more paranoid residents believed that a Communist invasion was imminent.[73] Such fears were not unfounded. On March 1, 1950, the Communist commander-in-chief, General Zhu De, declared that eradication of the Chiang regime from Taiwan had become "the most pressing task of the entire country."[74] After the Chinese Civil War, the People's Liberation Army was poised to invade Taiwan and unify China with a far larger army than Chiang's Nationalist forces. Morale was low, and Chiang's smaller army was

China Youth Corps   87

also relatively undisciplined and disorganized. If an invasion were to occur, a swift People's Liberation Army victory would be almost assured.

Ironically, the threat of military invasion on the island was minimized with the outbreak of another armed conflict. Two days after the Democratic People's Republic of Korea Army crossed the thirty-eighth parallel on June 25, 1950, and engaged South Korean forces, US President Harry Truman ordered the US Seventh Fleet into the Taiwan Strait. Declaring that "the occupation of Formosa by Communist forces would be a direct threat to the security of the Pacific area and to United States forces performing their lawful and necessary functions in that area," Truman's decision was one of the first instances in which the ideology of containment became a reality on the ground.[75] It was a timely and auspicious relief for Chiang's struggling regime. Overnight, the arrival of US forces stifled any plans on the mainland for an overt military invasion of Taiwan.[76]

Nonetheless, the two sides remained in a heightened military state well into the 1960s, including direct night raids and clashes on neighboring islands. The Battle of Dachen Archipelago was part of the First Taiwan Straits Crisis (1954–1955), which forced the ROC to abandon the islands and prompted thousands of civilian refugees to evacuate. The Second Taiwan Straits Crisis, also known as the Jinmen-Mazu Crisis, occurred three years later in 1958, when the People's Republic of China shelled the small but important offshore-island outposts in an attempt to seize them from the GMD.[77] The Communist army had also attacked these islands in 1954–1955—a PRC takeover might have succeeded then if not for Chiang's order to heavily fortify both islands. These two key footholds were not only strategically important in detecting and trying to thwart a Communist invasion across the Strait but stood as symbols that Chiang's domain extended beyond Taiwan and Penghu. During these (and other) periodic crises with the PRC, the CYC sponsored youth campaigns to boost morale.[78] Mao Cheng-how, a CYC member in the 1950s, recalled that students entertained military personnel (*laojun*) on Jinmen Island by singing and performing folk dances and theatric plays, but he did not participate because of his "lack of interest and talent."[79]

Thus, throughout the 1950s both the ROC's education system and the CYC were key to mobilizing military campaigns. The CYC was constantly active in Taiwan's public lower and upper middle schools, implementing compulsory military training for upper middle school and college students.[80] On campuses, regular CYC ceremonies gathered all students into the schoolyard to instill GMD propaganda. Lectures to strengthen students' patriotism usually focused on five major themes: principles, leader, country, duty, and honor.[81] They emphasized the Three People's Principles as the guiding ideology for youth revolution. Furthermore, the CYC taught that if one supported the leader (Chiang Kai-shek), he or

88   Chapter 3

she also supported the GMD government.[82] In this way, the organization guaranteed the strengthening of the party's regime and its policies.

The CYC also tried to "mold" young people when school was out of session, especially with popular training activities held during the summers. Not only did students receive training, they also participated in public service activities within military units (*junzhong fuwu dui*) and in civilian rural communities (*nongcun fuwu dui*).[83] These CYC student activities among the troops echoed what the Anti-Communist and Anti-Russia League of the Chinese Youth had previously organized; "the students would teach basic literacy courses to the soldiers, help them write letters, comfort the troops in hospitals, and provide entertainment."[84] CYC students also aided rural farmers by actually working on the land and harvesting crops during the summer. One of the goals was to provide urban youth with farming experience, and thus build character through agrarian labor.[85] To participate in these service endeavors, young people registered their interests with the CYC, completed a physical examination, and were assigned to a specific activity. Selection criteria included students' talents or interests and the ability to speak Taiwanese (for those wanting to join rural service teams).[86]

One 1954 handbook, *How to Develop Rural Service Work* (*Zenyang zhankai nongcun fuwu gongzuo*), was printed in Taiwanese by CYC's publishing company, Young Lion. It was meant for CYC youth traveling to the countryside and contained a chart indicating that more high school teams participated than college teams.[87] It also included childhood stories about Chiang Kai-shek, obviously meant to promote his personality cult. A popular legend was a story about Chiang as a boy, in which he observes many fish swimming upstream in a river. The fish are pushed back by the current, but they ultimately succeed in swimming against the current, symbolizing Chiang's lifelong struggle against adversities and the way in which his work ethic allowed him to prevail.[88] According to the handbook, swimming upstream represented life's situations getting better and improving. Another story claimed that "when President Chiang was young, he and many young children played outside together, no matter whether they were older or younger than he was, he always wanted to be the leader of the children."[89] This account was meant to convey to students that Chiang was destined to be the leader of the ROC even as a child.

In 1895, when Chiang was eight years old, he read two of *The Four Books* (of Confucianism)—the *Great Learning* (*Daxue*) and the *Doctrine of the Mean* (*Zhongyong*)—the other two were the *Analects of Confucius* (*Lunyu*) and *Mencius* (*Mengzi*). The CYC pamphlet described how

his head hurt because it was difficult to study the *Great Learning* and the *Doctrine of the Mean* but he continued to read it because his teacher told him to. This occurred soon after Japan defeated China in the First Sino-Japanese War (1894–1895) and the signing of the Treaty of Shimonoseki, which gave Taiwan to Japan. The treaty infuriated people and some called for the end of the Qing dynasty. Zhang Zhidong's published *Exhortation to Study* (*Quan Xue Pian*) discussed why the Japanese defeated China and encouraged people to study and learn from Western civilization. The emperor ordered that Zhang Zhidong's work be disseminated throughout the country for people to read.[90]

How to Develop Rural Service built on Chiang's personality cult by claiming that "his mother bought a copy of *Exhortation to Study* and often read it to him." According to the pamphlet, "*Exhortation to Study* and the defeat in the First Sino-Japanese War led to Chiang's decision to become a soldier for his country."[91] CYC youth publications aimed to convince readers that Chiang was not only hardworking when he studied Confucianism but also very patriotic even as a young child.

While the ability to speak Taiwanese often determined whether a student would serve in rural areas, one's major in college or secondary school interests also suggested a particular activity. Some with artistic talent were assigned to the military service team, where they put on performances. Medical students were likely to take part in military medical service teams, while those with particular trade skills were sometimes sent to military factories for apprentice training.[92] Yet regardless of the differences between the activities students were assigned, virtually all of the programs centered on the military.

On middle school campuses throughout Taiwan, the military organized students into "big teams," similar to divisions, which were then broken into corps and units by county. All participants received "patriotic education," which consisted of four themes: the Three People's Principles, Anti-Communism and Resist Russia, *The Fate of China* (Chiang Kai-shek's 1937 book), and the five beliefs of principles, leader, country, duty, and honor.[93]

According to Taiwan's National Educational Materials Center's *Manual of Educational Statistics*, 70,549 young people attended summer training during the CYC's first nine years (1953–1962)—including 15,688 college students, 46,854 middle school students, 4,649 nonstudents, and 3,358 non-CYC members.[94] The "nonstudents" or "social youth" were mostly school teachers, the sector Wu identifies as sharing "the same pattern of consumption on leisure activities" as students.[95] These nonstudents enjoyed similar extracurricular activities as students. This group must have also included youth who did not enroll in formal education institutes. On the mainland, the SQT had recruited "social youth," defined as young people outside the school system.[96] Wu states that the CYC's recruitment

90   Chapter 3

of the nonstudent population was less successful than its efforts with students because nonstudents lacked "an organizational fabric such as the school" from which the corps could rally and enlist potential members.[97] If that is true, it probably indicates that teachers comprised the majority of the nonstudent group.

National Educational Materials Center statistics for the early years of the CYC also include a group categorized as "non-Youth Corps," indicating that some participants who were not CYC members were still allowed to attend. Unfortunately, more concrete information about the identities of these "non-Youth Corps" participants is unavailable. The figures also provide a stark look at the gender imbalance within these 1950s summer programs. For every year, males outnumbered females anywhere from 3:1 to 5:1.[98] It is possible that by 1970 some two hundred thousand youth had attended a CYC summer training activity and been exposed to its political content, considering that participation continued to increase after 1962.[99]

In June 1953 the CYC mobilized its members throughout the island to participate in preparatory drills during summer vacation in case of invasion from the mainland. To chronicle the activities, the organization's in-house press published an English-language leaflet entitled *China Youth Warriors March*. It indicated the CYC's desire to publicize its activities outside Taiwan and mobilize youth to cultivate foreign support for Taiwan as the "legitimate" China. Even Chiang Kai-shek himself tried to circulate his message to a broader audience in the West during the mid-1950s, securing the English-language publication of *Soviet Russia in China* in 1957. (Such attempts could just as easily backfire: "The 'Chinese Communists' are throughout referred to as if they were a race apart, a bogey people," lamented one Western review of Chiang's book.[100])

Whether in English or Chinese, CYC pamphlets were full of promotional photographs and celebratory descriptions of outgoing teenagers in Taiwan who enjoyed participating in fun camp activities. According to *China Youth Warriors March*, the CYC called on youth to "make use of the leisure period" during summer and engage in activities "in air, at sea, into the forest, and amid the frontlines that they might realize their book knowledge through actual life."[101] In 1953, student leaders at the major institutes of higher learning emphasized support for that summer's program throughout the country. When 25,339 youth registered within five days after enrollment was open, the CYC tried to accept the maximum applicants within its ability to accommodate. After "strict physical examination and intelligence tests," 8,625 of the applicants were admitted. Most (6,808) took part in the In-Camp-Service, which focused on military drill as well as medical, engineering, and agricultural services for two weeks.[102] Several college professors voluntarily participated with the students.[103] In-Camp-Service was divided into

230 groups, each consisting of thirty people: 194 high school student groups, four youth of society groups (or "social youth," referring to those not enrolled in school), and thirty-two college student groups. The other seven activities included scaling the 3,950-meter peak of Yushan and hoisting the national flag on the summit while singing patriotic songs, exploring the Central Mountains, sea warfaring, cycling, seaside swimming, gliding, and parachuting. Among these seven activities, nearly 90 percent of the participants were male (1,310) and 10 percent female (147).[104] In terms of education level, 86.3 percent were high school students (1,257), 4.7 percent were youth of society (69), and 9 percent were college students (131).[105] The majority of the participants were Taiwanese and the remaining youth were mainlanders. Unfortunately, the percentages provided in *China Youth Warriors March* do not add up to 100 percent. The leaflet notes that "participants consisted of 86.8% of Formosans (1,001 persons) and 32.2% of mainlanders (147 in number)," when the total number of participants for the seven activities was 1,457.[106]

The CYC leadership used the pamphlets to justify the summer camps in a number of ways, most importantly by insisting that students across the island were clamoring at the idea. The announcement of the inaugural 1953 summer camp was an "impressive youth activity and epoch-making call," proclaimed *China Youth Warriors March*. "When the plan for drill was proclaimed in the papers, it was, as if it were, like a ringing bugle sounded to the youth of China. Every young man and woman stirred in the mind, and every mind resounded with the call. It soon won the approval of the society and the support of the youth."[107]

While CYC publications lauded students for wholeheartedly accepting the summer programs, there were plenty of young people who were more apathetic, if not outright skeptical; yet even many of these eventually participated in camp activities during the decade. One student, Mao Cheng-how, never heard a "ringing bugle." Instead, he remembered how he and other upper middle school students were required to attend CYC activities. As a freshman at National Taiwan University in 1953–1954, Mao was chosen to participate in the CYC's first winter camp, held at Taipei's National Taiwan Normal School (Guoli Taiwan Shifan Daxue), an institution that trained teachers to work in elementary schools. Mao explained that normal school (*shifan xuexiao*) was "equivalent to a junior college" in the US.[108] "There was no specific location for CYC activities in the early years," Mao recalled. "We used that campus for that winter activity. We were gathered together for training. In each class you have, say, fifty students, so you separated into ten people per group. I was selected as a squad leader because I was tall. When we had military training, I was responsible for making certain that everyone was there. Just the leaders had to attend the camp for one week. At least a hundred people came from all colleges in Taiwan."[109] Mao surmised that only boys attended

92   Chapter 3

because they lived in the school dormitory (thus, it could not have been co-ed). They slept in large rooms without beds, similar to military training.[110]

During winter camp, Mao and other students attended classes such as the "Three People's Principles," "Anti-Communist," and "Anti-Soviet" sessions. There was even a course entitled "Youth Rules" (Qingnian shouze), which included memorizing the Twelve Maxims of the GMD Code.[111] These maxims were a set of guidelines for citizens to cultivate habits of virtue and responsibilities, and over a decade earlier Chiang Kai-shek had personally inserted them into the curriculum. In 1939, Chiang insisted at the Third National Educational Conference that "the twelve Party Maxims [were] maxims for Youth." The following year, on February 20, 1940, he telegraphed the maxims to principals at every university, middle school, and primary school in GMD-occupied China.[112] Over fifty years later, Mao could only remember one he memorized at CYC winter camp in 1953: "helping others is the foundation of happiness."[113]

Like many students in 1950s Taiwan, Mao attended camp because his school decided that he participate. "[I was] probably like the typical student, not interested," he recalled. "We were in the CYC because the government said we had to be there . . . I did not have a choice. If I said no, it was not good. Besides, it was a new and interesting thing so I thought, 'why not?'"[114] During winter camp, the CYC also filmed some participants. Throughout the 1950s, local movie theaters ran newsreel footage before feature films, and audiences sang the national anthem. For a period of time, CYC's winter camp film was included as part of the pre-film footage; on one occasion, Mao's friends even recognized him on the big screen and told him that he had been filmed at winter camp. Because it was compulsory, Mao participated in the CYC for one year in upper middle school and all four years in college.

In addition to indoctrination, camps, and outdoor activities, another important function of the China Youth Corps in the 1950s was the mobilization of political support from youth during times of national crisis. The CYC encouraged young people to demonstrate their support of the government and help build public morale.[115] In 1954, the Chinese Communists sunk a battleship in the Taiwan Strait. A week later, on November 15, the CYC established the "Committee for Building Battleship and Revenge by Chinese Youth."[116] According to Wu, the goal of the movement was to encourage the youth to enlist in the army. Within three months, about five million Taiwanese dollars were donated, along with a pair of golden earrings, two golden rings, eight watches, twenty-two fountain pens, and a radio.[117] The enlistment effort was even more successful—over twenty thousand students signed up to quit school and immediately join the army. However, only a little more than one thousand actually followed through with the commitment.[118]

Another national crisis used by the CYC to galvanize youth support was the PRC's attempt to take over the islands of Jinmen and Mazu in 1954 and 1958. Throughout the 1950s, the CYC organized youth groups to visit Jinmen and launch "psychological warfare balloons" to the mainland.[119] Jinmen is located no more than two kilometers from Xiamen, the nearest major city on the mainland's coast from Taiwan. The balloons held banners with the image of the ROC flag and written propaganda messages. The CYC also mobilized large-scale efforts across Taiwan, organizing youth parades, marches, and demonstrations at various assemblies. It employed "seat displays," in which students were seated before an assembly in elaborate arrangements, holding up large cards that spelled out messages or intricate designs.[120] According to Brindley:

> The CYC contacted school principals and CYC representatives in schools and county offices, who in turn put up notices and made plans to assemble the students and community youth and CYC volunteers at designated points. The military likewise alerted its soldiers and sailors. Government officials, KMT party members, factory officials and laborers, as well as the business groups, like the Rotary and Lions Clubs, and others in officially allowed organizations and clubs, all joined to participate in demonstrations and assemblies. Selected speakers, chosen or acknowledged by the KMT, were asked to speak at these public rallies.[121]

Besides the Building Battleship to Revenge Movement and Protecting Jinmen-Mazu Island Movement, the CYC sponsored other youth campaigns, including the Overcoming Difficulty Movement from 1950 to 1959, the Supporting Wuhan Students Anti-Communist Movement in 1956 (a confrontation between the students and the Communist regime in Wuhan), the Supporting Anti-Communism of Tibetan Patriots Movement from 1959 to 1960 (following a riot in Tibet), and the Youth Culture Movement in 1960.[122]

During the Overcoming Difficulty Movement, the government wanted to, in the words of Bullard, "psychologically . . . eradicate any feelings of dependence" within the populace.[123] In his 1953 publication *Ziyou Zhonggguo shijian kenan yundong* (Free China's practice of the Overcoming Difficulty Movement), Wu Manjun explained the origins of the movement. In 1950, army officer He Guozhu held a "How to Overcome Difficulty Meeting" with his soldiers.[124] He told them that "there are many difficulties right now but we cannot allow them to hold us back," and asked for solutions. For example, people faced the problem of getting bitten by mosquitoes while they slept. He Guozhu wanted to buy mosquito nets, but the army could not afford them. Therefore, the soldiers needed to solve the problem

94   Chapter 3

with their own capabilities. Wang Bisheng, a soldier of Army Company 4617, developed a method to prevent mosquitoes from biting him. He shared how he dried grass and burned it, using the smoke to drive away the mosquitoes. Wu described how Wang's "overcoming difficulty" story spread throughout the military and everyone was "encouraged" by his brilliant solution. The year was 1950 and the army had just arrived in Taiwan. At the time, people were psychologically defeated and dependent on the government for help, yet Chiang Kai-shek called upon residents to rely on themselves to fulfill national reconstruction and defeat the Communists. On October 1, 1950, the Ministry of National Defense started the Overcoming Difficulty Movement. However, Army Company 4617 could be credited for spreading the movement throughout the island.[125]

Wu Manjun also reported that another problem soldiers faced was harsh military life, since the government could not afford to provide them with a large budget. The military owned land on which the soldiers had to plant vegetables and take care of livestock to grow their own food.[126] Soldiers also had to make their own clothes and wash them. "They had to do everything themselves," he wrote. "They even built their own housing out of mud, bamboo, and straw."[127] In terms of transportation, they had to construct roads and cargo carriages out of bamboo. Wu even claimed that "when the soldiers practiced target shooting, they studied the target very carefully so they could get a good aim and not waste all the bullets."[128] They were very protective in maintaining their equipment. Of course, Wu's account may have been exaggerated for propaganda, but it did provide a glimpse of what soldiers achieved on their own as part of the Overcoming Difficulty Movement.

Supporting the government's aims, the CYC likewise encouraged people to work hard by finding creative ways to be frugal and save resources. Since scarcity was common throughout Taiwan, individuals who found imaginative ways to conserve were lauded as "overcoming difficulty heroes" (kenan yingxiong).[129] The government honored them and displayed their achievements island-wide as examples for society. However, the Overcoming Difficulty Movement never reached the level of intensity or influence of the mainland's Communist movements such as the Cultural Revolution (1966–1976).

In addition to national causes and patriotic events, Brindley writes that the GMD also called on the CYC "to foment . . . support [for its domestic] policies in line with the government and . . . Party or to show displeasure and censure of policies contrary to the ROC."[130] During parades and demonstrations, young people waved the CYC's symbolic green flags and placards in tandem with the red, white, and blue ROC flag. According to Chiang Ching-kuo, green symbolized young Chinese people's eternal youthfulness, representing the Chinese race's springtime—a time of growth and renewal. At a ceremony in Taipei on December 1, 1952, Ching-kuo commented on the flag's symbolism:

> The blue sky and white sun represent the people's soul, the three national principles, the Republic of China . . . The three red horizontal lines symbolize the revolutionary determination of fearing no pain, fearing no difficulty and fearing no sacrifice, red symbolizes youth's blood and passion, we need to give our lives to the motherland, which is worthy of adoration yet turbulent. Green symbolizes our Chinese youth's eternal youthfulness, Chinese youth is the Chinese race's springtime, never grows old, never feels discouraged, ever victorious.[131]

The term for "people" that Ching-kuo used was *minzu*, and in this case some have translated it as "ethnic." Yet, since he later referred to the nation by mentioning "the Republic of China," and since "ethnic" does not make sense in the context, the logical translation is "people" or "race." As for the ethnic composition of CYC participants, the organization included both mainland-born youth and Taiwanese students whose families had lived on the island before the 1945 retrocession (some for several generations). However, the GMD considered both mainlander and Taiwanese to be "Chinese," belonging to the Han ethnicity. The word that Ching-kuo used for "race" was also *minzu*.

CYC Ideology and Membership Guidelines

In part, the China Youth Corps also operated as an educational institution with a moral component, representing Chinese culture much like the ROC government did.[132] It taught youth that abiding by traditional Confucian values was the mark of being truly Chinese. In the 1950s, Confucian values and ideas of family unity dominated Taiwanese society. These social values were the underlying belief system for most GMD loyalists, especially the vague term "Chineseness." The GMD wanted to ensure that schools taught what it meant to be Chinese to Taiwanese students, especially since the island had been subjected to Japanese education for the previous fifty years. In addition, before the lifting of martial law in 1987, the government urgently believed it needed to educate the public in Confucian expectations of social behavior and acceptable values. The entire value system represented "Chineseness," as understood by Chiang Kai-shek and the GMD during the 1950s, an ideal that the government and its secondary education policy

96   Chapter 3

constantly propagated. The CYC aided GMD efforts by advocating the values of group cooperation, service, citizenship, patriotism, and loyalty—along with respect for parents, teachers, leaders, and, most importantly, Chiang's government.[133]

Yet along with its key role in defining traditional Confucianism for young Taiwanese, the CYC also incorporated "modern" values with its social agenda. Modern principles were drawn especially from Sun Yat-sen's teachings, including the "Three People's Principles" (nationalism, democracy, and people's livelihood).[134] The CYC even published four books full of political and social indoctrination: *The System of the Three People's Principles and the Procedure of Its Implementation, Elementary Anti-Communism, The Fate of China* (authored by Chiang Kai-shek in 1937), and *Principles, Leader, Country, Duty and Honor*. The organization widely distributed the books to students and its social youth members. To ensure that students carefully read and memorized the doctrines, the CYC managed to get portions of the books into textbooks used for Chinese, history, and civics courses in Taiwan's middle schools. To the chagrin of most young people, they had to actually memorize the doctrines to pass examinations.[135]

In the initial years after the CYC's formation, many middle schools across Taiwan mandated that all students join the group. According to the CYC's official Laws and Regulations ratified in September 1952, "all young people who believe in the Three Principles of the People, adhere firmly to an anticommunist, anti-Soviet viewpoint, are willing to accept every kind of training and work from this organization, and who are more than fifteen and less than thirty years of age" could apply for membership.[136] The United Nations' 1953 *Demographic Yearbook* included figures of this cohort (excluding aborigines and foreigners) for 1952. Altogether, 2,210,051 people fell between the ages of fifteen and twenty-nine years of age: that is, fifteen to nineteen years (848,122), twenty to twenty-four years (736,525), and twenty-five to twenty-nine years (625,404).[137] Therefore, the CYC had a large group to appeal to. In some schools, the organization staged elaborate enlistment ceremonies for incoming students featuring games, food, and singing. The event would end with members of an entire class reciting a loyalty oath on the spot, signing a membership list, and being presented with a badge.[138]

Mao Cheng-how, who was a senior at Taipei's Jianguo High School, recalled participating in the first CYC oath-swearing ceremony on December 1, 1952.[139] It was held at the only large-scale indoor basketball court in Taipei, the Three Armed Forces Basketball Arena (Sanjunqiuchang), where Mao himself often played. All upper middle school students in Taiwan, 9,500 in total, including those from Jianguo, Fuzhong High School, Chenggong Boys' School, First Taipei Girls' School, and Second Taipei Girls' School, were in attendance.[140] A fascinating photograph of this first CYC oath-swearing ceremony shows a myriad of students—the boys standing on the floor in the foreground, while the girls stand in the bleachers behind them, everyone with his or her right hand raised in allegiance, left hand holding the oath, and mouth open in recitation. The girls and boys were segregated during the ceremony. However, since CYC activities were co-ed, while most schools were gender segregated (out of the three boys' schools, Jianzhong and Fuzhong had a token number of girls who made up a tiny percentage of the schools' rosters), Mao recalled that students were excited by the chance for boys and girls to mingle, despite noting that "Taiwan was very, very conservative. There was no such thing as dating in high schools and in general, so I'm pretty sure some students viewed [CYC activities] as an opportunity."[141] At the opening ceremony, parties were not held before or after the event, but Mao surmised that "there were maybe welcoming parties for some officials, not the students. Because the CYC was a government entity, I'm pretty sure there were some kinds of celebration somewhere. I'm not aware of any involving the students—at least I do not know of them." For students like Mao, even the enjoyable events came with an understanding that larger, political forces were at work: "[We] were just like pawns. We did not have a choice. The government said we are going to have the CYC."[142]

CYC members were expected to attend and participate in all special rallies and nationally sponsored activities in support of holidays or patriotic events. And regardless of whether they were in schools or county groups, all members received basic military training, usually close-order drill and rifle training.[143] As a student at Shida Fuzhong Upper Middle School in the late 1950s, Yu Jian-ye recalled how "the CYC established military training because Chiang Ching-kuo believed that the youth should receive military education. Students needed to learn literary and military skills (*wen* and *wu*)."[144] However, by 1961 the CYC had acquired enough status for the organization to cancel compulsory membership. Nevertheless, strong recruitment continued. The organization still held elaborate welcome parties in schools and local communities, even though young people no longer had to sign membership papers or recite an oath during the festivities.[145]

Whether or not the CYC mandated registration or recruited heavily, some young people were eager to join the organization throughout the 1950s and into the 1960s. In particular, students enthusiastically registered for popular, exciting recreational activities such as target practice, horseback riding, and paragliding. In all, the organization recorded 79,850 participants (on 1,497 "teams") who completed summer camping programs from 1953 to 1962.[146] Although there were certainly students who signed up for multiple events (and in multiple years), it is an impressive statistic that indicates the CYC's impact on a generation of youth on Taiwan. Indeed, not everyone who signed up for an event was guaranteed a spot. Yu Jian-ye recalled that the CYC determined who was able to participate in

98   Chapter 3

its activities through "raffle tickets"—individual names were drawn. Yu later joined CYC's staff in 1968, serving as deputy director of recreational activities before retiring in 2005.[147]

Yet contrary to Yu and other CYC participants' accounts, Monte Bullard and George Bowie's studies of the CYC maintain that strict government guidelines—including age, educational background, and physical health—determined enrollment.[148] Perhaps in the initial years of the CYC's establishment, certain eligibilities had to be fulfilled to join activities and the practice of random drawings was not implemented until later. The CYC's 1953 pamphlet, *China Youth Warriors*, also stated that the organization admitted applicants through "physical examinations and intelligence tests."[149] Another possibility is that the CYC lied to those who had signed up and used the "raffle" as a front while it chose who could participate. Regardless of how students were selected to take part in the most popular activities, interest in joining the CYC swelled. Roughly two-thirds of applicants to the 1953 summer programs were rejected.[150]

Because the GMD government exercised tight security and authoritarian control over the island during the 1950s and 1960s, there were limited opportunities for young people from different schools to meet each other. Very few public or youth-oriented programs were available—Taiwan was largely rural and impoverished, life was difficult, and entertainment and amenities scarce. Moreover, homework consumed most of students' time outside the classroom. Wu Cai-e, who migrated to Taiwan from the Dachen Islands off the coast of Zhejiang province, recounted "not being able to attend upper middle school because I had to work to support my family."[151] Many 1950s Taiwanese teens lived under similar circumstances. According to Brindley, for many of these students CYC activities became a popular, welcoming outlet that provided opportunities to meet new friends, have fun, and gain new experiences that were simply unavailable otherwise. It also allowed students to travel within the country at very little cost, since the organization paid for most expenses.

Some students found that only through the CYC could they forge relationships with other young people from different parts of the island. Moreover, the level of poverty pervading Taiwan in its first twenty years after the 1945 retrocession discouraged leisure and recreation—both of which the GMD (and the League) considered luxuries. Whereas the League had patrolled the streets, publicly condemning leisure and conspicuous consumption, the CYC became a GMD-sanctioned organization that arranged and sponsored virtually every opportunity for young people to meet across campuses and participate in recreational activities. In these ways, it became an important, quasi-official, extracurricular branch of Taiwan's education system.

It is important not to overstate the uniqueness of CYC-sponsored events and travel programs. Although 1950s students had limited opportunities to meet young people outside of their schools, contrary to Brindley's assessment they certainly traveled outside of CYC-sponsored activities. Mao Cheng-how recalled schools organizing an excursion every semester:

> In the Taipei area, either you go by train or bike—twice a year, once during the fall semester and once in the spring. We called it an "excursion" (*jiaoyou*). Typically, it was on a Sunday because we had six days of school. It had nothing to do with the CYC. Each class had a separate activity. At that period of time, my high school year started with four classes of fifty students each. They were labeled as A, B, C, and D. We took entrance exams. Typically, if your score was high, you were in group A. In the Taipei area we went to Danshui. Another place was Bitan. We would swim there. Sometimes we would go to Shitoushan. It was a little bit south of Taipei so we took the train. One time we rode bikes to Danshui. Four or five of us said "let's go to Keelung" and that was a long trip. [Keelung is located at the northernmost tip of Taiwan.] The teachers allowed us to do this without a chaperone. Our parents paid for the trips. Everyone brought his lunch (*biandang*); typically it was packed in an aluminum box. During that period, most people were not rich. They could not afford to go to other places. Certainly, the CYC opened up opportunities.[152]

Thus, contrary to Brindley's assertion that youth's extracurricular activities were limited to those arranged by the CYC, Mao's recollections demonstrate that middle school students had chances to travel around the island with their schoolteachers in excursions that were separate from CYC-sanctioned events.

The CYC attempted to publicize itself around the world. In particular, it tried to recruit young overseas Chinese into the organization so they would form a political base of anti-Communist activities abroad.[153] At the Overseas Chinese Affairs Conference in Taipei in late October 1952, a resolution was adopted which "called on young Chinese living abroad to volunteer for service in support of the Nationalist government."[154] In addition, the CYC sponsored visits to countries like the US. On September 23, 1957, one hundred young CYC men and women toured the New York City Hall in Manhattan after spending three weeks at the Moral Re-Armament (MRA) Assembly on Mackinac Island, Michigan.[155] Their trip, covered in national outlets like the *New York Times,* introduced many Americans to the CYC for the first time. During the 1940s and 1950s, the right-wing MRA movement met on Mackinac Island upon Michigan governor Murray Van Wagoner's invitation. According to its own history, "The MRA was a multi-national

100   Chapter 3

group . . . [which] promoted the philosophy of love, unselfishness, purity and honesty in a world-wide evangelistic campaign." It is interesting to note that the MRA "was the ideological alternative to the post World War II spread of Communistic influence," which partly explains why CYC delegates spent three weeks at its conference.[156] The MRA was primarily made up of young volunteers. For example, from 1965 to 1970, its *Up with People* television show sent at least 2,500 young idealists on singing tours all over the world. This was similar to how the CYC dispatched its young people to spread political support during times of national crisis in the 1950s.

Exams on Chiang Kai-shek and Sun Yat-sen's doctrine aside, many students generally enjoyed the CYC, especially its summer and winter camps. Moreover, their parents were willing to send them because they believed the camps were safe and wholesome environments. The organization established activity centers in many of Taiwan's most beautiful natural settings—"resort areas," according to some accounts.[157] These included camps built in the island's depopulated interior, which contributed to the prosperity of rural areas deep in the mountains (most of Taiwan's population was, and still is, concentrated along the west coast). This also may have been a concerted effort by the GMD to solidify support among minority groups and residents outside the cities, as the vast majority of Chinese mainlanders who retreated to the island in 1949 still remained in the coastal cities during the 1950s and 1960s. By 1964, four youth hostels were built in the beautiful Central Mountain Range: Lishan, Dayuling, Ci'en, and Tianxiang.[158] Furthermore, sixty youth recreational centers were established throughout the cities of Taiwan, with at least one in each of the island's fifteen counties.[159] There was even a recreational center in the city of Magong on the offshore island of Penghu. CYC camps and recreational centers gave young people the opportunity to travel around the islands, participate in fun activities, and make new friends. The activities were also popular because they were well planned and well managed. Positive word of mouth from previous participants encouraged more young people to sign up for subsequent trips.[160]

The opportunity to engage in co-ed social interaction at CYC events also contributed to the organization's popularity in the 1950s. Young boys often teased girls for enjoying the military training, since females were only learning the skills for fun and would never actually have to participate in battle. In general, the fact that many CYC activities were co-ed is quite interesting. Unlike Western organizations (like the Boy Scouts, designed to instill masculinity with camping and mountain experiences), the CYC relied on similar activities yet consciously operated them in a co-ed environment to allow young people an opportunity to explore the natural, rural parts of the island and recruit local youth for membership. In fact, the CYC was heavily dependent on female participation to maximize its impact, even at a time when virtually all of the island's schools were gender segregated.

In certain instances, student participants also became team leaders, camp counselors, and paid instructors in subsequent years. Yang Zhen, who came to Taiwan from Hubei province in 1949, recalled participating in the CYC for the first time when he was eighteen years old. From 1954 to 1958, he served five consecutive years as a horseback riding instructor for the organization. The CYC invited him to return each summer to work at a horse stable in the central city of Houli. For his services, he was paid and stayed at one of the many CYC activity centers built throughout the island. According to Yang, "the CYC deserves praise because it brought positive experiences and happiness to many young people."[161]

Ironically, even though the CYC sought to indoctrinate youth with GMD politics and ideology, some students still considered the organization an attractive outlet for freedom. After all, Brindley notes that the CYC was the only major political club that allowed space for youth to assemble, discuss ideas (albeit within expected doctrine), and have some independence away from school or family.[162] Yet the CYC controlled most of the extracurricular activities at all levels outside of school, and it also held the power to permit (or deny) new associations or clubs created between schools. For example, the organization could choose to subsidize certain extracurricular groups, associations, or school functions with money awarded through each school's administrative office.[163] In fact, GMD policy before 1988 completely forbade intercollegiate or interscholastic association in Taiwan except those established through contacts arranged by the CYC. Throughout the period of authoritarian rule and martial law (1949–1987), officials feared the formation of political groups that might speak against the government or advocate for Taiwanese independence. Thus, students could meet with those from other schools only by engaging in the many CYC activities that recruited from throughout Taiwan. In the 1950s, this was the only way that students from one district could meet with those in other localities or towns.

A number of students even met future spouses through such intercollegiate meetings, and many went on to be very successful in government service, the GMD party, and the CYC staff. One crucial CYC goal was to identify and recruit bright and enthusiastic future leaders in the GMD, government civil service, and military.[164] The organization trained its leaders to possess charisma—to rely upon personal charm in leading a group. The CYC not only discovered and trained talented youth who it identified as potential GMD leaders, but it also selected promising artists and film directors. From 1952 to 1960, a number of members later

102   Chapter 3

became successful and well-known figures in Taiwan, including journalist Li Wenzhong, film director Li Xing, film director Bai Jinrei, and doctor Cui Jiu. On July 16, 1958, Chiang Ching-kuo sent Zhang Xucheng to serve as a CYC representative at the International Youth Meeting, held in France. At the time, Zhang was a student at National Taiwan University. Later, he became an international relations scholar and, ironically, an overseas legislator of the Democratic Progressive Party, the island's main opposition party to the GMD.[165]

In addition to the activity programs that directly involved youth, the CYC also heavily impacted media in the early ROC. On October 10, 1958, the organization combined a network of publishing houses, journals, and youth radio stations to become the "Young Lion Youth Cultural Enterprises Corporation" (*Youshi,* also known as Youth Book Company).[166] Young Lion had first formed on January 1, 1953, and issued a biweekly journal called *Corps Affairs Correspondence* (*Tuan wu tongxun*). Completely run by the CYC and still thriving today, Youth Book Company offered many publications for sale or donation, depending on the sponsor.[167] Various leaflets, pamphlets, and workbooks—such as *How to Develop Rural Service Work* (for CYC members who spoke Taiwanese and were planning to work on activities in the island's southern and eastern regions)—were routinely distributed to students. Even more important, the CYC was able to insert messages into formal textbooks and classroom material that students had to memorize. The organization used its powerful influence in the island's publishing world to acquaint youth with its messages in the 1950s, in particular the call to defend Taiwan by force against Communism and the Soviet Union.

Moreover, throughout the 1950s government officials controlled radio and newsprint on the island and the GMD articulated all media policies. This helped the CYC publishing house exert an even larger influence on young students and workers, for censorship was pervasive and CYC-sponsored literature was a legitimate (and often sole) source for news, fiction, and human interest stories told by young people, for young people. Besides these media channels, the CYC also used radio broadcasts to reach a large number of youth, and listeners in the 1950s reported that CYC radio messages were particularly effective in propagating both the organization and the GMD.[168]

Music was also an important tool for socializing young people in postwar Taiwan, cultivating "Chineseness," and generating political support for anti-Communist reunification. One 1950s CYC record (produced by Young Lion) was entitled *Happy New Year, Merry Christmas.* The album also featured titles such as "Congratulations Everyone, Happy New Year!" "Victory is Coming Soon," "In a Far Away Land," "Embroidered Pouch," and "Dudu Dang." Interestingly, the CYC included "In a Far Away Land," a folk song about Uighurs in Xinjiang province, and "Dudu Dang," a Taiwanese folk song. By incorporating traditional ethnic tunes, CYC music celebrated both traditional (pre-Communist) China and a vision of the future, in which more modern, diverse Chinese students would reestablish the true China under the banner of anti-Communism. Not surprisingly, then, CYC albums also featured songs with explicitly patriotic lyrics, such as "Victory is Coming Soon": "Look, the national flag is waving in the wind. Hear the war drum vibrating to the clouds in the sky . . . it already lights up to fight back the mainland's fire, for our countrymen, to save our country, we should clean up ourselves. For the revolution, to reconstruct our nation, we want to rebuild our country."[169]

The China Youth Corps' Critics

For all its popularity with some teens and centrality in shaping 1950s youth culture on Taiwan, the CYC did not avoid criticism during the decade. Immediately after its formation, Provincial Governor Wu Guozhen (also known to Americans as K. C. Wu), who had denied Chiang Ching-kuo's request for League funding, was a particularly vocal opponent, especially after he resigned on April 10, 1953, and emigrated to the US, never to return to the island. Although Chiang Kai-shek had included Wu among the twelve senior government and party members in the CYC's Central Guidance Committee (Tuanwu zhidao weiyuan) to support his son and legitimize the organization, Wu became a harsh critic.[170] On March 27, 1954, he sent a letter to the GMD National Assembly charging that the "undemocratic" government "violated human rights."[171] Furthermore, he even accused Chiang Ching-kuo of organizing "a Youth Corps modeled after Hitler Youth and the Communist Youth"; Ching-kuo, of course, denied the charges.[172] Wu also attacked Ching-kuo for using "police-state techniques he learned from the Communists," a reference to Ching-kuo's study at a Soviet military academy in Moscow and his twelve-year stay in the Soviet Union.[173] Furthermore, Wu lamented that it was unclear whether the party or government controlled the CYC.

Another public denouncer of the CYC was Lei Chen, the chief editor of a biweekly political journal called *Free China* (*Ziyou zhongguo*). Lei had studied in Japan and held a deep understanding of constitutional government and Western political thought. He was a GMD member who had served in prominent positions in the Nationalist government on the mainland. Lei initially had a fairly close and cordial relationship with Chiang Kai-shek, who assured him that he would support *Free China*. In November 1949, Lei launched the first issue in Taiwan, and during the magazine's early days the GMD government even provided financial support because the journal printed anti-Communist propaganda and did not

104   Chapter 3

directly discuss Taiwanese politics. It is noteworthy that Wu Guozhen, while he served as provincial governor from 1951 to 1953, annually supported *Free China* with 20,000 New Taiwan dollars. When the Garrison Headquarters' deputy chief of staff, Peng Mengji, eventually issued a warrant for Lei Chen's arrest, Wu overruled it, thus protecting and preventing him from imprisonment.[174]

However, by 1954 *Free China* had begun to turn its critiques towards the GMD's authoritarian policy and Chiang Kai-shek's personal power.[175] For this Lei was expelled from the GMD party the same year. He argued that martial law denied people basic rights and freedom, and the CYC served as a perpetrator of these violations. He ran articles criticizing the CYC for possessing too many functions and failing to articulate its main goal. One editorial, penned by Fu Zheng and published on January 1, 1958, alleged that the CYC took advantage of its power to control many aspects of students' lives. In addition, Fu asserted that "there were factions within the GMD that utilized the CYC to develop their individual political power."[176] This accusation, in particular, was a thinly veiled criticism aimed at Chiang Ching-kuo, whom many already believed had used the CYC to achieve his political ascension. Fu argued that the GMD cliques' struggle over the CYC was only natural, since the youth organization was a political institution.

Moreover, Fu sharply criticized the CYC for mandating upper middle school students to join. Statistics for the year leading up to the January 1, 1958, article indicated the impact this had. That year, a total of 81,642 students attended upper middle school in Taiwan, with 1,082 in national schools (*guoli xuexiao*), 49,411 in provincial schools (*shengli xuexiao*), 16,605 in county and municipal schools (*xianshili xuexiao*), and 14,544 in private schools (*sili xuexiao*). Of the 81,642 students, 43,992 enrolled in regular upper middle school (*gaozhong xuexiao*), 7,272 in normal school (*shifan xuexiao*), and 30,378 in vocational school (*zhixiao*).[177] Meanwhile, the United Nations' 1957 *Demographic Yearbook* reported a total of 950,853 residents between the ages of fifteen and nineteen years in Taiwan.[178] Traditional upper middle school students fell into this cohort. What is striking is that only 81,642 out of 950,853 in that age group attended upper middle school, less than 10 percent. Therefore, the CYC was guaranteed to reach just a small minority since most of its participants were students and only a few were "social youth."

Still, Fu Zheng argued that coercive policies, especially upper middle school students' compulsory membership in the CYC, were similar to the GMD's past behavior of "forcing young people to take part in the Three People's Principles Youth Corps (SQT)." He claimed that on the mainland the SQT also made students participate in the organization, but the GMD "did not control their minds and opinions." After the War of Resistance, many former members of the SQT opposed the institution. According to Fu, "they had the freedom and ability to reject the SQT because their minds had not been fully manipulated by the GMD. Following the war, the GMD had many internal struggles, which was one of the reasons that led to the dissolution of the SQT."[179]

Meanwhile, the CYC's mission was to oppose Communism and the Soviet Union. To Fu, such a purpose forced students to participate in politics instead of concentrating on their schoolwork. He called on the GMD to dismantle the organization if it "numbs" and lies to the youth.[180] It is appropriate that he used the verb "numb" or "to apply anesthesia" (*da mazui*), because youth were particularly prone to have vocal opinions. "To numb" was (and still is) commonly used in Chinese to describe a person, group of people, or power that seeks to control others by causing them to lose their strength and senses. This numbing leads to their defenseless state, thus rendering them unable to criticize and fight back against the party that injected the "anesthesia." Using such vivid allusions, Fu and other CYC opponents charged that the government sought to indoctrinate students with party ideology (*dangyi*) to stifle their freedom of thought and the possibility of directing criticism and protest at the GMD.

Fu Zheng also noted that the CYC was "not a mass organization, but rather one that belonged to the Ministry of National Defense (Guofangbu)," a government institution that was "outside the law"—another reason why critics called for an end to the CYC.[181] Fu maintained that the organization's work did not produce results. He asserted that the CYC had harmed society in two different ways—"by destroying law and order, and wasting money." Its establishment was outside the confines of the law, and since the CYC was a political organization, "its practice of military training in school had to cease completely."[182] In the early years of retrocession, Taiwan's laws were not firmly established, and the CYC had benefitted from the lack of oversight and regulation. In addition, Fu argued that the Ministry of Education should handle students' education, not the CYC or the Ministry of National Defense.

Furthermore, it was Fu who circulated the rumor that the CYC spent "around three hundred million new Taiwan dollars" (*sanyiyuan zuoyou*) in 1956. He maintained that this budget information was "certainly something that the CYC kept highly confidential—an outsider would not be able to verify" (*zhe dangran shi qingnian jiuguotuan de gaodu jimi, fei juwairen suoneng zhengshi*).[183] Six months later, *Free China* published another editorial, also presumably from Fu (it featured a similar title assailing the CYC once more), again attacking the organization and calling for it to be dismantled.[184]

For these assertions, *Free China* incurred the wrath of GMD leaders. Along with other publications critical of the party and Chiang Kai-shek, the government soon considered *Free China* taboo. Furthermore, the journal also tried to push

106   Chapter 3

the GMD towards democracy. In 1959, when Chiang decided to amend the 1946 constitution to extend his presidency to a third term, Lei became involved in plans to establish an opposition party with activists engaged in local elections. In 1960, he was charged with sedition after forming the China Democratic Party with other liberal politicians that same year. Unlike before, when he avoided authorities with help from Wu Guozhen, who was the provincial governor from 1951 to 1953, this time Lei had nowhere to turn. Chiang Kai-shek personally ordered his arrest and the command was followed through immediately. The GMD arrested Lei for treason on September 4, 1960, and sentenced him to ten years in prison; Fu Zheng received a six-year sentence. Soon after, *Free China* was shut down.[185]

In response to CYC critics like Fu, Lei, and Wu, Chiang Ching-kuo was careful to downplay the organization's relationship with the GMD, instead shaping public perception of CYC youth activities as depoliticized, harmless, and nonthreatening. On July 1, 1960, the military training program and personnel came under the aegis and budget of the Ministry of Education.[186] Even before the lifting of martial law and as early as the 1960s, Ching-kuo authorized the CYC to change its mission to serve the social, cultural, and educational needs of Taiwan's youth, and to shed its political, ideological image to do so.[187] Fifty years later, the CYC's former director of recreational activities, Yu Jian-ye, defended the CYC, noting that during the martial law period "there was only one political party" and people had few alternatives. According to Yu, when the CYC was established, "Chiang Ching-kuo wanted it to be an institution that was not associated with the GMD, but everyone, even to this day, believes that the organization is a GMD unit because many young members of the CYC later became involved in the party's politics."[188] Yu noted that some directors of CYC county branches later ran in county elections and became county committee members or legislators. Moreover, former CYC volunteers continue to take part in GMD elections to this day, indicating that the party and the CYC maintained an intimate relationship well beyond the 1950s and 1960s. Yu admitted that he himself was a member of the GMD but did not participate in any "political activities." He also recounted how some CYC members purposely strove to become acquainted with many people through the organization because they had the aspirations of running for political office. Often the GMD and CYC shared administrators and staff, one being the stepping stone for the other.[189]

During the 1950s, the CYC emphasized military training because GMD leaders feared an imminent attack by the Communists. By the 1960s, however, the organization began to broaden its scope, expand its mission, and incorporate more overt, educational activities meant to build individual character and develop well-rounded adults. Today, its overt political ties are minimal, but the Democratic Progressive Party still remains suspicious of it for having ties to the GMD and receiving government contracts.

Still, in its first eight years the CYC was an overt mouthpiece for the GMD's strict, authoritarian regime, and its primary goal was to instill patriotism and martial spirit in youth. From its inception in 1952, the organization gradually succeeded in tackling other aspects of its original mission to educate and provide social services and activities for the nation's youth, which explains why it has far exceeded the shelf life of its predecessors. Whether or not it articulated a vision of the Chinese past, present, or future, the CYC certainly reached more young Taiwanese than any other youth organization in the island's history. Under Japanese colonial rule (1895–1945), there were organizations formed around *kokugo* (national language), sumo wrestling, baseball, and wartime service labor "volunteer" groups (which the Japanese also instituted in Korea). These served the purpose of scouting organizations, yet the Japanese never established a youth group that reached the scale and longevity of the China Youth Corps. The CYC and its contribution to the political socialization of youth in the early years of GMD rule in Taiwan cannot be underestimated, especially its role in shaping young minds and lives during a pivotal decade in which the island's youth forged a unique identity and culture. Meanwhile, this generation of Chinese on Taiwan would also face a renewed militarism; in particular, compulsory military training in upper middle schools throughout the 1950s. While the CYC itself sponsored much of this military training, the insertion of military teachers (*jiaoguan*) into upper middle schools across the island and the fusion of military-themed courses into Taiwanese curriculum had far-reaching significance beyond just the CYC.

CHAPTER FOUR

Military Training and Instructors, 1953–1960

In early postwar Taiwan, the threat of Communist invasion prompted the Guomindang regime's Ministry of National Defense to establish a strong link between the military and upper middle schools on the island. Anti-Communist fervor also contributed to the GMD's desire to cultivate among youth a sense of duty to combat Communists, which the state successfully accomplished via mandatory military training (*junshi xunlian*) in upper middle schools and colleges. From its inception in 1953, the GMD tasked the Ministry of National Defense Political Department (Guofangbu Zhengzhibu, or MNDPD) with such training. In particular, Chiang Ching-kuo directed the Political Department, which fell under the aegis of the Ministry. Chiang Kai-shek had appointed Ching-kuo to the position in 1950, intentionally establishing it for his son in order to bolster Ching-kuo's status within the military. As director of the MNDPD, Ching-kuo oversaw the training of military instructors (*jiaoguan*) from both the Political Warfare College and the army before dispatching them to secondary schools across the island. Ching-kuo's Political Department also controlled the China Youth Corps, which under his leadership helped inculcate martial spirit in young people, indoctrinate students in GMD ideology, and implement systematic military training in Taiwan's upper middle schools. Once the imminent threat of Communist invasion gradually began to subside, the government transferred both the CYC and its military training programs to the Ministry of Education in 1960.

It is important to examine the motivations behind this systematic implementation of student military training during the crucial years after the Nationalists arrived in Taiwan, including the recruitment and training of military instructors throughout the 1950s, the instructors' backgrounds and experiences, and the way in which overt militarization impacted the day-to-day life of Taiwanese middle school students. There were, of course, lingering martial and educational influences from Republican-era China (1912–1949) and Taiwan's colonial period under the Japanese (1895–1945). In addition, tensions between instructors and students reveal how and why critics opposed the program's implementation. Finally, an illustration of the impact of military training on student activism and protest in

1950s Taiwan is the Liu Ziran Incident (Liu Ziran shijian), a sensational 1957 murder case that prompted student riots, only this time not against the Nationalist government but rather the US. Because the incident involved both CYC leadership and military instructors acting on the ground level, it appeared to occur with the complicity of the GMD authorities, culminating in street violence and significant damage to the US Embassy in Taipei. The Liu Ziran Incident had major implications, for it sparked the first anti-American riot on Taiwan, one seemingly sanctioned by the Nationalist government and fueled by the CYC's compulsory military training.

A long tradition of youth military training, mobilization, and activism in Republican-era China foreshadowed the dynamics that developed later in 1950s Taiwan. Wen-hsin Yeh's study of the radicalization of youth in Zhejiang province's middle counties during the early Republican years (1912–1927) explores middle school and college students' united attack on traditional authority.[1] Robert Culp notes that military training was a feature of many physical education programs in mainland middle schools as early as the 1910s.[2] According to the *Historical Materials for the Modern Chinese School System,* "at those schools that held military training in the 1910s and 1920s, it generally occupied no more than an hour or two of students' time each week, since it split time with regular physical training or physical education classes."[3]

After 1927, state policy on in-school military training evolved through student demands, state directives, and administrators' desire to accommodate both. During the Jinan Incident in May 1928, Japanese troops interfered with the advance of the Nationalist Party's Northern Expedition in Shandong province. This event prompted patriotic students and social groups to call for more extensive military training in schools.[4] A group of citizens from Shanghai petitioned the University Council to start a military training program in all the nation's schools, arguing that Japanese students had received training since the end of World War I.[5] Meanwhile, the Shanghai Student Union went so far as to organize a student army trained by school athletic instructors.[6]

According to the China Youth Corps' official history, formal military training officially began in China's upper middle schools and colleges in 1928, when the First National Education Congress unanimously passed an act establishing the Ministry of Training and Supervision.[7] That summer, the University Council and the First National Educational Congress responded to student demands by enacting a military training program, which included army training at least three times a week at all schools above the primary level.[8] According to Jeffrey Wasserstrom's study of student protests in Shanghai, when the Japanese invaded Manchuria in September 1931 (also known as the Mukden Incident), "one of the first

110   Chapter 4

demands youths made when news . . . reached Shanghai was they be allowed to form 'student armies' (*xueshengjun*) to help defend their country."[9] Wen-hsin Yeh also notes that the Mukden Incident marked "a turning point in revolutionary nationalism."[10] When college students demanded military training on campus to help prepare for China's armed resistance against Japan, the GMD "moved swiftly to co-opt the students and 'nationalize' their patriotism." "It quickly introduced compulsory military instruction of college students along with political training in the Nationalist Party doctrines."[11] The Military Affairs Commission, headed by Chiang Kai-shek, oversaw military training in schools. Students were required to wear military-style uniforms during their hours of weekly drill; the same would be echoed in Taiwan two decades later. Within a year after news of the 1931 Mukden Incident reached Shanghai, youth from twelve local schools had joined together to establish a student army and more than eight thousand local students had enrolled in military training programs.[12]

The Rationale for Student Military Training on Taiwan

Even before the 1949 retreat the party had established its rule following Japan's surrender to the Allied forces in August 1945. On October 25, 1945, Japan "returned" Taiwan to China and the island became part of the Republic of China.[13] Two new social groups emerged: *waishengren* and *benshengren*. *Waishengren* literally meant "people from other provinces of China," referring to the mainland Chinese who migrated to the island after the retrocession and their children (hereafter "mainlanders"). *Benshengren* referred to the people of ethnic Han origin who lived on Taiwan before 1945 (hereafter "Taiwanese"). Distinguishing them from the newly arrived mainlanders, *benshengren* literally meant "people of this province" and did not include non-Han aborigines. During the 1950s, the GMD controlled schools for both mainlanders and Taiwanese, which played a central role in maintaining sociopolitical stability. One of the areas of education that contributed to this stability was compulsory military training in upper middle schools.

When Chiang Kai-shek and his troops retreated to Taiwan in 1949, the generalissimo worried that his soldiers were already too old and uneducated. On November 1, a group of Japanese military officers arrived on the island at Chiang's invitation, all of whom were assigned Chinese names to avoid strong anti-Japanese public sentiment following World War II. The head of the Japanese Military Advisory Group, General Bai Hongliang, was a former Imperial Japanese Army major who immediately recommended that Chiang implement a plan for establishing reserves. Yi Zuoren, another Japanese officer, arrived in June 1951 and was charged with training the existing army on the island, but he too insisted that Taiwan needed reserves. Particularly, Yi suggested a recruitment system based on the United States' Reserve Officers' Training Corps (ROTC), a program the Americans successfully implemented in public schools.[14]

Both Chiang and his Japanese advisers had legitimate reasons for concern. By 1950, nearly six hundred thousand troops had arrived in Taiwan from the mainland. Many had already reached the age of retirement, having served in the Nationalist Army since the late 1920s.[15] In December 1951, 20 percent of soldiers in the armed forces were over thirty-five years old, and 10 percent were over forty years old. The fact that there were too many officers and too few soldiers posed an additional problem; by the end of 1951, the ratio of officers to soldiers was 1:3.[16] There was also no reserve army, prompting Chiang to accept the Japanese recommendations and seek to build a strong recruitment apparatus in Taiwan's upper middle schools and colleges. Yet, from the beginning, the GMD's militarization programs (particularly in middle schools) differed dramatically from both the American ROTC model and Japanese interpretations, a decision that would have a strong and lasting impact on future generations of Taiwanese youth.

The generalissimo wanted to build a new force by simultaneously retraining the existing army while recruiting and equipping Taiwan's reserves.[17] Under Chiang's plan to revitalize his armed forces, the army forced old soldiers to retire and promoted younger ones to officers. Chiang also desired more youth in the reserve system, including more fresh, young soldiers and more "nonprofessional" (i.e., reserve) officers.[18] These he wanted trained and prepared for mobilization at a moment's notice. During a November 21, 1951, meeting, Chiang announced that the Nationalists would have to rely on Taiwanese manpower to counterattack Communist China, for there was insufficient time to train Chinese on mainland soil since soldiers were supposed to receive at least half a year of preparatory drills. To meet his ambitious goal for the GMD's reserve army, the government had little choice but to implement compulsory military training in schools. However, it would be a program quite different not only from those of the Japanese or American, but also from the Nationalists' own precursor on the mainland.

Besides training soldiers to serve as reserve frontline troops, the Ministry of National Defense also wanted to train students to become reserve officers. Officer training occurred not only in schools but also in military academies, where male students went after graduating from upper middle school. In the 1950s the GMD mandated that all males serve two years in the military after graduation, and it also required those who were college bound to complete reserve officers' training and serve a minimum of one year. In this way, the MND did experiment a bit by drawing on the US ROTC as an early model for in-school military training.[19] In January 1952, the Ministry drafted an order dictating how upper middle

112   Chapter 4

school students would train to become reserve officers. Initially, the plan was for all instruction to take place within the schools themselves, simulating life in the barracks and offering extensive extracurricular military exercises on school grounds. However, since most students did not live on campus (with the exception of normal schools), the Ministry soon decided that military instructors would train students only for three hours per week, during class time.[20]

While Chiang Kai-shek and the Ministry of National Defense established student military training to build a reserve army, the Ministry of Education supported the program for a different reason: discipline. During the early years of retrocession, the MOE was concerned with juvenile delinquency, especially growing GMD concerns about "thirteen teenage male gangsters, thirteen teenage female gangsters" (*shisan taibao, shisan taimei*) from the mainland. Most of these students came from wealthy backgrounds, with parents who were often government officials. In particular, Minister of Education Cheng Tianfang was furious over the rising number of gang fights in Taipei and directly supported organized militarism as a way to combat the growth of juvenile delinquency. It was actually Cheng—not Chiang, the army, or the Ministry of National Defense—who implemented some of the most memorable, visible signs of militarism in 1950s Taiwanese schools, including his order that all students wear uniforms and all males shave their heads. Throughout the decade, the MOE, led by Cheng, insisted that the implementation of compulsory military training would resolve the problems of delinquency, irresponsible youth, and overprivileged students.[21]

Recruiting Military Instructors

The competitive and rigorous selection process for military instructors was a cooperative effort between the Ministry of Education and the Ministry of National Defense, both of which recruited mostly from the Ministry of National Defense Political Department's Political Warfare College, which was founded on January 6, 1952. The GMD designed the college to prepare officers in their specialty, offering a core curriculum that included "spiritual education," "revolutionary theory," "enemy situations," "political warfare," "military science," and "social science."[22] At the time of its establishment, cadets trained for eighteen months while divided into two groups: middle school students and college graduates. Most of the secondary school students were mainlanders already serving in the military, all of whom the MNDPD intended to become officers in company-level units and divided into two further classes: "political science" (which numbered 385 students in 1952) and "professional" (368, including 52 female students). Finally, the college also subdivided the professional classes into five majors: journalism, fine arts, music, film and drama, and physical education. As for the college graduates (most of whom were active in the military before entry), the college placed them in upper-level research classes, expecting that they would eventually serve as higher officers in the military. In addition, reserve officers, officer candidates, mid-level career officers, and China Youth Corps cadres also participated in courses at the Political Warfare College. In fact, by January 1959 more than forty thousand people had received training at the institution.[23]

In addition to the Political Warfare College, the CYC also recruited and trained military instructors on its own. In September 1954, the organization selected and trained 188 instructors (158 males and 30 females) and sent them to the Taiwan Provincial Government's Department of Education for placement in secondary schools. Of the 188, the CYC asked the Ministry of National Defense to recommend ninety-three to receive training for eight weeks and requested the Political Warfare College to select sixty-five male graduates for one week of intensive training. Meanwhile, it recruited the thirty females from among two pools: the Warfare Cadre Training Class and the MNDPD's female staff.[24] Interestingly, these initial female military instructors received six weeks of training, while their male counterparts only one week—perhaps it required more time to train them in nursing skills. However, other female instructors recalled undergoing a full year of training, while Monte Bullard maintains that all men and women also attended a four-week training course at the Political Warfare College.[25] A possible explanation for these contradictory estimates and recollections could be that both men and women were required to receive training at the Political Warfare College. However, after four weeks they were separated so that female military instructors had to undergo one more year of training to be certified. Hence, Bullard refers to the four-week training of both men and women, while former female military instructors recall one year.

Regardless of the length of time spent in training, from 1953 to 1960 only 20 percent of applicants passed an initial exam qualifying them to begin military instructor education. Recruits who made this first cut next had to attend a course at the Political Warfare College, which an additional 30 percent failed to pass—one qualification was "knowledge of GMD ideology" and the ability to convey it to students.[26] But the CYC also dropped applicants for a variety of arbitrary, even inane reasons. In 1953, Zhang Ruiqing made it through the first cut but not the second. She took the exam for recruiting female military instructors and did quite well, but during training the officers who made selections deemed her too young and short, claiming that students would not take her seriously when she stood in

114   Chapter 4

front of them. They cut her on the spot and ordered her instead to work at the CYC headquarters. Zhang refused and returned to join the MNDPD's female staff.[27]

Not only did the CYC reject a majority of potential military instructors who volunteered to apply, it actively recruited some who did not. In 1953, the first year of CYC recruitment, members learned that Guo Wencui was experienced and qualified—they even paid a visit to her home after she refused their offer several times. Guo did not want to be a soldier, but after some convincing she finally submitted an application. The CYC decided that she did not even need to take the exam because of her qualifications, yet the organization still required her to receive one year of training. According to Guo, the CYC dismissed many recruits from training because they had "stayed at home too long" (*zai jia dai jiu le*) and were thus deemed "not sharp" (*bu lingguang*) enough.[28]

It is important to examine how secondary school teachers were hired in China before the Nationalist government retreated to Taiwan as a comparison with the recruitment of military instructors on the island. Before 1930, most middle schools had been located in provincial capitals, big cities, and sometimes county seats. The development of teachers' schools led to the expansion of secondary education at the county level and below, especially in inland China, where teachers' schools made up a large part of local secondary education. In some cases, virtually the only secondary schools women could attend in their local counties were female teachers' schools. Due to the scarcity of teachers, no regulations governed teachers at middle schools, and school principals were permitted to hire teachers they believed were qualified. Under a new regulation in 1934, the Ministry of Education stipulated that both graduates of teachers' schools and secondary school teachers should take unified comprehensive examinations for certification: this was a strategy for the Nationalist government to control the teachers' schools. Secondary school teachers in villages also had to enroll in summer in-service training programs. Waivers were only given to those who had some years of teaching experience.[29]

In the initial years of student military training, Chiang Ching-kuo devoted much effort and money to hiring military instructors. The MND provided the budget for instructor education, including salaries and dormitory lodging. Once military instructors began teaching on campuses, the individual schools assumed the responsibility for their salaries, as determined by an instructor's most recent job title and military rank in the MND. Meanwhile, the CYC paid those at normal schools two grades above the basic entry-level wages of normal school teachers. However, if the salary offered by the school was higher than what the military would pay (based on rank), a military instructor received the lower of the two salaries.[30] Regardless of who paid them, the CYC still considered all instructors active-duty military officers while they taught.[31] They also were ineligible for promotion but instead had the option of returning to the military after two years of teaching. Many, however, chose not to return to troop units, regarding life as a military instructor much easier than an austere soldier's life.[32] Still, the MND was actually happy to send military instructors to schools and have them stay, for it meant that public schools were taking a heavy financial burden off the military, since the Ministry did not have to be concerned with instructors' salaries once it dispatched them.[33]

The implementation of military training in upper middle schools and colleges came at a time when Taiwanese public schools were expanding rapidly. In 1956 alone, the government added fifteen new upper middle schools and four new colleges.[34] During the 1950s, the total number of middle school, vocational school, and college students on the island increased at an astonishing rate: from 6,241 in 1951 to 144,424 in 1960.[35] Taiwan's general and student populations were exploding and its new government vigorously encouraged public education. During the decade, the number of military instructors also increased roughly in proportion to the student population, from 28 in 1951 to 509 in 1960.[36]

A substantial number of females became military instructors serving in all-girls schools, and the CYC drew many from the same source: the Women's Corps (Nü qingnian dadui). On July 15, 1947, the GMD had bestowed on General Sun Liren the title of acting vice commander of the Chinese Nationalist Army. He became the vice commander in July 1948. That winter, Sun returned to Nanjing from Taiwan and observed that the people "seemed anxious and frightened" (renxin huanghuang). He recommended that the government "gather" (zhaoshou) them and the GMD soon implemented his suggestion, recruiting seven thousand males and four hundred females. The females underwent gender-segregated training, forming the Women's Corps that same month.[37]

From June 1948 to May 1949, the Women's Corps continued to recruit females between the ages of fifteen and twenty-five years old from all provinces, and Sun sent them to Taiwan between March and June 1949. There, the Women's Corps resumed training in the southern city of Pingdong: the school's opening ceremony took place on March 8, 1949. Two more training locations opened in Tainan and Jiayi around 1955.[38] (Meanwhile, male recruits trained at Fengshan in Kaohsiung, a major port city located in southwestern Taiwan.) A Women's Corps cadet's first six months centered on basic training, while the following year participants underwent more advanced "professional" training. The Women's Corps separated girls into three different groups, with students given an option between military service, social service, and first aid. The corps further divided social service into two subcategories (social education and child welfare) and after graduation each of the girls also received political training.[39] Academia Sinica historians Chen

116   Chapter 4

San-jing, Chu Hong-yuan, and Wu Mei-hui interviewed twenty former Women's Corps members from two groups: a group that went on to become MNDPD staff, and another consisting of those who had simply been Corps members. Eight of the twenty eventually became military instructors in female upper middle schools and colleges in Taiwan.

Among the interviewees was You Huaiyan, a woman who worked as a recorder and adviser at the MNDPD in 1953, routinely recording meetings and conflicts between military officers.[40] In 1956, she left the MNDPD and returned to the Women's Corps, serving on offshore Mazu Island as a small-group leader. There she taught singing, ethnic dance, and politics, and helped publish works for three months.[41] Finally, in late 1956 Chiang Ching-kuo personally sent You to Taipei's Jinling Girls' Middle School (Jinling Nüzhong) to become a military instructor. Since Jinling was brand-new, You informed the school's administrators that she could substitute teach other courses if they did not have enough staff. Thus, she also became a teacher (*bandaoshi*) of first-year upper middle school students as well as a military instructor. Under her guidance, You's class won first place in competitions in writing and sports. Because she was also a teacher, You realized that most people viewed her differently from other military instructors, recalling that "Director Chiang selected me to serve at Jinling Middle School. I couldn't let him lose face!"[42] You felt she was representing not only the military but also Ching-kuo himself. In 1957, Taichung Jingyi Yingzhuan College was preparing to open and the CYC wanted You to supervise the school's establishment. She had no desire to go, afraid that the daunting responsibility would be "quite tiring" because she would have to lead the task of developing the school. You thus retired from the military in 1959.[43] This particular case demonstrates how female military instructors played prominent roles in upper middle schools, training girls to become dutiful citizens who would serve their country if the Chinese Communists were to invade the island.

Student Military Training

Military training in Taiwanese schools technically began in September 1951 on an experimental basis at eight normal middle schools.[44] In July 1953 the MND formally implemented training in all upper middle schools and, six months later, all colleges.[45] Since the government paid all expenses at normal schools, students lived on campus under more rules, constant surveillance, and harsher discipline. Because of this, the experiment with normal schools generally produced more "positive" results.

In a speech at the Political Warfare College on September 22, 1952, Chiang Ching-kuo stressed the differences between military training on the mainland and the new program on Taiwan. Many in the audience were preparing to be military instructors, and they listened as Ching-kuo criticized the past GMD program: "On the mainland, we did not have time to organize and train youth . . . Frankly speaking, mainlander students received bad influence from military instructors who were of poor quality. They only knew how to eat and were incompetent. You cannot be like them. If you are like the past military instructors, I would rather not send you to the schools."[46] He continued, "I think that people's opinion about military training in the past was incorrect. They thought military training was simply 'stand up straight' and 'run.' This is wrong. We have to pay attention to training the character of military instructors. My definition of military training is to train the country's youth to be patriotic and modernize them. 'Attention' and 'to stand at ease' are only part of the training."[47]

To meet Ching-kuo's vision of "modern" compulsory training, the new program incorporated two types of pedagogy: classroom learning (*xueke*) and outdoors learning (*shuke*). For males, classroom knowledge included basic training for infantry, weaponry, maintaining one's sleeping area (*neiwu shouce*), military hygiene, military salutes, flag-raising, GMD revolutionary and military history, military terminology, martial law, map-reading, and enlistment laws.[48] Classroom instruction also covered battlefield activities, which included how to protect oneself during air raids, resist poisonous gases, counter spies, help with military transportation, propagandize after occupying enemy territory, organize and train, help refugees, and handle prisoners of war.[49] Basic training for outdoors learning included lining up and standing straight, combat, target shooting, digging foxholes and trenches, bayoneting, and night combat.

The number of female military instructors in the 1950s was certainly significant, but perhaps even more surprising was that female students participated in nearly all of the above activities along with boys, with the exception of saluting, map-reading, transportation, dealing with prisoners of war, digging foxholes and trenches, and bayoneting. In place of these, the program substituted nursing, personal hygiene, military hygiene, CPR (cardiopulmonary resuscitation), bandaging, and female and pediatric hygiene. Ideas about gender surely informed the decision to add nursing and medical training to the standard pedagogy for girls, but nevertheless females and males alike shot rifles and participated in combat drills. Both boys and girls also visited military bases.[50] Overall, the curriculum in the classroom and outdoors was virtually the same as that used in the military: nothing was designed especially for middle school students.

118   Chapter 4

Military training soon influenced general standards of behavior and dress codes in Taiwanese schools. Minister of Education Cheng Tianfang changed all upper middle school uniforms to khaki on September 6, 1953 (some schools' uniforms had been gray before this). After much discussion, in February 1955 the MOE and MND announced that college students would also wear khaki uniforms, but only during occasions when they were undergoing military training and participating in special events (parades, holidays, all-school CYC activities). The MOE actually assigned students to specific tailors, who custom-made all uniforms. The rest of the time it allowed college students to wear the clothing of their choice.[51]

Parent and Student Response to Student Military Training

Even before the government implemented mandatory military education in all Taiwanese middle schools, citizens began to anticipate the changes and respond in different ways. Many who opposed the idea began voicing their concerns immediately. On May 30, 1952, Cheng Tianfang issued a statement to calm the fears of parents and students about the one-year mandatory training after college graduation. "While students are in school, they are unable to receive full-time training," he explained. "This one year is to complete what was not done at school. It is only training to be a reserves officer, not service in the armed forces. Our training is the same system as the ones in England and the U.S."[52]

From February 12–14, 1953, the GMD's official newspaper, *Central Daily News* (*Zhongyang ribao*), published the CYC's response to fifty-seven questions sent in by readers, some of which indicated fears that the youth organization and military instructors would negatively interfere with schools. Question 40 (referring to training on the mainland) posed: "Is the CYC's military training style the same as the past?" Since the program was not yet fully implemented in 1953, the organization provided a rather lackluster response, noting that "in the past military training's contents were boring, the method was always the same. It lacked equipment, thus it was not effective."[53] Another question inquired: "What does it mean to militarize extracurricular activities?" To some readers, the CYC's reply was again vague and inadequate, attempting to promote militarism by linking it to manners, behaviors, and dress—in essence, military instructors would teach Taiwan's children to act like respectable young people. "Students' life must meet military standards," the answer began. "For example, when students gather, they need to line up. When class is dismissed, they need to line up and walk as a group according to military standards. Their gestures, speech, and behavior must meet military standards."[54] In this way, the CYC attempted to downplay overt militarization and direct links between compulsory military training and the armed forces, choosing instead to focus on the fight against delinquency and convincing skeptical parents that the pedagogy would teach the island's youngsters how to be proper citizens as well as soldiers.

Still, when the MND first implemented the training, most students' families were suspicious of the program and very few encouraged or praised the idea. According to Xiao Xiqing, head of CYC military training, parents soon "observed that student discipline gradually improved so they were pleased about it."[55] Yet Xiao's sentiments, like the CYC's own reports, were naturally biased, and both had a vested interest in expanding the program and convincing the public that parents welcomed military training. On the other hand, one GMD publication— the biweekly journal *Free Youth* (*Ziyou qingnian*)—actually criticized the instruction vehemently. It routinely argued that students rejected military training not out of delinquency but because they viewed it as a waste of time that interfered with their schoolwork. Some students and their families believed in more elaborate conspiracy theories, including the idea that the government had dispatched the military instructors to spy on students and control them. Despite Xiao's words and the usually upbeat CYC publications, a September 13, 1953, CYC report recognized these fears, concluding that "schools, families, and the social environment" were all influencing students' negative attitude towards the military programs.[56]

Overall, the CYC's official publications were important tools that celebrated military training.[57] One influential writer was Liu Yifu, a CYC representative who conducted a survey in the 1950s to gauge popular opinion about the training. Liu interviewed the former Pingdong county magistrate, Lin Shicheng, who had served under Japanese colonial rule (1895–1945). Lin recounted that "under Japanese occupation, we had military training every day. Now it is only three hours a week? How could it be so little? All the Taiwanese received military training under the Japanese. After retrocession, military training ceased. We all felt that was strange. Why didn't our country have military training? Now everyone is happy that military training is reinstated."[58] According to Liu's account, the Taiwanese public welcomed the pedagogy because residents had experienced it under the Japanese and were accustomed to the "military training lifestyle" (*junxun shenghuo*).[59] He noted that parents were especially interested in the program for their sons and daughters because they themselves had received the training as students.

According to Liu, the Japanese training of the past was far more intense than any CYC program, including discipline: Japanese military instructors were known to kick students with leather boots, slap them across the face, and demean them by forcing students to kneel down. Many 1950s Taiwanese parents felt military

120   Chapter 4

instructors under the GMD government were actually quite soft, no longer beating or berating—indeed, even treating students like friends. To some parents this was a great improvement, and they only wished that more school hours were devoted to compulsory training.[60] Liu also interviewed Chen Wanguo, a history teacher from Hualian Middle School who himself had once been a student at the school. Chen also recalled the strictness of Japanese military training, noting that "when students were berated and beaten, they were very afraid" (*xueshengmen zai dama zi xia jiu shi zhidao pa*) and hailed the new program as a refreshing break from the past. He opined "nowadays, people teach and learn with ease, and improvements are faster even though less time is spent on military training" (*xianzhai dajia dou shi qingsong yukuai de jiao he xue, suiran shijian shao, jinbu fan'er genkuai*).[61]

In many ways, Liu constructed his 1950s interviews around similar themes as CYC official reports. He was, after all, acting as a CYC representative and he clearly framed the interviews to support his other publications, including a 1955 article entitled "Revival's Opportunity, Victory's Guarantee" in the CYC's *Chinese Youth's Military Training Life*.[62] Liu argued that the Taiwanese embraced military training, yet he carefully selected quotes from interviewees that supported the organization's cause and he contrasted the Japanese program with that of the GMD's to convince readers of the greater humaneness and productivity of the latter.

Yet by other accounts, military training in 1950s Taiwan still occasionally slipped into older patterns of harsh discipline and physical punishment. Li Taihan documents how CYC military instructors punished students by forcing them to kneel if they did not salute the national flag, and Chiang Ching-kuo himself had to address the issue at times during the decade, especially after he was informed that military instructors were using corporal punishment on students, which he flatly prohibited.

Regardless of how widespread these instances were, CYC military training was definitely not as positive and rosy as Liu's publications insisted. In addition to renouncing corporal punishment, Ching-kuo also reprimanded military instructors for dating, "pompousness," and other behaviors he deemed "inappropriate." In Yilan county, one instructor took his students to the movie theater and demanded a discount for the tickets. When the theater staff refused, the disgruntled man threatened to bomb the theater, prompting frightened employees to call the police.[63]

Mao Cheng-how (1935–) recalled when his military program began in 1953 during his senior year at Jianguo High School in Taipei. "Military training started as a result of the China Youth Corps . . . In the beginning it was very primitive.

The government didn't have a well-planned, thought-out program. It was sort of like basic training—'line up,' 'stand at attention,' 'turn left.' Students did not like the military instructors."[64] Mao witnessed one incident in which students even challenged their instructor directly: "The military instructor was picking on a class representative (*banzhang*). He wanted to possess complete control and the *banzhang* tried to reason [with the instructor] rather than be controlled and that was a 'no-no' in the military. We all ganged together to support the schoolmate." The instructor tried to use the student as a scapegoat to teach them all a lesson. In the morning, they held the flag raising ceremony. Over fifty years later, Mao could still vividly recall: "It was raining that day so the ceremony was indoors. We had to do some military-style activities. We gave our best performance so the military instructor could not find trouble with the *banzhang*. So we saved the student from embarrassment." He also recounted that each class had fifty students: "Everyday they had one student who called 'Stand at attention! Salute!' (*Lizhen! Jingli!*) He gave the order and everyone followed. The military instructor was always on the platform. That student led us to do it in front of the military instructor. We saluted the flag after we raised it."[65]

Public Criticism of Military Training

In September 1952, the CYC first published its laws and regulations before its formal establishment on October 31. Xu Fuguan was a professor at Tunghai University in Taichung and a friend of Lei Chen, editor of *Free China* (*Ziyou zhongguo*)—a journal initially sympathetic to the GMD regime. In response to the CYC's proclamation, Xu posed some suggestions and critiques pertaining to student military training in a *Free China* article published on October 16, two weeks before the organization's official establishment. Reacting to the CYC's indication that it would enter schools, Xu recommended that "the CYC Deputy Director should be from the MNDPD and be in charge of the social youth and student military training," while all military instructors "be under the authority of the school principal and be part of the faculty, not an independent group."[66] Xu argued that compulsory training should only be a temporary wartime program, and he also suggested that the minister of education serve as the CYC director. Chiang Chingkuo accepted many of Xu's recommendations, with the exception that Chingkuo himself became the organization's first director. Also, the fact that the CYC remained housed under the MND until July 1, 1960, continued to bother critics of overt militarism, including Xu.

Yuan Shi, another contributor to *Free China,* cautiously criticized both military training and the CYC in mild tones, recognizing the danger in denouncing

122   Chapter 4

GMD programs during the 1950s. Still, Yuan maintained that the CYC's "most unsatisfactory aspect" was the compulsory military training, a program that to him stemmed from a government afraid of previous college student protests and anti-hunger and anti-suppression campaigns. (Notably, Yuan used the term "anti-suppression" (*fan pohai*) strikes instead of the stronger term "anti-civil war" (*fan neizhan*) strikes that occurred on the mainland.) In one 1957 column, Yuan wrote that this was the reason why "today everything has to be under 'leadership' for approval." (Again, here Yuan utilized the milder term "leadership" (*lingdao*) instead of the loaded term "control" (*kongzhi*).) "Perhaps there is a reason for it," he continued, "but sometimes the correction is overboard . . . Every summer the CYC has training for youth. Some young people enjoy it, but other than that, it is useless." Yuan also criticized the futility of sporadic combat training in schools: "Students practice target shooting only once a semester. Just because someone shoots the target a few times does not mean he is familiar with the weapon or increases his combat experience. The guns that they practiced with are very old and outdated."[67]

Free China's influential and liberal contributors soon ramped up their critique of the GMD, eventually leading the regime to denounce and dismantle the publication in 1960 following the government's arrest of Lei Chen on sedition charges for trying to establish the Chinese Democratic Party.[68] Throughout the 1950s military training continued to be one of *Free China's* primary targets. In a January 1, 1958, editorial, Fu Zheng charged that the training was neither systematic nor scientific. Fu emerged as one of the CYC's most vocal critics, especially condemning compulsory training. He attacked the organization for using the program to infiltrate upper middle schools and sending unqualified military instructors, noting that many had not completed upper middle school themselves, while others had no formal military training. Fu also criticized the imposition of the program in schools for having "too many negative side effects," including interference with students' learning.[69]

In response to these (and other) critics in the press, student negativity, and the skepticism of some parents, Chiang Ching-kuo himself echoed CYC publications by vigorously defending compulsory military training throughout the 1950s. During the China Youth Corps Work Meeting on February 27, 1958, Ching-kuo responded directly to Fu's critique with ten points justifying the CYC. The fourth pertained to military training, arguing that the "CYC's military training in school is part of education. The principals are the CYC's supervisors. Military training is independent from school administration. The CYC cooperates with schools and has never interfered with nor superseded their administration."[70] Two years earlier, on December 4, 1956, Ching-kuo had even started warning military instructors to pay attention to *Free China* articles penned by "liberal writers."[71]

Later that summer, Fu Zheng again blasted CYC training in another editorial, criticizing the organization's claim that the GMD had formed it for the sole purpose of student military training.[72] According to Fu, the CYC had poorly planned the program and should not have implemented it without formal legislation. To Fu, the organization had initially wanted to train reserves and low-level officers; however, it was now simply disciplining students, abandoning the idea to recruit and train soldiers for the reserve army. Fu also noted that the organization had already established formal armed forces training for graduating college students, thus there was no need for such programs in both upper middle schools *and* colleges. Most significantly, Fu further increased the rhetoric linking military training to a repressive government, attacking the CYC for "appearing to be a government organization established for military training, however it is actually meant for the one-party reserves so it can control schools' education and more completely interfere with academic freedom and independence . . . It wastes much of students' time and effort, hindering their pursuit of education."[73]

While critics like Fu attacked the program as part of a larger critique of the CYC, the two Chiangs, and the Nationalist regime, others (including many students and parents) simply directed frustration at military instructors themselves. In a June 16, 1958, letter to *Free China*, one contributor charged that many instructors suffered from inferiority complexes because they felt threatened by students and came from "poorly educated backgrounds." Thus, instructors used the excuse that students had to obey them in order to prove their power over young people—and students simply had to tolerate the situation because they did not want any trouble. The contributor also condemned the military pedagogy for being "meaningless and riddled with mistakes." It was "a ridiculous political class," s/he opined, "if you want to improve military training, military instructors with modern knowledge and education need to teach the courses." Still, even when critiquing the instructors or the pedagogy, students and parents easily found themselves making larger assessments about the one-party government. The author's letter ended with a reference to Chiang Ching-kuo, who was "behind the implementation of military training and thus, the system could not be dismantled . . . since the organization backing is very strong, so other legislative members dare not oppose it."[74]

The Liu Ziran Incident

As *Free China* contributor Yuan Shi suggested, one of the reasons why the government implemented military training in schools was to curb potential student protests, and on that front the program succeeded remarkably well for the first

124   Chapter 4

three decades of GMD rule—with one notable exception.[75] In 1957, China Youth Corps members at Chenggong High School, along with thousands of other young people, staged a dramatic anti-American riot at locations across Taipei. The US had sent the Military Assistance Advisory Group to provide aid to the National-ist government and contain Communist expansion in 1951; and by 1957 there were ten thousand American military personnel and civilians on the island. The ad-visers enjoyed diplomatic immunity. (The Military Assistance Advisory Group did not leave Taiwan until 1978.) This particularly violent demonstration, dubbed the "Liu Ziran Incident" by the Chinese and the "Reynolds case" by Americans, is sig-nificant not only because of its links to the CYC and compulsory military instruc-tion, but also because those very connections made the student protest appear to be sanctioned by the GMD.

On March 20, 1957, US Army sergeant Robert Reynolds fatally shot a main-lander, Liu Ziran, outside of the Reynolds family residence in the American military housing community of Yangmingshan's Shantzuhou, eight miles outside Taipei.[76] There were no witnesses, and during his American tribunal hearing Reynolds testified that Liu had been peeping at his wife while she showered and he had shot the man in self-defense (he claimed that Liu was brandishing a pipe). When a court martial acquitted Reynolds on May 23, the sergeant received a rous-ing ovation from the American audience. The Chinese, however, expressed outrage at the verdict. According to US State Department records, rumors spread throughout Taipei that "there had been black market dealings between Reynolds and the deceased and that Chinese and American authorities were in collusion to cover up evidence which might embarrass either Government."[77] According to the most prominent rumor, Reynolds had employed Liu for a long time to smuggle controlled products (such as imported tobacco and liquor) out of the Army Co-op for sale on the black market, with both men pocketing the profit: Reynolds had fatally shot Liu over a financial dispute between the two.

On May 24, an air force plane quickly flew Reynolds, his wife, and daughter back to the US. Figure 4.1 shows them departing from the plane that landed at Tra-vis Air Force Base near Fairfield, California. At noon the same day, Liu's widow began a hunger strike and started picketing the US Embassy. A radio reporter from the Broadcasting Corporation of China recorded an interview with her and played it back through a loudspeaker for the gathering crowd.[78] According to the *New York Times,* around 1:30 p.m. "a youth clad in blue jeans hurled a stone at the Embassy window."[79] The crowd cheered and more stones flew. By 2:00 p.m., the mob had grown to three thousand, smashing through the embassy's gates and climbing over the walls. Another youth scaled the flagpole, tore down and shredded the Ameri-can flag, and hoisted the Chinese Nationalist flag in its place.[80] The rioters next

Figure 4.1. Sergeant Robert Reynolds, his wife, Clara, and daughter, Shirley, aged seven years, arrive at Travis Air Force Base near Fairfield, California, on May 27, 1957. Reynolds's acquittal of the murder of Liu Ziran by a military court sparked one of the largest anti-American protests in Taiwan's history. Courtesy of the Associated Press.

stormed the embassy building itself, smashing furniture, tossing classified documents out the windows, setting a truck on fire, and overturning fourteen vehicles.

The disorder soon spread to other parts of Taipei. Figure 4.2 displays a crowd watching the destruction of the US Information Service (USIS) building. Another crowd tried to infiltrate the US Military Communications Center.[81] (Interestingly, the USIS sold subscriptions to *Free China*, which had begun, by 1954, to publish articles critical of Chiang Kai-shek and the GMD.[82]) Officials called in troops, but thirty-three thousand Chinese soldiers did not arrive until after the violence had injured nine Americans, killed one Chinese, and injured thirteen others.[83] The seven-hour riot ended after the troops established order and the government imposed martial law from midnight to 5:00 a.m.[84] In the US, the Reynolds case and the subsequent riot made front-page headlines around the country.

Figure 4.2. On May 24, 1957, an office chair is tossed from a window of the US Information Service (USIS) building as a crowd watches during anti-American riots in Taipei. China Youth Corps members from Chenggong High School participated in the protests, including the ransacking of the USIS building and the US Embassy. Courtesy of the Associated Press.

Not only were China Youth Corps members among these anti-American rioters, but Chenggong High School's military instructor actually led the core contingent of students from the school. They had sought Chiang Ching-kuo's approval to demonstrate before the embassy, which he granted with an understanding that the students would keep things peaceful.[85] Fifty students wearing uniforms and CYC armbands arrived at the embassy.[86] However, the demonstration became increasingly violent, especially as outsiders joined the crowd. Lee Huan, a top aide to Ching-kuo, alerted him, and both men sped to the CYC headquarters to monitor the situation. Still, according to Jay Taylor, a retired Foreign Service officer, Ching-kuo "declined to send in a nearby antiriot squad."[87] Taiwan's foreign minister George Yeh soon pressed Ching-kuo for immediate action, and when the Garrison Command officer in charge of the riot squad requested permission to restore order, Ching-kuo "instructed him not to use force . . . [and] ordered plainclothesmen to infiltrate the mob to try to contain the violence."[88] Lee claimed he contacted schools to persuade students to return to their campuses and asked principals to stop students from surrounding the embassy. However, about thirty Chenggong High School students still "voluntarily" gathered there.[89]

Ching-kuo and Lee worked all through the night to manage the situation. Meanwhile, rumors spread that Ching-kuo himself had arranged for CYC members to initiate the riot. Ching-kuo later told Lee, "Others say the CYC planned the anti-American May 24th Incident behind the scenes. We went through a lot of trouble to handle the problem but there are still people who slander us." Two days after the riots, a dejected Ching-kuo remarked to Lee that some people proposed that the government dismantle the CYC because of its connection to the violence. "This is too unjust," Lee responded, and suggested that he publicly issue a statement on behalf of Ching-kuo outlining their course of action in handling the situation. However, Ching-kuo refused, telling Lee, "No, this will create complications . . . In the future, the truth will be revealed."[90]

Ching-kuo probably could not imagine that a small group of middle school students would help precipitate a riot ultimately destroying the US Embassy. As Taylor writes, he also "worried about his 'enforcer' image in Taiwan and his future leadership role . . . [and] would not have wanted to turn the anti-riot police against members of his own Youth Corps."[91] Former Taiwan president Ma Ying-jeou, a senior aide to Ching-kuo in the 1980s and former CYC member, recalled that Ching-kuo believed the Americans could afford a new embassy and remarked, "better that than have the police in Ching-kuo's name shoot down citizens in the streets."[92]

Yet, whether officially encouraged by Ching-kuo and the CYC or not, students were the heart of the anti-American protest and were directly influenced by their military instructors. Even the Americans recognized the connection and its implications. Undoubtedly referring to Chenggong High School, the *New York Times* reported under the headline "Riot Link Denied By Chiang Regime" that "a junior high school in Taipei seems to have been the focal point of the unrest before and after the controversial court-martial verdict was announced." The *Times* went on to note that "many students were among the apparent leaders of rioters, generally believed to be about equally divided between mainlanders and Taiwanese. The leaders were identifiable by their school uniforms."[93] The paper also described how "a throng of 10,000 besieged the Taipei Police Headquarters to demand the release of students arrested in the disorders."[94] US State Department authorities who subsequently investigated the incident also observed that "in the attack on the USIS building, the riot was led by a small group of students who apparently were responsible for most of the damage done."[95]

Despite the role of students, many US officials and Americans in Taiwan did not believe that the riot was "spontaneous." On May 25, the US Military

128   Chapter 4

Communication Center informed the US Department of Defense that it had obtained evidence that the rioters planned the protest in advance. The CIA also received reports indicating that the day before the incident many foreign Catholic priests had received cryptic phone calls warning them not to go out the next day. If they had to go out, the mysterious callers advised them, they should avoid the US Embassy.[96] In addition, one CIA officer reported to the *New York Times* that "he received at least twenty telephone calls from Chinese the afternoon and morning preceding the riot, warning him that a dangerous situation was developing."[97]

In a remarkable confrontation on May 26, US ambassador to the Republic of China Karl Rankin arrived at Chiang Kai-shek's residence unannounced and interrogated the president directly. According to the Taiwan Central News Agency, Rankin spoke frankly with Chiang: "You did not send the army and police earlier. You allowed the embassy to fall into the hands of the mob." He implied that Chingkuo himself instigated the riot, asking the elder Chiang, "is this because the person who initiated the attack is very powerful and influential? Powerful enough to stop any police action?" The generalissimo denied everything.[98] According to Rankin's autobiography, Chiang then asked the ambassador "to express his profound regrets to President Dwight D. Eisenhower and Secretary of State John Foster Dulles; also to assure them that the incident [did] not reflect anti-American feeling but simply resentment at the verdict of the court-martial."[99] Rankin concluded that widespread antipathy towards Americans existed because of the living standards flaunted by an American community that numbered ten thousand, and because of the immunity from Chinese laws (reminiscent of extraterritoriality) that all Americans connected with the US military enjoyed.[100]

On June 14, Premier O. K. Yui's (Yu Jongjun's) cabinet gave its report on the Liu Ziran Incident to the Legislative Yuan. This official Chinese version of what happened addressed the accusation that middle school students or the CYC were the primary protesters. The report explained that the eleven injured protesters ranged in age from sixteen to forty-six and their occupations varied from "office boys, salesclerks, pedicab drivers, printing shop workers, to editors, students and trades people."[101] Of the 111 arrested, their ages also ranged from sixteen to forty-six, and consisted of "lower-level government employees, tailors, workers, drivers, farmers, trades people, office boys, peddlers, reporters, students, and a number of unemployed."[102] (In fact, historian Stephen Craft points out that two students, ages thirteen and fourteen, were arrested but later released.[103]) Taiwan officials could not see how it was possible that such a diverse group of individuals could organize and implement a preplanned protest.

The report acknowledged the presence of students at the May 24 riot and admitted that they were "almost unanimously dissatisfied with the not-guilty verdict."[104] However, it claimed that most students limited their protests to speeches and writings. Both the Ministry of Education and the CYC "advised students on the Reynolds case and tried to channel their feelings in order to prevent disturbances."[105] Internal Taiwan government documents show that the night before the riots, a warning went out to the CYC that any protests could damage US–Taiwan relations.[106] Nevertheless, fifty students from Chenggong High School left school premises without permission (supposedly their principal was ill) and marched by the embassy carrying placards, but they did not shout slogans nor did they join the mob.[107] This account contradicts Jay Taylor's claim that Chenggong students received permission from Ching-kuo to demonstrate peacefully at the embassy. Premier O. K. Yui's report further explained that high school students who were unable to reach their campuses because of a previously scheduled air raid drill stopped at the embassy, as did students who left school to go home for lunch. These students, who wore uniforms and carried satchel bags, "out of curiosity at first and later under the spell of the mob psychology, followed the crowds into the Embassy and participated in their senseless acts of violence."[108] In an attempt to counter the American accusation that the CYC organized the embassy riot, the report asserted that all students in upper middle school and above wore the CYC insignia on their sleeves. This was true since it was mandatory for all upper middle school students to become CYC members in 1957. The report further argued that the facts presented "should serve to prove that the students' participation in the riots was not pre-arranged or organized."[109]

In mid-September, President Eisenhower appointed Special Assistant James Richards to investigate the incident. Richards wrote to Dulles that Chiang refused to comment when he informed the generalissimo "that it was widely reported in the United States that members of the Youth Corps (which is commanded by his son, Chiang Ching-kuo) were active in inciting the riot and the destruction of [the] Embassy and the USIS Office."[110] Dulles' brother, CIA director Allen Dulles, also believed that the riot was not spontaneous, but he told the National Security Council that the extent of the convulsion had probably exceeded official expectations. Despite the assertions of other American and Chinese observers, Allen Dulles discounted speculation that Ching-kuo himself instigated the riot.[111]

Based on reports that the destruction went on for some seven hours despite Taiwan's reputation for tight police control, Americans suspected that the GMD government at the very least condoned the violence. If so, there were at least two possible motives. First, many Taiwanese indeed resented the wealth and privilege that the American community enjoyed in Taiwan, including immunity from the local legal system. According to the State Department, "the acquittal verdict of [the] court martial had touched Chinese National feeling at a very tender spot—namely,

130   Chapter 4

hatred of extraterritoriality."[112] The incident was thus an opportunity for the public to blow off steam. However, at a higher level there was another good reason to suspect GMD leaders of complicity. According to Nancy Bernkopf Tucker, in May 1957 they were unhappy with John Foster Dulles' "efforts to get Beijing to renounce the use of force in the Taiwan Straits so that U.S.–China relations could be improved. They felt disappointed by the unwillingness of the U.S. government to commit its power to the defense of the offshore islands or to endorse their efforts to return to the mainland."[113] Tucker argues that, when faced with a dominating superpower, "Chiang Kai-shek sought to impress upon American military authorities his determination to retain full, autonomous control of his armed forces," as well as Taiwan's political and economic affairs.[114]

In the end, the Liu Ziran Incident did not seriously damage US–Taiwan relations. Apologies immediately followed and Chiang Kai-shek dismissed and imprisoned three high-ranking public security officers.[115] The GMD also repaired the damaged facilities and the US remained, as Tucker writes, "Taiwan's most generous and dominant benefactor."[116]

As for Ching-kuo, in the aftermath of the Liu Ziran Incident he further consolidated his power by obstructing challengers' attempts to thwart him from succeeding his father's position or threaten the elder Chiang's rule. In early 1959, Vice President Chen Cheng met with a group of generals who had long-standing ties with him. One of the topics discussed was the arrangements for President Chiang Kai-shek's succession if the elder Chiang were to adhere to the constitution and not seek another term in 1960. Ching-kuo's intelligence people had bugged the meeting, and the senior officials involved soon found themselves retiring or assigned to noncommand positions.[117] Meanwhile, in 1960 Lei Chen, the editor of *Free China,* began planning his formation of the new China Democratic Party in a direct challenge to the GMD regime. In response, Chen Cheng advocated tolerance: perhaps he and, more importantly, those around him hoped to build a future base of political support among Taiwanese. Lei interpreted this endorsement as a green light. In contrast, Ching-kuo took a tough position against Lei's initiative. He gave permission for internal security officials to suppress the China Democratic Party. Bribes and threats persuaded one of the new party's leaders to leave the country, two were beaten by unknown persons, and several had their business licenses revoked. In September security police arrested Lei, who was sentenced to ten years in prison.[118]

Still, the Liu Ziran Incident demonstrated the power of nascent compulsory military instruction in Taiwan's middle schools, and how GMD leaders simultaneously used the CYC's program to stifle student activism and enforce discipline while allowing a "spontaneous" student riot to escalate into a full-scale, anti-American demonstration in an authoritarian police state. However, officials probably did not foresee the degree of magnitude and violence that students eventually manifested over Reynolds' acquittal. If the students had directed such a riot at the GMD itself, it would have undoubtedly drawn a stiffer response and been stifled immediately.

Compulsory military training was a powerful force in Taiwan's classrooms and campuses throughout the 1950s, preventing student protests via discipline and fear, as well as attempting to instill in students a sense of patriotism and loyalty to the Nationalist government. According to Ching-kuo, the new state expected its military instructors to "develop student's physical fitness and enthusiasm, help them follow a proper lifestyle, and teach them to behave properly."[119] Overall, despite its hesitant origins, sometimes flimsy organization, vocal critics, and student activists, compulsory military training in Taiwan's upper middle schools and universities successfully helped maintain social order under the GMD's evolving authoritarian state. Another factor contributing to relative peace was the fact that Taiwan was much smaller than the mainland and there were not significant political parties, militias, or civil society organizations that could mount a real challenge to the GMD. Moreover, there was no hot battlefield war raging between the GMD and CCP after the Nationalist withdrawal to Taiwan. The GMD learned the lesson of restricting the CYC to youth instead of allowing older members to make up the majority of organizations such as the SQT and ignoring issues that pertained to young people. The CYC also incorporated many enjoyable extracurricular recreational activities that appealed to youth instead of purely party indoctrination, which undoubtedly made student military training and the presence of military instructors more palatable for some students and their families.

CHAPTER FIVE

Civics Textbooks and Curricular Standards, 1937–1960

The Sino-Japanese War's disruption not only prompted the Guomindang to exert stronger administrative control over some middle schools, it also opened the door for the central government to further influence actual curriculum and implement more specific classroom policies. It is impossible to understand Nationalist youth mobilization in secondary schools without examining the role of civics (*gongmin*) courses in GMD-occupied areas of China and Taiwan, from the beginning of Japan's invasion of China in 1937 to the end of the first decade of Nationalist rule on Taiwan in 1960. Civics class was offered one to two hours per week in both lower and upper middle schools. Based on civics curricular standards and textbooks, one can compare the material used in pre-1949, mainland classrooms to those used in post-1949 Taiwan. In both locations, the civics curriculum provides a unique look at what GMD education officials thought secondary school students should be learning to become citizens, including how the government sought to indoctrinate students with party ideology. According to Peter Zarrow, "textbooks are central to political socialization and knowledge formation in all modern societies, precisely because they represent the best opportunity for state elites to shape children."[1] Educators and scholars crafted textbooks to reach large audiences as quickly as possible. Whether for the lofty goal of educating the masses, or for the pragmatic aim of earning extra money, many leading GMD educators and academics wrote them. By the 1930s these men had already found the textbook market, in addition to classroom teaching, to be an important avenue for expressing views and disseminating ideas. However, as Zarrow rightly reminds us, "textbooks themselves tell us what elites hoped to impart to children but not what children actually learned or what they thought about their texts."[2]

Self-cultivation was a central theme emphasized in Chinese schools, beginning in the late Qing dynasty (1902–1911) and continuing into the early Republican period (1912–1927). Yet civics replaced self-cultivation in a series of curricular reforms initiated in 1923, a dramatic break that shifted curriculum away from emphasizing personal, moral character and more towards understanding social conditions.[3] "Nonetheless," writes Zarrow, "even after 1923, social life was predicated on the inculcation of 'good habits' which suggest moral training."[4] During the late Qing dynasty, classes in self-cultivation were designed to supplement the moral lessons educational leaders thought the traditional "Four Books" and "Five Classics" would provide. Textbooks in self-cultivation, a complete innovation in the late nineteenth century, were therefore meant to help students practice the principles and models covered in much older texts: "Educators first saw them in use in Japan, which . . . had adopted them from Western models even while maintaining the centrality of Chinese classics."[5] When the Qing government first proposed a self-cultivation curriculum in 1902, upper-level students were to begin with the *Classic of Filial Piety* and the *Analects* (records of conversations with Confucius written by his students) before moving on to classics focused on ritual, ethical philosophy, and history.[6] As Zarrow notes, "[t]his curriculum existed mostly on paper, as the actual schools were not yet operating, and it was soon superseded. But it clearly showed that Qing officials believed that the heart of self-cultivation lay in the Four Books and Five Classics that they themselves had studied."[7] By the late Qing, self-cultivation textbooks thus emphasized traditional concepts of personal morality—including filial piety, trustworthiness, and loyalty. But they also did so within a context of teaching students how members of a modern nation-state should act. "They did not speak of 'citizens,'" writes Zarrow, "because of course they were designed to educate 'subjects' of the emperor. But a new view of the virtue of loyalty was emerging: in this view the highest loyalty was not owed to any individual . . . but to the state, or perhaps even to the nation, to the Chinese people."[8]

The new curriculum began to be implemented in 1904, and it called for self-cultivation classes to be held two hours per week, separately from classics reading. Their goal was to foster children's moral nature, teaching them to avoid bad habits and acquire good ones.[9] In middle schools, self-cultivation was based on the *Five Sets of Bequeathed Guidelines* (*Wuzhong yigui*) of Chen Hongmou (1696–1771), which students were charged with reading systematically over five years. Emphasizing Chen's work was an effort to popularize orthodox morality and provide practical guidelines for specific classes of people, ranging from women to merchants.[10]

Following the 1911 Revolution, Cai Yuanpei—minister of education under the Nanjing revolutionary government of 1912—proposed a new set of principles to replace Qing education. Cai completely rejected the Qing principles of "loyalty to the monarch" and "reverence for Confucius"; in his eyes, the former were incompatible with a republic, the latter with religious freedom. Instead, Cai proposed a curriculum that would teach a new generation of Chinese students the French Revolution's principles of liberty, equality, and fraternity.[11] Yet this new, republican

134   Chapter 5

self-cultivation curriculum, like the old, began first with filial piety and fraternal duty, conceiving of a child's world of concern as gradually moving from family and immediate relatives to, eventually, the nation and the world. For all the radical features of Cai's ultimate vision of education, his specific ideas about a self-cultivation curriculum were as much a continuation as a break from late Qing practice.[12]

By approximately 1920, civics classes had begun to replace courses in self-cultivation, at least in progressive middle schools. In 1914, one Chinese education writer noted that nationalism formed the core of civics education in foreign countries. Whereas Western nations made civics a required course, Japan taught both civics and morality, he noted. But the issue facing China was particularly urgent, he claimed, because China—having just become a republic—needed civics education to qualify its people as citizens.[13]

As China descended into warlordism after President Yuan Shikai's death in 1916, regional power holders provided little support for schools. Nonetheless, civics still replaced self-cultivation in the curricular reforms of 1923. This new curriculum diminished Confucianism yet did not completely eliminate it, and in lower middle schools it reduced the attention paid to moral behavior in favor of more academic understanding of state and society. Curricular goals spoke of the "spirit" of constitutional government and "fostering citizenship morality."[14] Graduation standards included basic knowledge of hygiene, the legal system, and economics and society, as well as the relationship between self and others and the rules of collective living.

The Nationalist government that took power in 1928 inherited these 1923 reforms. As Zarrow notes, educator Sheng Langxi (1901–1974) "framed the 1923 reforms as a rejection of the narrow 'self-cultivation' emphasis on self-control in favor of a broader 'civics' knowledge of self and society, practical reforms, and habits suitable for modern life."[15] Classes in Party Principles and the Three People's Principles acted more to supplement and update the civics curriculum than replace it. Educators, intellectuals, and the GMD sought to use civics to relate to students' fundamental ideas about the meaning and practice of citizenship. As Robert Culp writes, students were now supposed to learn how "to relate contemporary ideas about modern society, social membership, and civic culture and morality."[16] Teachers also explained to them the institutions of political participation and patterns of self-government.

Once the GMD established its government in Nanjing, it sought to instill a new and stronger sense of patriotism across the entire nation. According to Zarrow, the party accepted that the Chinese people were not ready for democracy and instead "sought to create new citizens simultaneously capable of self-control and active participation—but participation only within the bounds drawn up by the Nationalists."[17] Schools were soon filled with a variety of textbooks on "Party Principles," the "Three People's Principles," "Civics," and "Society."[18] There was a good deal of overlap among these subjects. Generally, Party Principles represented an attempt to systematically inculcate students with Nationalist ideology. In the wake of the founding of the Nanjing government in 1928, civics education, like other subjects, underwent "partification" (*danghua*).

By 1930, civics materials were being reshaped to fit into classes on the "Three People's Principles" and "Party Principles." And later that decade the Nationalists changed the rubric's title for the course back to simply "Civics."[19] Nonetheless, regardless of the course name, the importance of citizenship training only increased under the Nationalists. Their curriculum included materials on the life of their party's founder, Sun Yat-sen, and various versions of his writings. Following Sun, the Nationalists also tried to make room in the curriculum for what they considered the positive aspects of "traditional morality."[20]

The first curricular goal listed in the GMD's 1932 civics curricular standards for lower middle schools was "to enable students through actual life experiences to understand the relationship between self and society and to foster the moral qualities of cultivating the self and serving others." The Three People's Principles came second and traditional morality last. None of this constituted revolutionary change to the existing curriculum. If the Nationalists brought back "loyalty and filial piety," they emphasized that this was loyalty to the nation, to the people, and not the traditional "loyalty to the monarch." The result was to sharpen lessons by directly inculcating patriotism through, for example, teaching respect for symbols of state and party.[21]

In the early twentieth century China's three largest publishers were the Commercial Press (Shangwu yingshuguan, founded in 1897), Zhonghua Book Company (Zhonghua shuju, founded 1912), and World Book Company (Shijie shuju, founded 1921). From the late Qing through the start of the Sino-Japanese War, the combination of these publishers accounted for the vast majority of books approved by the government and sold to students.[22]

The Challenges to Continuing Civics Education in Wartime

Before the outbreak of the Sino-Japanese War, Chiang Kai-shek constantly urged Chinese to save their country by strengthening education. According to Chiang, education was the nation's most powerful weapon. Yet the outbreak of the Marco Polo Incident in July 1937 saw this potential weapon lose its effectiveness, as many

136   Chapter 5

schools were soon bombed by Japanese forces, textbooks and equipment lost, and teachers and students forced to flee inland. Immediately after the invasion, the Chinese media, intellectuals, and educators associated with the GMD all addressed this crisis in education. How should China's education system change to cope with special wartime needs? What would be the role, principles, and goals of education during wartime? How should these goals be achieved? Such questions swirled for nine months until GMD education policy was formally addressed at the Extraordinary Congress, held in Wuchang in March 1938.[23] The government continued to insist that there was no difference between education during war and during peacetime: all it sought to do was correct defects in the peacetime system and attempt to apply those reforms while the nation remained at war.[24] This concept of treating wartime and peacetime education as equivalent was based on the views of two senior GMD members, Jiang Baili and Wu Zhihui, leading educators Hu Shi and Fu Sinian, and the GMD's new minister of education, Chen Lifu.[25] Jiang, an intimate friend of Chiang Kai-shek, and Fu Sinian, a Peking University history professor, opposed any changes to China's educational system at the Second Defense Advisory Meeting (Guofan canyi hui) held that same year.[26] Jiang asked the government not to mobilize middle school and university students for war, but rather to encourage them to continue their studies in order to contribute to the development of science and industrial production, which he insisted would be needed if the war ended up lasting a long time. Chen, who became minister of education on January 7, 1938, and served for seven years, agreed. To him, it mattered little what specific human resources were needed to fight the war: all necessary skills still depended on conventional school education, which therefore needed to continue.[27]

In March 1939, Chiang Kai-shek declared that the most serious defect in Chinese education was the lack of "common belief" (*gongtong xinyang*). He explained that "the educational problems of a country . . . were how to establish the issue of common beliefs. In short, it is how to make people believe one ideology . . . and to save the country under one 'ism' (*yige zhuyi*), the Three People's Principles, and one coherent national policy (*yige guozhe*)."[28] These three points were the central tenets of Chiang's wartime education policy. Any educational system centered around a single ideology involves some form of control, and during a grave national crisis the GMD obviously attempted to control education. One motion passed by the Extraordinary Congress ordered all history, civics, and geography textbooks to be standardized and promote nationalism.[29] As Hu Kuo-tai argues, this standardization of textbooks was just one example of how the GMD asserted control over education (which Chen Lifu vigorously denied later) because it provided a forum for the indoctrination of GMD ideology. Other examples, Hu notes, included the investigation of teacher qualifications. These policies and practices were originally designed to promote the quality and quantity of education, but when implemented some were blatant measures of control. In the case of identifying and rectifying poorly qualified teachers—a problem even before the war—some teachers later accused the GMD of using subject matter examinations to rid the system of teachers suspected of being disloyal to the government.[30] Such GMD policies centered on control measures were a reaction to a perceived threat of teacher and student radicalism fueled by communism.

According to the GMD, the goal of education during the war was to build up the strength of national defense to defeat the Japanese, and to foster human resources for the development of China.[31] During the Sino-Japanese War the administration thus improved middle schools and their curricula with respect to wartime needs. As Chen wrote in 1942, textbooks for "courses on citizenship were modified to fit actual conditions and instructive passages were selected from the teachings of . . . Sun Yat-sen and other great leaders."[32]

When war broke out in 1937 there were 627,000 middle school students in China, making them a relatively small proportion of the country's total population (four hundred million). In the 1930s, middle school was still an elite level of education, as the cost alone made it prohibitively expensive for all but wealthy families. The combined cost of tuition, fees, and room and board at one middle school in Jiangsu province during the 1931–1932 school year ranged between approximately 52 and 130 yuan a year.[33] Thus, middle school students generally came from relatively privileged economic backgrounds, and the exclusivity of secondary education imbued middle school graduates with elite social status. However, during the war most refugee students were totally destitute when they managed to arrive in Chinese-controlled areas (or "free zones" unoccupied by the Japanese). For them, tuition was free and the Ministry of Education offered generous loans to cover their living expenses. Later in the conflict, as serious inflation and impoverishment in the middle class worsened, the Ministry provided financial aid to almost every student. And eventually all students in national middle schools were given full scholarships covering tuition, room, and board.[34]

One of the government's most important education reforms was its revised secondary education curriculum. Besides increasing its special wartime curriculum, the MOE in 1940 started regulating which subjects needed to be taught in each grade and how many hours per week each subject deserved. Specific subject contents were determined the following year, and lower middle school students began to be split into categories dubbed Group A and Group B. Group A students graduated and worked, while Group B students went on to continue their education by enrolling in upper middle schools. There students were once again split

138   Chapter 5

into Group A and Group B. This time Group A studied science, math, and technology, while Group B studied humanities subjects. By the third year of upper middle school vocational curriculum was available for students who planned to work and not pursue higher education.[35]

The printing and publishing of school textbooks was badly impacted in the second half of the 1930s. After the outbreak of war in July 1937, primary suppliers of school textbooks did not quickly relocate to GMD-controlled areas. Worse, in 1938 all textbooks previously endorsed by the Nationalist government were banned in Japanese-occupied areas; therefore, publishing houses in both Beijing and Shanghai stopped printing and distributing them. Despite the restructuring of the curriculum by the Nationalist government to meet wartime needs in 1941, no private publisher in GMD-controlled areas had the resources to prepare a new set of texts in line with the changes.[36] All textbook publishing companies were left behind in Japanese-occupied areas except for one, Zhengzhong Press, which had managed to relocate its headquarters when the Japanese invaded.[37] The MOE used all the Zhengzhong books it could, but there was not enough inventory and the texts were incomplete. As a result, areas controlled by the GMD suffered from a severe lack of textbooks during this period. According to Minister of Education Chen Lifu, the inability to print new books compelled most schools in those areas to use older textbooks published during the early Republican period (1912–1927) and the Nanjing decade (1927–1937).[38] In some remote areas, teachers ran out of textbooks completely and were forced to distribute their own crude lecture notes to students. Responding to the grave situation, provincial and municipal commissioners of education jointly petitioned the MOE for more resources. In response, the Ministry decided during the latter years of the war that the National Institute for Compilation and Translation, under its direction, would prepare a complete new series of history, geography, civics, and Chinese literature textbooks for primary and secondary education.

According to Jenny Huangfu Day, most schools still used commercial textbooks approved by the MOE at the outbreak of the war. It was not until 1943 when the national standard textbooks (*guodingben jiaokeshu*), the first mandatory national textbooks edited and supplied under complete government oversight for students enrolled in public and private schools under the GMD government's administration, replaced other commercial and private textbooks in elementary and secondary schools.[39] The office mainly in charge of writing the *guodingben* was the Textbook Compilation Committee for Elementary and Secondary Textbooks (Zhongxiaoxue jiaoke yongshu bianjuzu), established in September 1938 in the Chongqing suburbs and relocated to Beipei in April 1939. This policy continued after the Chinese Civil War in both mainland China and Taiwan. Between 1938 and 1940, the committee's main responsibilities were to inspect existing textbooks to determine their compatibility with the government's wartime policies, and compile supplementary wartime education readers and a set of standardized textbooks of the Chinese language, history, geography, and civics, intended for universal adoption in all primary and secondary schools.[40] From 1943 to 1945, the government sponsored a joint monopoly of seven publishers, known as the Seven Alliance (Commercial, Zhonghua, Zhengzhong, World, Dadong, Kaiming, and Wentong) to coordinate textbook supplies with local agencies. The *guodingben's* end came in 1947 when the contract between the Ministry of Education and the Eleven Alliance (the original seven publishers later added four smaller companies) expired.

As Helen Schneider notes, the MOE had already established a system of primary- and secondary-school textbook review before the war: however, this process became more rigorous after the invasion, when the MOE increased its effort to solicit, compile, edit, "and review textbooks for use at all levels when the National Institute of Compilation and Translation took over the Committee for the Compilation of Textbooks in 1942."[41] In particular, the Ministry "appointed experts to edit works in order to standardize what teachers taught and to make sure that certain disciplines" met the needs of China and the GMD.[42] In addition, the MOE released detailed outlines on how to implement Sun Yat-sen's Three People's Principles in primary schools, middle schools, institutes of higher education, normal schools, institutes of social education, overseas Chinese education, and in the education of Mongolian and Tibetan youth. The Three People's Principles were the GMD party's guiding political ideology of nationalism, democracy, and livelihood. The MOE therefore designed a curriculum centered on Sun's theory of "revolutionizing China."

Once the National Institute for Compilation and Translation prepared the books, the MOE granted final approval and the textbooks were published and distributed, with teachers and experts asked to provide feedback. In response the MOE revised the books, distributed again, and solicited a second round of feedback, followed by more revision. There were thus three different textbook designations: "temporary," "revised," and "standardized." The final printing of new books was contracted to private publishers, which received MOE subsidies in the form of loans and special allotments of paper rations to meet the massive demands.[43]

One of these contracted publishers, Commercial Press (Shangwu yinshuguan), quickly adjusted to the political demands of the period. Unlike other presses, such as Zhonghua, Commercial Press was far less nationalistic and pro-GMD in the 1920s. Yet it changed in response to demand, publishing a number of writings to

140   Chapter 5

arouse nationalism after the Japanese bombed Shanghai in 1931.[44] The Japanese even targeted the press's building precisely because it was the primary publisher of anti-Japanese textbooks in China.[45] After 1941, Commercial Press again publicly sided with the Nationalist government in hopes of securing publishing contracts. Its editor-in-chief, Wang Yunwu, became one of the leading pro-GMD publishers of the 1940s.[46] Other private presses contracted to produce textbooks, such as Zhengzhong Press, employed writers and editors who were relatively free from government intervention. Nevertheless, their political stance was generally pro-GMD.[47]

Staff editors produced and managed textual material. Major publishing companies such as Commercial Press, Zhonghua, and World Books recruited recent middle school and college graduates as staff editors who made up most of the commercial publishers' editing departments (*bianjibu* or *bianyisuo*) during the 1920s and 1930s.[48] This group had the basic skills for translating, researching, and writing for the publishers' major projects. These homegrown scholars with modern Western learning worked relatively cheaply.

The MOE hired many experts to revise textbooks. During the latter years of the war, it compiled standardized textbooks for primary and secondary schools in Chinese-controlled areas. Before the conflict, these schools had the freedom to choose their own books with MOE approval. While the prewar books thus varied in scope and content, as the war dragged on textbooks became far more uniform. Critics immediately noticed, some attacking the MOE and its minister Chen Lifu for having the GMD "control students' thoughts" (*tongzi sixiang*) with "party education" (*danghua jiaoyu*) and not allowing other publishers to produce textbooks by using subsidies "to compete in civilians' business" (*yumin zhengli*). In his 1973 memoir, Chen defended the decision to standardize textbooks by arguing that these critics misunderstood the situation at the time. According to him, the move was more about cutting costs than political indoctrination. Paper was scarce and printing was difficult and expensive in Chinese-controlled areas during the war. Chen thus insisted that the MOE decided to standardize textbooks in order to save money and produce uniform texts on better-quality paper (along with including different content, older textbooks were often produced with different kinds of paper). He argued that neither he nor the MOE ever profited financially from books but rather partnered with private publishing companies that were "happy to have the business."[49]

July 1929 thus marked the first time that the Guomindang standardized middle-school textbooks in China, and it would continue to do so in areas it controlled through the revision of curricular standards in August 1932, November 1936, September 1941, and December 1948.[50] The GMD also planned another

Civics Textbooks   141

revision that was cancelled after civil war broke out with the Communists. A fifth revision was completed in December 1952 in Taiwan, revisiting curricular standards for middle school civics, Chinese literature, history, and geography specifically because the government believed that the course material dictated by the previous revisions performed on the mainland did not fit the new circumstances of a people in exile, nor did they reflect new GMD platforms dictating the struggle against communism and the Soviet Union. In particular, the 1952 revisions sought to forge curriculum that reflected the new national policy of pacifying the Communists while nation-building on Taiwan.

Since textbooks were the primary vehicle for transmitting civics curricula to students in China's modern schools, a recurring theme in them—both in pre-1949 China and post-1949 Taiwan—was urging students to learn, as Culp writes, that "individuals' thoughts and actions should not be 'for themselves' but rather should, to varying degrees, be oriented toward the general social welfare."[51] The books thus "included a variety of socially productive personal behaviors and ethical orientations that they expected students, as future citizens, to embody."[52]

One such title, *Gongmin keben* (Civics textbook), was a lower middle school civics textbook published by Commercial Press in Shanghai in June 1937, one month before the outbreak of the Sino-Japanese War. Reviewed by the MOE the same year, *Gongmin* introduced students to a discussion of what defined a country. It defined healthy nationhood, or state power, as a group of people living for a common purpose, with four essential elements: (1) a regard for people as paramount, fundamentally more important than anything else; (2) territory/land; (3) a government for the people's common will; and (4) sovereignty. Students learned how all four elements were integral, as a country could not form without all of them. A nation was composed of a group of people living within a certain territory and organizing a government to exercise a supreme and independent state power.[53]

Gongmin then asked students to consider the following: "Why do we have a country? What does a country mean to people's lives?" In answering, the textbook did not reference a classical, or even traditional, text but instead Sun Yat-sen's *Democracy and People's Livelihood,* from the GMD founder's series of lectures. According to the book (and Sun), a country was the product of social evolution and people's livelihoods were at the center of that evolution. As Aristotle said, "the purpose for human beings is to establish a country and people's livelihood." The purpose of a country was therefore little more than ensuring survival, beginning with prehistoric "countries" that formed in order for tribal people to ward off invasion from other tribes. Guarding peace and fighting foreign invasion were the primary responsibilities all countries carried from the start. Moreover, *Gongmin*

142   Chapter 5

indicated that a country's perpetual survival depended on its ability to serve another ultimate purpose: "contributing to the upward progress of human civilization."[54]

Beyond discussing the early origins of nationhood, civics teachers were also charged with emphasizing the three functions of a "modern" country. First was the protection of the people, built on Chiang Kai-shek's notion and policy before the outbreak of the Sino-Japanese War in July 1937 that a nation's primary task was "first internal pacification, then external resistance" (*xian annei, hou rangwai*). Students explicitly read and understood that this meant to "suppress the Communist rebellion and then fight against the Japanese." And the primary tool to guarantee domestic peace was the law, without which a country quickly descended into anarchy—a place where people could "do whatever they want" and general livelihood would be "impossible." To ensure domestic peace, students first had to have "the spirit" of obeying the law and uphold the dignity of law. Armament and national defense were the only tools to guarantee national peace. Without them a country could not protect itself—as the textbook noted, from the moment states evolved in social history no one could escape "the elimination of the weak by the strong," nor the rule that "the fittest survives" (the curriculum clearly drawing from Social Darwinism).[55] Civics textbooks taught students that peace would be impossible without strength. To ensure the survival of their nation, China had to have enough armaments and a solid national defense system, the primary forces that supported international diplomacy.

The second function of the modern state was to "nurture people" (or their "livelihoods") with clothing, food, shelter, and transportation. Students learned that modern countries all tried to support agriculture, essential for food and clothing. Through education, successful nations taught their citizens to use appropriate and scientific ways to produce crops and engage in animal husbandry. State-run national banks also helped by providing low-interest loans to alleviate peasants' adversities, while developed transportation networks ensured agricultural products reached where they were needed. *Gongmin* pointed to import taxes as important tools for encouraging domestic agricultural production—as well as commerce and industry—so that livelihoods were not "squeezed by foreign goods." Successful countries also paid attention to issues like clothing and food because they established criteria for public hygiene to improve the health of their citizens. For similar reasons all modern states also intervened actively in people's shelters, including regulating architectural forms, internal structures, and maximum capacities. Students learned that, because most "common people" could not build houses themselves, governments either built homes directly or encouraged

Civics Textbooks   143

private construction, leasing shelters with low prices to those in need to ensure against homelessness.

Finally, *Gongmin* outlined a third essential state function: addressing transportation problems. Students were taught that transportation was of high importance and that all modern states featured governments that took full responsibility for providing transportation—be it by land, air, or water. Human transportation, technologically progressing every year, not only provided a great convenience but also exemplified how education "civilizes people." Since the people were a nation's central resource, making a country civilized, wealthy, and powerful required those citizens to have good qualities, or at least meet basic criteria, so that the nation could become "healthy" and "proper." According to the textbook, "people are living in a very competitive world nowadays. If they do not have certain knowledge and independent skills, and still live an ignorant life, they would certainly be eliminated by the strong. Thus, education is outstandingly more important nowadays than before." *Gongmin* emphasized that the purpose of education was not just to enrich personal morality or enhance people's spiritual life, but also to strengthen people's survival skills and producing abilities. Physical exercise and public hygiene were also important: "half of the strongest in the world today are those with physically strong citizens."[56] In this way, the third essential function of the state once again incorporated Social Darwinism—the struggle for survival and selection of the fittest in a nation's struggle to thrive in a competitive world.

In terms of liberty, GMD civics courses for lower middle schools on the mainland emphasized the independence of the state, not the individual. That included the 1932 curriculum, which targeted "imperialist aggression" and "unequal treaties" as examples of the infringement of liberty.[57] Likewise, *Gongmin* in 1937 taught students that stronger and larger countries often oppressed their weaker, smaller counterparts, damaging the independence and freedom of smaller nations with superior force and status. Here it noted the 1839 Opium War as the starting point for imperialist powers to invade China, which was subsequently burdened by a series of unequal treaties.[58] The theme of the stronger ("imperialist aggressors") eliminating the weak (China) was central to the lesson, and students were reminded that Sun Yat-sen routinely called China's history of signing such treaties "a contract of selling yourself." *Gongmin* taught that Western powers ceaselessly imposed unequal treaties on China after the Treaty of Nanjing (1842) ended the First Opium War: "China's independence and freedom were completely lost. China fell into a nation with the status of a semi-colony."[59] The textbook went on to explain that China's freedom and independence had been violated in three major arenas: law, politics, and the economy.

Implementing the Three People's Principles in the Curriculum

According to the National Government's (Guomin zhengfu) internal documents, the MOE encouraged middle schools to "put Sun Yat-sen's principles into practice," noting that the first goal was to "establish the Three People's Principles as the young people's belief" and "cultivate a national morality of honesty, filial piety, benevolence, and peace."[60] The second purpose was to "pay attention to young people's character, their health condition, and psyche" and to "give them proper guidance and training."[61] The last goal was to provide youth with "professional guidance and cultivate their knowledge of the profession" in preparation for a career.[62] In order to put the Three People's Principles into practice, the MOE also insisted that administrators emphasize nursing skills for female students, military training in upper middle schools, and scouting in lower middle schools. Robert Culp indicates that Chinese educators and the GMD had first adopted scouting in the 1910s, just a few years after Robert Baden-Powell created the organization in 1908 in Britain.[63] According to Culp, "advocates favored Scouting because it provided students with opportunities to enact and practice many new forms of civility and civic action."[64] Chinese educators embraced the British program and "combined instruction in forms of etiquette and hygiene rooted in Euro-American culture with skills training and the promotion of social service."[65] The MOE also called on youth to cultivate patriotism, promote the "national spirit," and take part in the effort of "national reconstruction" (*jianguo*).[66] Sun wrote of this urgent need for the national reconstruction of China, which became part of GMD wartime discourse reiterated in secondary education curriculum. Furthermore, the MOE suggested that Sun's words become mottos for schools— including his slogans "People should exist harmoniously together, be honest and faithful," "wisdom, mercy, and valor," and "be moral"—recommending that students make posters with such messages.[67]

Although no significant number of refugee students fled to Mongolia and Tibet, MOE wartime policies also tried to transform primary and secondary schools in these peripheral regions with large minority populations. Andres Rodriguez has argued that "the wartime period provided an exceptional opportunity for the GMD state to experiment with a series of projects that sought to further its nation-state project in the borderland regions of China."[68] In particular, the MOE's recommendations for education in Mongolia and Tibet warrant a closer examination because they were quite different from anywhere else in the country and included even stronger suggestions that educators cultivate national identity. The Ministry exhorted these schools to recognize Sun's emphasis on equality, recommending that language and goals in Mongolia and Tibet be uniform to fulfill Sun's wish for "the unity of the five major ethnic groups."[69] During the war, the GMD sought to bring ethnic minorities into the fold as part of an integral and unified modern Chinese nation-state. Thomas Mullaney has shown that Chiang Kai-shek and GMD authorities, unlike Communist leaders, actually prohibited Chinese ethnologists from "all talk of 'ethnic groups'" because they felt it was divisive, and instead promoted a homogeneous China in the war against Japan.[70] The official position was that ethnic minorities formed a singular *Zhonghua minzu* ("Chinese people" and/or "Chinese state").[71] The GMD's education policy for non-Han peoples in turn demonstrated an attempt to gradually sinicize them over the course of their education. For example, the MOE designed a curriculum that allowed for multilingual primary-level textbooks in Mongolian, Tibetan, and Chinese but required that only Chinese-language textbooks be used in all secondary schools. The MOE also called on Mongolian and Tibetan schools to study the history of "the assimilation of China's ethnic groups," "the geographical relationship between the core and periphery," "the history and facts of imperialist aggression" in Mongolia and Tibet, the "relationship between people" in Mongolia and Tibet, "the relationship between local autonomy and democracy," and the economic relationship between the two regions.[72]

In addition, the MOE outlined what it called "training education," explaining that "people in Mongolia and Tibet should study scientific knowledge in order to get rid of their superstitions about nature." In order for that to be accomplished, the government directed schools to invoke "the national spirit" so they could help "get rid of tribalism."[73] Here the MOE believed it was improving the lives of non-Han peoples by calling for a change in their traditional beliefs, customs, and lifestyles to reap "the benefits of modernity and Chinese civilization."[74] The MOE also insisted that secondary schools educate Tibetans and Mongolians in international affairs, calling on youth to "cultivate the spirit of patriotism." As for resources, MOE policy held that school facilities and supplies "should follow the spirit of the Three People's Principles and meet the local needs of Mongolia and Tibet," as well as "provide all kinds of books and charts about Mongolia and Tibet, and cultural and historical relics from the core."[75] Here, "core" referred to the nonperipheral regions of China inhabited predominantly by Han Chinese.

Although clearly denouncing "superstitions," "tribalism," and local languages, these initial GMD curriculum guidelines nevertheless created the potential for some intriguing pedagogical uncertainty. Undeniably, teachers were implored to teach about a mono-*minzu* China, yet at times students were still allowed to celebrate local (and ethnic) identities, as well as read books and study charts specifically about their regions. And students still found opportunities to learn in their

146   Chapter 5

local languages even in GMD-controlled primary schools. It is not hard to envision how some Mongolian and Tibetan students cultivated notions of autonomy even in classrooms where the GMD wartime curriculum was meant to indoctrinate the concept of a singular *Zhonghua minzu*.

The Twelve Maxims in Civics Education

Military training curriculum also went hand in hand with the GMD's revised civics curricular standards on Taiwan, which had actually changed relatively little in the previous fifteen years. In February 1938 on the mainland, the MOE had begun circulating a list titled Twelve Maxims (or Twelve Youth Regulations, Qingnian shouze), which it formally published the following year on September 25, 1939. Based on Confucianism, the list would become central to the Nationalists' evolving education policy both before and after the war. On December 10, 1948, the list was published in Nanjing as part of the GMD's curricular standards' "Outline for Teaching Civics in Lower Middle School Civics Curriculum." Two revisions of the list were later released on Taiwan, the first on June 28, 1952, and again on September 25, 1968. By 1957, they were also part of some upper middle school standardized textbooks published by Taiwan's Provincial Department of Education (Taiwan sheng zhengfu Jiaoyuting). Minister of Education Chen Lifu considered them so important that he included them in full in an appendix to his 1973 memoir on wartime education.[76]

How to Implement Training

1. Teach the Three People's Principles and the speeches of the Father of Our Country (Sun Yat-sen) and Chiang Kai-shek to enhance the youth's belief in the Three People's Principles. Use civics and morality courses' Twelve Youth Regulations to instill in them morals and a spirit of loyalty, bravery, obedience, and sacrifice.
2. Regarding youth training and guidance, it is divided into horizontal and vertical aspects. The horizontal aspect is one's daily life. The individual is the base of your family, society, country, and world. The vertical aspect is from your past primary school days to the present middle school days as a continuity.
3. Use family ethics to develop how youth become responsible to their family. You cannot rely on one's family. Contribute to your family.
4. You need to understand history, geography, and civics courses plus current news. (Especially be aware of communist bandits who destroy the country.) Teach nationalism. Build up your state and na-

tion's utmost confidence. Let them know how to love your country and revive your nation. Be responsible to your country and nation.

5. Physical exercise, games, contests, skills, mountain climbing/hiking, and swimming. Use these sports for a healthy, strong body. Have a habit of moving and reacting fast. Train for team life with these sports.

6. Crafts and experiments courses, vocational training, joint business, and society business. Train students to eat bitterness, endure hard work, and be diligent and persistent. These characteristics become your habit. You perform these activities in groups so you must have team spirit. You must develop the passion to serve society.

7. Guide students to be involved in self-governing activities and other group activities. Use this to train the Four Rights (Siquan).

8. Have students conduct all kinds of research by themselves to cultivate their interest in studying and research. Have recreational activities to guide them after school. Pay attention to music and singing to train them to appreciate art.

9. Execute your military and Boy Scout training. Build up the habit of simplicity, frugality, neatness, cleanliness, seriousness, and nimbleness. Be responsible and disciplined.

10. Normal middle schools should teach that education saves the nation. Speak about the educational spirit of famous Chinese and foreign educators. Normal school students should use them as examples for their lifetime careers in education. Take care of children.

11. Vocational middle schools. Sun Yat-sen's *The Outline of National Reconstruction* (1918), includes material infrastructure. You need to teach them the meaning of production and saving the nation and the importance of military industry. Students can start their own entrepreneurial business related to the above.

12. Girls middle schools. Girls need to be taught the status of females in family and society. They need to be taught the correct concept of marriage and family. Regarding training females, they need to be passionate toward family.[77]

In the same vein, four goals listed for civics courses in the 1948 curricular standards on the mainland, then again in 1952 in Taiwan's lower middle schools, remained mostly similar, with a few revisions. Both lists featured the same first goal: to train students to form habits in the "four supports" (*siwei*) and "eight classical virtues" (*bade*). The four supports likened society's morals to four ropes

148   Chapter 5

of a net: ritual, justice, honesty, and sense of shame. Meanwhile, the eight classical virtues, which Sun Yat-sen identified in his Lecture Six ("Nationalism"), consisted of loyalty, filial piety, benevolence, love, truthfulness, righteousness, harmony, and peace. The second goal was similar on both the mainland and Taiwan, with one important exception. Initially, the goal was to ensure that students cultivated "correct attitudes" in their relationships with "family, school, society, and the world." An individual's relationship to "the nation" was not included in the 1948 curricular standards, but was added four years later on the island, an addition that suggests the GMD wanted to highlight students' loyalty to the new Republic of China in Taiwan and defend the island against the Chinese Communists. Even more differences emerged in the third goal: in 1948 it emphasized "teaching citizens politics, economy, law, morals, knowledge, and society life," while by 1952 it called for "teaching citizens cultivation and common knowledge." The fourth goal, which called for students to be aware of their rights and encouraged them to serve society and be loyal to their country, was unchanged.

Also similar across the 1949 divide was the time set aside for civics education in lower middle schools: one hour per week for a total of three years. Both curricular standards also included the Twelve Maxims chart, which was derived from the Twelve Youth Regulations based on Confucian teachings. The Twelve Maxims or Youth Regulations consisted of the following (with the intended result in parentheses): loyalty and bravery (patriotism), filial piety (family harmony), benevolence (interpersonal relationships), good faith (successful career), peace (conduct oneself in society), courtesy/etiquette (good performance at work), obedience (responsibility), diligence and frugality (service), cleaning (strength and health), helping others (happiness), knowledge (helping the world), and persistence/perseverance (success). According to Culp, the Nationalists made an effort "to recreate and integrate Confucian moral virtues and patterns of social interaction in these textbooks' formulations of a modern Chinese society [which] represented an effort to inject some degree of cultural distinctiveness into China's modernizing process."[78]

Each of these maxims was similar in 1948 and 1952, but Taiwan's 1952 curricular standards added "bravery" to the first (which had originally been just "loyalty"). Each maxim included instructions for how to cultivate, and overall these also remained relatively unchanged. In 1948, the first maxim (loyalty) called for students to "buy domestic products," while the 1952 list omitted that order and replaced it with "don't be afraid of bullies and don't avoid eating bitterness."[79] (It is curious that the 1948 curricular standards urged students to buy "domestic" products, considering the Sino-Japanese War ended in 1945 and China was in the midst of civil war.) Another difference came in the third maxim: benevolent love.

The 1948 standards included "charity," which was cut in 1952. Moreover, the 1952 maxims added a new instruction, imploring students "not to secretly harm people." Instructions for the fourth maxim (good faith/honesty) were also revised: in 1948 youth were urged "not to be prideful if one is good at something; not to gossip about others' shortcomings; and not to do unto others what one wouldn't like done to oneself." Yet the 1952 list did not include any of those commands, instead instructing students to "help others when they face disaster or danger." Finally, the instructions for the eleventh maxim (knowledge) were also altered: whereas the 1948 maxims told students to "respect well-known academics/scholars," the 1952 list specifically added that such academics could be "past and present as well as Chinese and foreign."[80]

Meanwhile, the four goals dictated for civics courses in upper middle schools in the 1948 and 1952 curricular standards remained almost completely the same: (1) understand and practice our existing moral standards (with the exception that the phrase "modern social ethics" was added in 1952); (2) acquire the basic knowledge of society, politics, economics, law, morals, and culture; (3) recognize our country's unique characteristics of society, politics, economics, law, morals, and culture; and (4) enhance your citizen's knowledge and morals in real life and take responsibility towards the nation and world. Just as they did in lower middle schools, the Twelve Maxims formed the outline for teaching civics in upper middle schools in both the 1948 and 1952 curricular standards. However, the instructions for each maxim differed, generally reconfigured for a more mature audience.

Education Policy for Indigenous Youth

In the 1940s and 1950s, the Nationalist government used Sun Yat-sen's written comments on minority people to explain its policy towards the indigenous people of Taiwan. The policy chosen for quotation was Sun's order to aid small and weak nations. To carry out his command, the government began by banning the terms "savage," "Formosan Race," and the names of tribes—all of which were seen as being inextricably tied to Japanese rule—as well as ordering that indigenous people be referred to as "mountain compatriots" (shanbao).[81]

At the time of retrocession, the GMD government was aware that the indigenous people of Taiwan were renowned for their warlike character and many had fought for the Japanese in World War II. It responded to this view of indigenous communities as a threat by adopting an assimilationist policy. In January 1946, the government renamed the earlier Formosan Education Centers run by the Japanese police and began calling them primary schools. It abolished their previous curriculum and replaced it with one emphasizing Chinese language, history,

150   Chapter 5

and citizenship. The aim of the new curriculum was to eradicate the effects of Japanese assimilation and military training. A 1953 government report on the administration of mountain areas detailed the aims of education in indigenous communities since 1947: (1) to promote Mandarin to strengthen a national outlook, (2) to teach production skills to create an economic outlook, and (3) to emphasize hygiene to create good customs. This was the beginning of a government policy that explicitly aimed to "make the mountains like the plains" (*shandi pingdihua*).[82] The Nationalists sought to make the mountain compatriots more like the plains compatriots because the latter were considered more acculturated, assimilated, and civilized than the former.

Before the arrival of the Nationalist government in 1949, the provincial government lacked the resources to effectively implement policy in Taiwan. Education was crucial to the government's assimilationist ideas at a time when Taiwan had a severe shortage of teachers. At the time of retrocession, almost all headmasters on the island were Japanese nationals: in the mountain districts schooling had been carried out entirely by the Japanese police. The Taiwan government advertised for a thousand new headmasters in Fujian and Chongqing, but even where individuals were willing, it was difficult for them to travel across war-torn China to Taiwan. Those teachers who did live in Taiwan were unwilling to reside in the mountains, where living standards were low, prices high, and the teacher shortage meant one might have to work at several schools simultaneously. Furthermore, there was nowhere for their families to live, their own children would receive an education so poor that it would prevent them from passing the exams to enter secondary school, and they might have to spend days transporting their payment (in rice) from whichever town was nearest.[83] Thus, through the 1950s, schools in indigenous communities continued to suffer from a shortage of teachers.[84]

The GMD was not able to pursue an effective assimilationist policy in the mountains until its defeat on the mainland and retreat to Taiwan. Along with the government officials and soldiers who arrived from the mainland in 1949 came a large number of teachers. In 1948, the first set of rules for the development of the Mountain Youth Service Corps (Shandi qingnian fuwu dui) was established, but little else was accomplished. The corps was intended to provide military training to members, who were encouraged to promote the use of Mandarin, improve customs and lifestyles, increase agricultural production, and promote frugality. The corps was reorganized the following year under the control of the police, and effective action began in 1950 when it was integrated into county self-defense forces. By 1953, the corps consisted of approximately 3,500 members across the island, out of a total population of an estimated ninety thousand indigenous people living in mountain areas.[85]

Additionally, in 1951 the government launched the Mountain People's Lifestyle Improvement Movement (Shandi renmin shenghuo gaijin yundong), which aimed to change indigenous language, clothing, food, housing, daily life, and customs. Many of the practices addressed were ones which had, obviously, long defined people as non-Han. Thus, indigenous people were urged to cover their bodies, rather than be "half-naked"; to eat with bowls and chopsticks instead of their hands; and to divide their living space into separate kitchen, sleeping, and toilet areas. In terms of language, Chineseness, and civics curriculum, teaching indigenous people to speak Mandarin was central to the GMD's assimilation policies and essential to the construction of a "national" outlook.[86] In turn, as Henrietta Harrison argues, indigenous individuals and communities adopted and manipulated nationality and ethnicity as functional attributes to suit political situations during the late 1940s and 1950s.[87]

Although civics education was a far cry from organizing youth in the CYC, and while each indeed had motivations that did not always overlap with the other, the underlying purpose of turning youth into political assets remained. While on the mainland, circumstances were such that the GMD took the approach of building up the strength of national defense to defeat the Japanese and trying to rectify the problem of textbook shortages. Once on Taiwan, postwar developments prompted some curricular change, such as focusing on national defense against Communist invasion. But despite these changes, many consistencies remained. After moving the government to Taiwan, the GMD found that it still needed to emphasize the Twelve Maxims based on Confucian teachings to middle school students, standardize textbooks, and adopt assimilation policies for ethnic minority students (Mongolians and Tibetans on the mainland, indigenous people on Taiwan). And while minor adjustments in these areas were sometimes necessary, the party (or government) did not have to start anew.

When the GMD retreated to Taiwan in 1949, it revised not only middle school curricular standards for the subject of civics, but also for Chinese literature, history, and geography. These post-1949 revisions in education reflected a new, national policy intent on pacifying the Communists and the urgent need to build a new nation on the island. Remarkably, for the most part civics curricular standards and textbooks changed little for students at GMD middle schools from 1937 to 1960—be it during war or peace, on the mainland or on Taiwan. In all cases,

152   Chapter 5

the standards included the most pressing knowledge that the GMD state wished to convey. In a critical, unstable period—during which the Nationalists fought fierce, bitter wars against Japan and Chinese Communists, which displaced them in their own land, then exiled them to Taiwan—civics textbooks conveyed to students the political values and behavioral norms of "modern" Chinese citizens. They provided clear definitions of "nation" and, eventually, emphasized the role students had to play in building one. They offered lessons in civic consciousness and Chinese nationalism, in which students learned about their relationships with family, community, nation, and world—that is, they helped students explore their identities at a critical juncture when those very identities were altered, or at times destroyed, by war and displacement. Amidst the conflagration—and despite the government's attempts at times to use civics education to silence political dissent, shore up its power, or demand loyalty—civics teachers nevertheless sought to teach their students a set of internalized skills that allowed young people to both understand a "modern society" and operate successfully within one.

Epilogue

When New York governor and former US presidential candidate Thomas Dewey visited Taiwan in the spring of 1951, Chiang Kai-shek told him he would "accept full blame for losing the mainland in the struggle against the Communists."[1] According to Minister of Education Chen Lifu, after the Guomindang reestablished its government in Taipei, "its leaders agonized, pondering what kind of lessons to learn from the mistakes."[2] Failures in the mobilization of youth was one critical fault the Nationalists sought to rectify.

On the mainland during the Sino-Japanese War, primary education was neither universal nor mandatory. Chen was aware that few students could afford to pay tuition in order to attend these schools.[3] Thus, when the GMD relocated to Taiwan, the MOE implemented six years of free compulsory education. By 1968, it had increased schooling to nine years, making lower middle school a requirement.[4] These reforms had major implications for keeping more youth in school (even though lower middle school students were required to pay tuition). From the beginning of GMD rule, the percentage of children in Taiwan enrolled in primary school was higher than that on the mainland. During the 1950–1951 academic year, 80 percent of school-aged children attended Taiwan's primary schools. By 1960–1961, 96 percent were enrolled. A total of 32 percent of primary graduates went on to enroll in lower middle school in 1950–1951, and by 1960–1961 over half (58 percent) of eligible youth attended lower middle school on the island.[5] Almost immediately, the GMD succeeded in providing education for more middle school youth in Taiwan than it ever had on the mainland during the war years.

While on the mainland, Chen Lifu contended that 53 percent of school-aged children attended schools in 1936, a year before the war, without specifying the percentage of primary graduates who enrolled in upper middle school. He also claimed that by 1946, 70 percent of children attended school. He arrived at the number by totaling some 34,110,000 school-aged children in the nineteen provinces and municipalities outside Japanese-occupied areas. Chen calculated that "the number of those children attending school reached some 17,220,000. Those children not at school but who had already received some compulsory education

153

154   Epilogue

numbered as high as 25,000,000."[6] However, these percentages seem unreasonably high, and Chen was probably trying to bolster his image as minister of education. In addition, it is unclear what level of education Chen referred to—whether it was all school-aged youth or only school-aged children attending primary school. But he admitted that "the war had greatly set back our public education, especially in the enemy-occupied areas," referring to Japanese-controlled regions.[7] These territories consisted of north China (where the main educational centers were in the Beijing and Tianjin regions) and the coastal areas, historically the most populated and educated regions. Also, the war certainly disrupted schooling for most students in these areas, lowering the percentage of children attending school in the whole country.

In terms of student military training, Chiang Ching-kuo in particular realized the party's mistakes on the mainland and sought to correct them after the exile to Taiwan. In a February 7, 1968, address to school heads, university leaders, and chief military instructors in Taipei, he admitted that "the student military training system did not begin in Taiwan. It was initiated on the mainland, but we did not do a good job then. Once we were criticized we dared not aggressively implement the system, therefore we ended in failure."[8] Ching-kuo also responded to foreign and domestic criticism of military training on the island, arguing that "we did not allow the disapproval to dissuade us. The purpose of political work is to restore the combat spirit to the army and the purpose of student military training is to calm campuses and to channel student energies in the proper direction."[9] Ching-kuo claimed that military training in mainland schools was not "aggressively implemented" because the GMD feared a backlash, yet in reality the party did not need military training in every school when manpower was abundant. With fewer resources (including people) on Taiwan, and under the threat of Communist invasion, the GMD mandated military training in all schools out of an urgent need to produce a reserve army. When he addressed the criticism of military training, Ching-kuo remained confident that the Nationalist policy would not succumb to such attacks on Taiwan. Throughout the 1950s and 1960s, he insisted that military training would continue unabated in all upper middle schools on the island. More importantly, he explained that the prevention of student protests was one of the reasons why he enforced the training.

The mandatory two-year military service for all eligible male citizens prevailed for many decades in Taiwan. Since the 1990s, the government has reduced its military service to four months for all eligible male citizens. Such compulsory service took on decreasingly "militaristic" forms. By the turn of the twenty-first century young men in uniform were working the desks and performing other community service jobs at places like the Taiwan Historica archival institute (in

Nantou, central Taiwan). In 2008, each day, at noon, an alarm rang, sending the youth scurrying down the halls and stairs to stand at attention in front of the main entrance of the complex. There, an instructor led them in a short drill before they returned to work. Images like these are common in contemporary Taiwan, a testament to the fact that the government has cut down its military manpower while still requiring alternative service. The number of males eligible to serve in the military (either not pursuing higher education, or college graduates) exceeded the actual demands of the forces. Thus, the surplus substituted true military service by working in a variety of government services, including libraries and historical archives. This was a stark contrast to the 1950s, when the GMD feared imminent Communist attack and mandated all young men of a certain age to serve in the actual military. Yet the fact that such service continues to take on militaristic dimensions (uniforms, flags and symbols, drilling, etc.)—even as participants perform duties completely unrelated to the armed forces—speaks to the government's ongoing commitment to the original ideals behind 1950s military training.

However, recent events, such as Russia's invasion of Ukraine and the frequent incursions of China's sea exercises close to Taiwan and warplanes in the island's air defense identification zone (ADIZ), have brought renewed attention to whether Taiwan's civilian population, including its middle school students, would be ready to defend the island if it ever faced an invading force from China. Analysts say that the incursions are warnings against Taiwan's government from moving towards a formal declaration of independence. The mandatory military service is seen by many as too short, and the reservist program insufficiently rigorous. Starting in 2024, President Tsai Ing-wen's administration will be extending the length of military service to up to one year for men born after 2005. In 2018 Taiwan began the transition to a voluntary military system even though four months of military training is still required for eligible male citizens. Experts say the military's authoritarian legacy and relatively low pay have made it difficult to attract skilled recruits. If tensions continue between China and Taiwan, Taiwan may have to increase its mandatory military service and possibly even reinstate military training in middle schools.

The commitment to military education remains, but even before 1960 it was clear that a new generation of teenagers on Taiwan was emerging, with cultural values, political notions, and youth identities that differed from the generation that faced the brutal war with Japan and hardship on the mainland. Some continuities were still obvious: Taiwan certainly remained economically poor during the 1950s, leading the Ministry of National Defense to champion the Overcoming Difficulty Movement throughout the decade. Yet living standards in the early years of retrocession were still better than the dire situation in war-torn China. Most

156   Epilogue

civilians who fled to the island were wealthy, educated elite, able to provide disposable income for their children. For mainlanders who had just arrived, their new home was a place to explore, and the island inspired some teens to travel for leisure in the unfamiliar environment: wartime youth, on the other hand, had relocated on the mainland just to survive. Similarly, the refugee generation migrated to southwest China and encountered local inhabitants and different terrain during the war. Instead of escaping Japanese attacks like their counterparts on the mainland, Taiwan's young people prepared themselves for Communist invasion. In essence, the fears of those on the mainland were more immediate, while the threat on Taiwan was always more abstract, or "imminent." The authoritarian GMD state realized this generational shift and adjusted its youth mobilization tactics accordingly. While the party tightened control on Taiwan more than it ever had on the mainland (imposing martial law from 1949 to 1987), its China Youth Corps represented a much softer appeal to youth than the Three People's Principles Youth Corps. This attempt to win over young people with recreational activities, as opposed to harsh indoctrination, represented a much broader recognition of (and acquiescence to) powerful new youth identities and the importance of youth culture, leisure, and consumption. Therefore, not only did the GMD leadership and its approach to secondary education change, but Chinese youth themselves also evolved dramatically in just one generation.

Before, the GMD had difficulty trying to mobilize youth on the mainland during the Sino-Japanese War and the civil war—having millions of people uprooted was especially destabilizing. Throughout the conflict with Japan, youth were spread across the vast country in three different areas—GMD-controlled, Communist-ruled, and Japanese-occupied territories—many of them dislocated from their hometowns. While the Nationalists mostly struggled to mobilize youth in regions they controlled, National Executive Yuan records reveal one important exception: the GMD provided stipends to SQT branches in provinces held by the Japanese, such as Shandong.[10] For the most part, the GMD's influence on youth education in territories beyond its control was extremely restricted, yet the Nationalists clearly saw these organizations as an important battlefront, and the SQT attempted to win the struggle for youth support in contested areas. Despite these endeavors to support students in Japanese-controlled regions, the GMD's mobilization of students was quite limited even within its domain. In 1939, the SQT's first full year of existence, only 8 percent of its nine thousand members were students. By 1947, the year it was dismantled, the percentage of students had grown to 47 percent out of 1.3 million members.[11] Despite this increase in the ratio of students, the SQT was often unwilling to emphasize student recruitment, and a majority of members belonged to other sectors of society. Perhaps that itself con-

Epilogue   157

tributed to the disillusionment some youth felt towards the GMD by the end of the war, many turning their allegiance to the Communists.

In contrast, the Nationalists established the CYC exclusively for young people, catering to youth interests with fun activities like swimming, cycling, hiking, and camping. However, it still devoted a significant amount of time for youth to receive party indoctrination and acquire military skills, recognizing what it considered the ultimate threat to the island: Communist attack. When they mandated that all upper middle school students join the CYC and undergo military training, the Nationalists found it far easier to mobilize in the smaller world of 1950s Taiwan. Those who had fled from the mainland and remained loyal to the GMD were a minority (two million in 1949) compared to the Taiwanese (seven million), yet both groups had to comply with orders, since military instructors closely monitored schools and GMD officials rigidly controlled the highest positions of government in Taiwan, a single-party state. The CYC was also able to dominate activities by establishing itself as the only government-sanctioned youth organization. Other than the CYC, one of the few opportunities for organized activities was short excursions on Sundays chaperoned by teachers.

While on the mainland from 1937 to 1949, the Nationalists maintained strict surveillance over anti-government activities. In 1950s and 1960s Taiwan, GMD crackdowns became even more extreme in order to prevent major demonstrations while the Nationalists consolidated power on the island. Thus, the government's 1953 introduction of strict military instructors in schools also forestalled youth from mobilizing against it. By the late 1980s and 1990s, Presidents Chiang Ching-kuo and Lee Teng-hui had gradually implemented policies towards liberalization and democratization in politics and society. In 1987, Ching-kuo finally revoked martial law, releasing government constraints on the media and public speech. As part of these reforms, military instructors and their authority in Taiwan's schools became increasingly marginalized, while the GMD's harsh suppression of student protest and political activity began to subside.[12]

Meanwhile, students in politics remained important on the mainland. The Tiananmen Square protests of 1989 provided a lasting, iconic image of student political activism that was recognized globally (and especially championed by the West), yet few Westerners noticed Taiwan's Month of March Movement (or Wild White Lily Student Movement), which occurred just one year later. Political scientist Teresa Wright notes that "in both cases, students relied on peaceful methods of protest, occupied the central square in the capital, and petitioned the government for political reform."[13] She explains that the Month of March Movement "arose as a response to the coming National Assembly election of a new president . . . many citizens were angered and alarmed by the factional struggle between more

158   Epilogue

traditional KMT elites [particularly Lee Huan and Hao Po-ts'un] and the reform-
ist Taiwanese Lee Teng-hui."[14] They were upset that "the existing method of choosing the president did not directly reflect the opinions of the people."[15] Fearing
that conservative elites would dominate once again, thousands of Taipei students
called for democratic reform. On March 14, students organized a sit-in of three
hundred people in front of GMD headquarters to protest the illegitimacy of the
National Assembly and electoral system. Two days later, the movement culmi-
nated with thousands participating in another sit-in in Liberty Square (originally
Chiang Kai-shek Memorial Square but renamed by the Democratic Progressive
Party after it took power with the election of President Chen Shui-bian in 2000).
According to Wright, on March 21, "news of Lee Teng-hui's nearly unanimous
election reached the square. The power struggle within the KMT appeared to
have been resolved . . . now Lee could speak with the students from a position of
strength." On the same day, Lee met with students in the Presidential Building
and affirmed their patriotism, supporting their demand for direct elections of
future presidents and agreeing to other reforms and democratization of the
political system. The next day, the last protester withdrew from the square.[16] Thus,
the 1990 Month of March Movement ended on a peaceful and positive note, while
the Tiananmen Square protests resulted in violence and failure. As Wright points
out, "a crucial difference existed in the manner of the government's response to
the demonstrators" and the "more open environment in Taiwan helped make
organizational difficulties less extreme."[17]

   In terms of youth and secondary education, a final link between the GMD's
mainland years and the Taiwan period is found in the personality cult of Chiang
Kai-shek himself. It emerged during the Nanjing decade (1927–1937) but grew
more intense on Taiwan as citizens sought favor with the GMD or commercial
benefits from producing sculptures of the generalissimo.[18] On the mainland, Chiang had actually forbidden statues of himself.[19] However, in the early decades of
retrocession the GMD actively built his personality cult, and secondary schools
(and students) were central to the process. Schools required students to memorize Chiang's speeches and writings. After his death, the GMD erected statues and
busts in virtually every schoolyard on the island. Since assuming power, the Democratic Progressive Party has deleted the hagiography of Chiang from textbooks
and taken down most of the statues in schools and other places around the island
(some still remain in public squares, schools, and parks). Today about two hundred
Chiang sculptures rest at the Cihu Memorial Sculpture Garden near his burial site
in Cihu, located in Daxi District in Taoyuan City. The majority are busts labeled
with the various elementary, lower middle schools, and upper middle schools where
they were first displayed, a testament to the importance of Taiwan's secondary edu-

cation system in forging his personality cult and the way in which Chiang remained prevalent in most students' lives, including their studies. Figure E.1 shows a Chiang Kai-shek bust that used to be displayed at a middle school in Taichung, with other CKS statues in the background. Figure E.2 exhibits a statue of the generalissimo on a horse with many statues of him behind it. Both photos were taken at the Cihu Memorial Sculpture Garden.

Some of the GMD's education goals remained constant or at least similar throughout its rule on the mainland and in postwar Taiwan. In the 1950s, the Nationalist Party continued to promote a military ethos by using the threat of Communist invasion as justification for military training in upper middle schools. Schools placed great emphasis on cultivating loyalty to leaders, culminating in devotion to Sun Yat-sen and Chiang Kai-shek, which echoed military training in the 1930s.

Another lasting effect of the GMD's approaches to Taiwan's secondary school students is assigning military instructors at upper middle schools to maintain discipline. In the 1950s, military instructors were responsible for persuading students

Figure E.1. A Chiang Kai-shek bust from a middle school in Taichung with statues of him in the background, at the Cihu Memorial Sculpture Garden. (Author's collection)

Figure E.2. A statue of Chiang Kai-shek on a horse with many statues of him in the background, at the Cihu Memorial Sculpture Garden. (Author's collection)

to join the GMD, policing students' appearance (length of hair, nails, or skirts/pants) along with students' thoughts on the government, reporting those who were not loyal to the party and the leader, and teaching basic military training at school. As Taiwan transitioned into a democracy, the military instructors' duties changed from policing students for the GMD to student counseling and campus security. Even today, they remain a presence in Taiwan's high schools, colleges, and universities. In 2013, the Democratic Progressive Party legislators proposed to replace military instructors with security guards, but the plan received backlash from parents who argued that the latter cannot be expected to stay on campuses after classes end and handle threats posed to students the way military instructors can. Military instructors used to be criticized as authoritarian symbols, but that has changed because many younger instructors do not have any political affiliations.

In China, the GMD initiated military training in upper middle schools in 1928 but did not aggressively implement it. In 1951, Chiang Kai-shek announced his decision to integrate military training in Taiwan's schools at upper middle level and above. It began on an experimental basis the same year before its implementation throughout the island in 1953. Students were expected to take on civil defense

Epilogue   161

duties in events of national emergency. In the early days the Ministry of Education, the Ministry of National Defense, the CYC, and the Taiwan Provincial Government's Department of Education inspected student military training with an emphasis on the physical (combat applicable) aspects. Boys and girls were taught to use firearms, but that is no longer the case. Military training in upper middle schools has evolved over time to regard character guidance as most important.

The function of the CYC continued to evolve as well. When it was established in 1952, upper middle school students' membership was mandatory, but by 1961 it was no longer a requirement since the organization had already gained status. The CYC's original purpose was to provide military training to young men before they were conscripted into the Nationalist Armed Forces. In recent decades it has lost much of its militaristic character, although military camps remain one of the many activities offered. By 1972, twenty years after the CYC's founding, the organization's goals had shifted from patriotism and anti-Communism to modern industrial development.[20] This new emphasis on vocational education was not only initiated by the GMD government and party but also by young people themselves who understood their future depended on training in occupation and practical skills. Another new approach, which began in 1969, was the CYC's formation of the counseling and guidance service called "Teacher Chang."

Democratic Progressive Party officials have since called for the CYC to rid itself of its close connection with the GMD and even labeled it the "KMT Youth Corps," reminding Taiwanese it served as the propaganda arm of the GMD in the past. Under Chiang Kai-shek, Taiwan's young people were controlled by the family, the school, the media, and, by extension, the CYC. The CYC advocated young people to be loyal, patriotic citizens and show respect to the GMD government and Chiang Kai-shek. It was founded as a government agency and remained under the control of the Ministry of National Defense from 1952 to 1969 before registering with the Ministry of Interior as a "social movement organization" in 1970. In 1989 the CYC became an independent nonprofit civic group. It worked towards breaking off its affiliation with the government and the GMD and removed "anti-Communist" from its Chinese-language name in 2000.

In the 1950s and 1960s, there were limited opportunities for a young person to meet others outside of one's own school. Very few public or youth-oriented programs were available. Life was difficult and entertainment and amenities scarce. The CYC became a welcome and very popular outlet, one that provided a young person the chance to meet new people, travel within the country, and have some fun with new experiences. The CYC was the only major organization that politically allowed an opportunity for youth to assemble outside of school and family.

162   Epilogue

After martial law was lifted in 1987, the organization no longer monopolized young people's leisure and recreational activities because other groups, businesses, and agencies offered competitive programs. Nevertheless, Taiwan remains full of these reminders of Cold War education policy—be it CYC mountain campgrounds or an eerie garden filled with Chiang Kai-shek statues that were removed from schools—and of course, teenagers today continue to be bombarded on a daily basis with news of "imminent" Chinese military incursions.

NOTES

Introduction

1. Guomin xingzhengyuan [National Executive Yuan], "Ge di zhongdeng xuexiao jiaozhi-yuan beikong" [Secondary school staff from different locales accused of crimes], file 5262, J-1275, vol. 2, Di'er lishi dang'anguan, Nanjing [Second Historical Archives of China; hereafter SHAC].

2. Guomin xingzhengyuan, "Ge di zhongdeng di zhongdeng xuexiao jiaozhiyuan beikong."

3. Valerie Hansen, *The Open Empire: A History of China to 1600* (New York: W. W. Norton Company, 2000), 141–142.

4. Jeffrey N. Wasserstrom, *Student Protests in Twentieth-Century China: The View from Shanghai* (Stanford, CA: Stanford University Press, 1991), 14.

5. Wasserstrom, *Student Protests,* 95.

6. Wasserstrom, *Student Protests,* 158.

7. Cong Xiaoping, "Localizing the Global, Nationalizing the Local: The Role of Teachers' Schools in Making China Modern 1897–1937" (PhD diss., UCLA, 2001), 341.

8. Jiaoyubu [Ministry of Education], *Di'erci Zhongguo jiaoyu nianjian* [The second yearbook of Chinese education] (1948; repr., Taipei: Zhongqing, 1981), 13.

9. John Israel, *Lianda: A Chinese University in War and Revolution* (Stanford, CA: Stanford University Press, 1998). Lianda was the common abbreviation for National Southwest Associated University.

10. Regarding the discussion of wartime higher education, see Hu Kuo-tai, "The Struggle between the Kuomintang and the Chinese Communist Party on Campus during the War of Resistance, 1937–1945," *China Quarterly,* no. 118 (June 1989): 300–323; Wasserstrom, *Student Protests*; Helen M. Schneider, *Keeping the Nation's House: Domestic Management and the Making of Modern China* (Vancouver: University of British Columbia Press, 2012); J. Megan Greene, "Looking toward the Future: State Standardization and Professionalization of Science in Wartime China," in *Knowledge Acts in Modern China: Ideas, Institutions, and Identities,* ed. Robert Culp, Eddy U, and Wen-hsin Yeh (Berkeley: Institute of East Asian Studies, University of California, 2016), 275–303.

11. Regarding recent studies of wartime middle schools, see Robert Culp, *Articulating Citizenship: Civic Education and Student Politics in Southeastern China, 1912–1940* (Cambridge, MA: Harvard University Asia Center, 2007); R. Keith Schoppa, *In a Sea of Bitterness: Refugees in the Sino-Japanese War* (Cambridge, MA: Harvard University Press, 2011).

12. Michael H. Kater, *Hitler Youth* (Cambridge, MA: Harvard University Press, 2004), 29.

13. Kater, *Hitler Youth,* 34.

164   Notes to Pages 5–10

14. The Socialist Youth League was established in 1920 and renamed the Communist Youth League at the Third National Congress in 1925.

15. "Zhongguo gongchandang di'erci quanguo daibiao dahui wenjian" [Chinese Communist Party Second National Congress document], *Chinese Communist Central Committee Youth Movement Compilations, July 1921–September 1949* (Beijing: Zhongguo qingnian chubanshe, 1988), 12.

16. Sanmin zhuyi qingniantuan dierjie zhongyang ganshihui gongzuo baogao, 89–90, cited in Wang Liangqing, *Sanmin zhuyi qingniantuan yu Zhongguo Guomindang guanxi yanjiu, 1938–1949* [A study of the relationship between the San-min Chu-I Youth Corps and the Kuomintang, 1938–1949] (Taipei: Kuomintang History Library No. 4, Historical Commission, Central Committee of the Kuomintang, Modern China Publishers, 1998), 116–117.

17. Guomindang Historical Commission, ed., "Kangzhan shiqi zhi zhongdeng jiaoyu" [Secondary education during the War of Resistance], *Geming wenxian* [Documents on revolution], vol. 61 (Taipei, 1953–present), 247–248 and 250–267, information originated from Jiaoyubu [Ministry of Education], *Disanci Zhongguo jiaoyu nianjian* [The third yearbook of Chinese education] (Taipei: Zhongqing, 1957).

18. Jiaoyubu, *Di'erci Zhongguo jiaoyu nianjian,* 13.

19. Ou Tsiun-chen [Wu Junsheng], "Education in Wartime China," in *Nationalist China during the Sino-Japanese War, 1937–1945,* ed. Paul K. T. Sih (Hicksville, NY: Exposition Press, 1977), 89–123.

20. Allen B. Linden, "Politics and Higher Education in China: The Kuomintang and the University Community, 1927–1937" (PhD diss., Columbia University, 1969); Hu Kuo-tai, "Politics and Higher Education in China: The Control and Development Policies of the Guomindang, 1937–1945" (PhD diss., Griffith University, 1987).

21. Peter Zarrow, *Educating China: Knowledge, Society and Textbooks in a Modernizing World, 1902–1937* (New York: Cambridge University Press, 2015); Cong Xiaoping, *Teachers' Schools and the Making of the Modern Chinese Nation-State* (Toronto: University of British Columbia Press, 2007); Evelyn S. Rawski, *Education and Popular Literacy in Ch'ing China* (Ann Arbor: University of Michigan Press, 2003); Barry Keenan, *The Dewey Experiment in China: Educational Reform and Political Power in the Early Republic* (Cambridge, MA: Harvard University Press, 1977); Wen-hsin Yeh, *The Alienated Academy: Culture and Politics in Republican China, 1919–1937* (Cambridge, MA: Harvard University Press, 1990).

22. "Christianity in China," *TIME,* April 28, 1941.

23. Cong, "Localizing the Global," 341.

24. According to John Cogan, Paul Morris, and Murray Print, "civic education generally focuses on three forms of learning: the knowledge, skills, and values that are perceived as important to become an effective citizen," John J. Cogan, Paul Morris, and Murray Print, eds., *Civic Education in the Asia-Pacific Region: Case Studies across Six Societies* (New York: RoutledgeFalmer, 2002), 4; Zarrow, *Educating China;* Cong, *Teachers' Schools.*

25. Culp, *Articulating Citizenship,* 2.

26. Culp, *Articulating Citizenship,* 216–217.

27. Lloyd Eastman, *Seeds of Destruction: Nationalist China in War and Revolution, 1937–1949* (Stanford, CA: Stanford University Press, 1984), 89–107; Huang Jianli, *The Politics of Depoliticization in Republican China: Guomindang Policy towards Student Political Activism, 1927–1949* (Bern: Peter Lang, 1996); Kristin Mulready-Stone, *Mobilizing Shanghai Youth: CCP Internationalism, GMD Nationalism and Japanese Collaboration* (New York: Routledge, 2015).

Notes to Pages 10–15   165

28. John Israel, *Student Nationalism in China, 1927–1937* (Stanford, CA: Stanford University Press, 1966).

29. Wasserstrom, *Student Protests*, 265–275; Suzanne Pepper, *Civil War in China* (Lanham, MD: Rowman & Littlefield, 1999), 42–93.

30. Paul A. Cohen, "Reflections on a Watershed Date: The 1949 Divide in Chinese History," in *Twentieth-Century China: New Approaches,* ed. Jeffrey N. Wasserstrom (London: Routledge, 2003), 27–36.

31. J. Megan Greene, *The Origins of the Developmental State in Taiwan: Science Policy and the Quest for Modernization* (Cambridge, MA: Harvard University Press, 2008).

32. Robert Culp, *The Power of Print in Modern China: Intellectuals and Industrial Publishing from the End of Empires to Maoist State Socialism* (New York: Columbia University Press, 2019); Margaret Mih Tillman, *Raising China's Revolutionaries: Modernizing Childhood for Nationalists and Liberated Comrades, 1920s–1950s* (New York: Columbia University Press, 2018); Janet Y. Chen, *Guilty of Indigence: The Urban Poor in China, 1900–1953* (Princeton, NJ: Princeton University Press, 2012); Susan Glosser, *Chinese Visions of Family and State, 1915–1953* (Berkeley: University of California Press, 2003); Gail Herschatter, *Dangerous Pleasures: Prostitution and Modernity in Twentieth-Century Shanghai* (Berkeley: University of California Press, 1999).

33. Li Tai-han, "Dangtuan, junshi, yu jiaoyu: yijiu wuling niandai xuesheng junxun jinru xiaoyuan zhi yanjiu" [Party corps, the military, and education: The study of 1950s student military training entering the campus] (Master's thesis, National Central University, 2002); Li Tai-han, "Dang'an yunyong yu lishi yanjiu: yi xuesheng junxun zai zhanhou Taiwan shi shi de yiti wei li" [Archive research and history study: Issues on the implication of student military training in postwar Taiwan], *Dangan jikan* 56, no. 4 (June 2004): 1–13.

34. Monte R. Bullard, *The Soldier and the Citizen: The Role of the Military in Taiwan's Development* (Armonk, NY: M. E. Sharpe, 1997).

35. Thomas A. Brindley, *The China Youth Corps in Taiwan* (New York: Peter Lang, 1999).

36. Rana Mitter and Helen M. Schneider, "Introduction: Relief and Reconstruction in Wartime China," *European Journal of East Asian Studies* 11, no. 2 (2012): 179–180.

37. As cited in Huang, *Politics of Depoliticization*, 108.

38. Jay Taylor, *The Generalissimo: Chiang Kai-shek and the Struggle for Modern China* (Cambridge, MA: Belknap Press of Harvard University Press, 2011), 379.

Chapter 1. The Relocation of Middle Schools during the Sino-Japanese War, 1937–1945

1. After the Japanese attack on Pearl Harbor on December 7, 1941, the Second Sino-Japanese War (or the "War of Resistance against Japan," as the Chinese referred to it) merged into the greater conflict of World War II as a major front in the Pacific Theatre.

2. Stephen R. MacKinnon, "Conclusion: Wartime China," in *China at War: Regions of China, 1937–1945,* ed. Stephen R. MacKinnon, Diana Lary, and Ezra F. Vogel (Stanford, CA: Stanford University Press, 2007), 338–339.

3. MacKinnon, "Conclusion," 337.

4. Lu Liu, "Imagining the Refugee: The Emergence of a State Welfare System in the War of Resistance," in *Visualizing Modern China: Image, History, and Memory, 1750-Present,* ed. James A. Cook, Joshua Goldstein, Matthew D. Johnson, and Sigrid Schmalzer (Lanham, MD: Lexington Books, 2014), 176.

166   Notes to Pages 16–20

5. Lu, "Imagining the Refugee," 176–177.

6. Schoppa, *Sea of Bitterness,* 190.

7. Danke Li, *Echoes of Chongqing: Women in Wartime China* (Urbana-Champaign: University of Illinois Press, 2010), 17.

8. See the special issue entitled "China in World War II, 1937–1945: Experience, Memory and Legacy," ed. Rana Mitter and Aaron William Moore, special issue, *Modern Asian Studies* 45, no. 2 (2011).

9. Rana Mitter, "Classifying Citizens in Nationalist China during World War II, 1937–1941," *Modern Asian Studies* 45, no. 2 (2011): 254.

10. Quoted in Mitter, "Classifying Citizens," 254.

11. Chen Lifu, *Four Years of Chinese Education, 1937–1941* (Chongqing: China Information Committee, 1941), 27; Jiaoyubu, *Di'erci Zhongguo jiaoyu nianjian,* 13. There is a discrepancy between Minister of Education Chen Lifu's figure of 571,800 and *The Second Yearbook of Chinese Education's* number of 627,000 middle school students. It is unclear what period of the war Chen is referring to, therefore this study retains the latter figure as more accurate in calculating the number of middle school students on the eve of the war. The total number of 627,000 middle school students includes those who did and did not relocate.

12. Jiaoyubu, *Di'erci Zhongguo jiaoyu nianjian,* 3.

13. Ou, "Education in Wartime China," 101–103. Ou's source is derived from Jiaoyubu, *Di'erci Zhongguo jiaoyu nianjian,* 1462.

14. Ou, "Education in Wartime China," 114.

15. Huang, *Politics of Depoliticization,* 29.

16. Culp, *Articulating Citizenship,* 27.

17. Huang, *Politics of Depoliticization,* 29.

18. Li, *Echoes of Chongqing,* 42.

19. Li, *Echoes of Chongqing,* 41.

20. Culp, *Articulating Citizenship,* 21.

21. *Zhejiang jiaoyu jianzhi* [A brief chronicle of Zhejiang education], December 1939, 102–103, 122, cited in Culp, *Articulating Citizenship,* 21.

22. Culp, *Articulating Citizenship,* 21.

23. *Zhejiang jiaoyu jianzhi,* 22, cited in Culp, *Articulating Citizenship,* 21.

24. Jiaoyubu, "Methods to Unify the Management of Various Levels of Educational Institutions by Government Agencies," issued on January 20, 1938, 9, and "Methods of the Ministry of Education to Manage Students Retreating from War Zones," Order #660 issued on February 25, 1938, 17, in *Jiaoyu gongbao* [Bulletin of the Ministry of Education] 10, no. 1–3 (March 1938), cited in Huang, *Politics of Depoliticization,* 118.

25. Jiaoyubu, ed., *Zuijin jiaoyu tongji jianbian* [A concise edition of the latest educational statistics] (Chongqing: Jiaoyubu, 1940), part of Table 10, no pagination, cited in Huang, *Politics of Depoliticization,* 119.

26. Chen Lifu, *The Storm Clouds Clear Over China: The Memoir of Ch'en Li-fu, 1900–1993,* ed. Sidney H. Chang and Ramon Myers (Stanford, CA: Hoover Institution Press), 169.

27. Schneider, *Keeping the Nation's House,* 129.

28. Guomin xingzhengyuan [National Executive Yuan], "Zhan di shixue qingnian zhao xun banfa gangyao jige fang zhi jianyi" [Proposal for registration and training solution for youth who do not have schools where war occurs], file 2293, 16J-1621, vol. 2, sec. 2, April 1939–July 1944, Di'er lishi dang'anguan, Nanjing [SHAC].

Notes to Pages 21–25   167

29. Jiaoyubu, *Di'erci Zhongguo jiaoyu nianjian,* 11.

30. The Mukden Incident, also called the Manchurian Incident, was the seizure of the Manchurian city of Mukden (now Shenyang) by Japanese troops. On the night of September 18, 1931, Japanese troops used the pretext of an explosion along the Japanese-controlled South Manchurian Railway to occupy Mukden. Japanese reinforcements eventually arrived, occupied the region, and established the puppet state of Manchukuo. In China, September 18, 1931, marks the official beginning of the Second Sino-Japanese War, but full-scale war did not break out until July 7, 1937.

31. Jiaoyubu, *Di'erci Zhongguo jiaoyu nianjian,* 55. Qi Hongshen, *Liuwang: Dongbei xuesheng* [Refugees: The northeast students] (Zhengzhou: Daxiang chubanshe, 2008), 14.

32. Qi, *Liuwang,* 14.

33. Qi, *Liuwang,* 70.

34. Qi, *Liuwang,* 14, 73, 108.

35. Jiaoyubu, *Di'erci Zhongguo jiaoyu nianjian,* 55.

36. Jiaoyubu, *Di'erci Zhongguo jiaoyu nianjian,* 31.

37. Jiaoyubu, *Di'erci Zhongguo jiaoyu nianjian,* 32.

38. Jiaoyubu, *Di'erci Zhongguo jiaoyu nianjian,* 32–33.

39. Hankou was a major city that merged with Wuchang and Hanyang to form Wuhan, the capital and largest city in Hubei province. Wuhan briefly served as the GMD's temporary wartime capital before Nationalist leaders moved to Chongqing in Sichuan province to flee Japanese attacks on the city.

40. The arrangement of state ritual below the emperor was coordinated exactly with the national administrative system. At each administrative level—province, prefecture, and county—there was a city or town serving as the administrative seat, where in addition to the government compound (*yamen*), which was the officiating magistrate's headquarters, there were several official religious establishments. Among the most important were the Confucian, or civil, temple (*wen miao*) and the military temple (*wu miao*), which were the ritual foci of the two major divisions in the Chinese bureaucracy; and also the City God temple (*chenghuang miao*). A city serving as both prefectural seat and county seat would have two *yamen* and two sets of state temples.

41. Jiaoyubu, *Di'erci Zhongguo jiaoyu nianjian,* 33–34.

42. Jiaoyubu, *Di'erci Zhongguo jiaoyu nianjian,* 53.

43. Guomin xingzhengyuan [National Executive Yuan], "Guomindang zhongyang junxiao tebie xunlianban yuanbing cansha Hechuan xian Guoli di'er zhongxue xuesheng Zheng Xuepu deng jingguo qingxing" [The stages of events that led the GMD Central Special Military Training class member to murder Zheng Xuepu of Number Two Middle School from Hechuan County], file 2300, 16J-1621, vol. 2, sec. 2, December 1942, Di'er lishi dang'anguan, Nanjing [SHAC].

44. Guomin xingzhengyuan, "Guomindang zhongyang junxiao."

45. Guomin xingzhengyuan, "Guomindang zhongyang junxiao."

46. Guomin xingzhengyuan, "Guomindang zhongyang junxiao."

47. Guomin xingzhengyuan, "Guomindang zhongyang junxiao."

48. Guomin xingzhengyuan, "Guomindang zhongyang junxiao."

49. Guomin xingzhengyuan, "Guomindang zhongyang junxiao."

50. Guomin xingzhengyuan, "Guomindang zhongyang junxiao."

51. Schoppa, *Sea of Bitterness,* 212.

168   Notes to Pages 26–33

52. *Geming wenxian,* vol. 61, 353. Information originated from Zhejiang Province Department of Education. *Zhejiang jiaoyu* [Zhejiang education] 3, no. 6 (December 1939): 29–34.

53. *Geming wenxian,* vol. 61.

54. Yuqian was a significant city because it became the military and governmental center of Zhejiang after the Japanese invaded Hangzhou.

55. *Geming wenxian,* vol. 61, 357.

56. *Geming wenxian,* vol. 61, 356.

57. *Geming wenxian,* vol. 61, 356.

58. *Geming wenxian,* vol. 61, 356.

59. *Geming wenxian,* vol. 61, 357.

60. *Geming wenxian,* vol. 61, 356–360.

61. Schoppa, *Sea of Bitterness,* 191–192.

62. Schoppa, *Sea of Bitterness,* 200.

63. Rebecca Nedostup, *Superstitious Regimes: Religion and the Politics of Chinese Modernity* (Cambridge, MA: Harvard University Press, 2009), 11.

64. Nedostup, *Superstitious Regimes,* 265.

65. Guomin xingzhengyuan [National Executive Yuan], "Ge di zhongdeng xuexiao jiaozhiyuan beikong" [Secondary school staff from different locales accused of crimes], file 5262, J-1275, vol. 2, Di'er lishi dang'anguan, Nanjing [SHAC].

66. Guomin xingzhengyuan, "Ge di zhongdeng zhongdeng xuexiao jiaozhiyuan beikong."

67. Guomin xingzhengyuan, "Ge di zhongdeng zhongdeng xuexiao jiaozhiyuan beikong."

68. Lower middle school students joined the Boy Scouts and Girl Scouts, which followed the British model.

69. Guomin xingzhengyuan, "Ge di zhongdeng zhongdeng xuexiao jiaozhiyuan beikong."

70. Guomin xingzhengyuan, "Ge di zhongdeng zhongdeng xuexiao jiaozhiyuan beikong."

71. Guomin xingzhengyuan, "Ge di zhongdeng zhongdeng xuexiao jiaozhiyuan beikong."

72. Guomin xingzhengyuan, "Ge di zhongdeng zhongdeng xuexiao jiaozhiyuan beikong."

73. Guomin xingzhengyuan, "Ge di zhongdeng zhongdeng xuexiao jiaozhiyuan beikong."

74. Guomin xingzhengyuan, "Ge di zhongdeng zhongdeng xuexiao jiaozhiyuan beikong."

75. Guomin xingzhengyuan, "Ge di zhongdeng zhongdeng xuexiao jiaozhiyuan beikong."

76. Guomin xingzhengyuan, "Ge di zhongdeng zhongdeng xuexiao jiaozhiyuan beikong."

77. Jiaoyubu, *Di'erci Zhongguo jiaoyu nianjian,* 380.

78. Guomin xingzhengyuan, "Ge di zhongdeng zhongdeng xuexiao jiaozhiyuan beikong."

79. Teenagers dating was frowned upon not only in 1940s China but also today. It is still common for young Chinese to never have had a boyfriend or girlfriend, and many teens were (and are) discouraged from having romantic relationships in middle school, instead told to focus on schoolwork.

80. Guomin xingzhengyuan, "Ge di zhongdeng zhongdeng xuexiao jiaozhiyuan beikong."

81. Guomin xingzhengyuan, "Ge di zhongdeng zhongdeng xuexiao jiaozhiyuan beikong."

82. Li, *Echoes of Chongqing,* 44. For a detailed discussion of the Green Gang, see Frederic Wakeman Jr., *Policing Shanghai, 1927–1937* (Berkeley: University of California Press, 1995).

83. Jessie G. Lutz, "Comments," in *Nationalist China during the Sino-Japanese War, 1937–1945,* ed. Paul K. T. Sih (Hicksville, NY: Exposition Press, 1977), 125.

Notes to Pages 35–37   169

Chapter 2. The Three People's Principles Youth Corps on the Mainland, 1938–1947

1. Chen, *Storm Clouds,* 142–145; Pichon P. Y. Loh, "The Politics of Chiang Kai-shek: A Reappraisal," *Journal of Asian Studies* 25, no. 3 (May 1966): 442.

2. Lloyd Eastman, *The Abortive Revolution: China under Nationalist Rule, 1927–1937* (Cambridge, MA: Harvard University Press, 1974), 32; Huang, *Politics of Depoliticization,* 108.

3. In the 1920s, China was fragmented into numerous regions controlled by warlords. The GMD and CCP jointly established the Whampoa Military Academy in May 1924 to train an indoctrinated army to defeat the warlords and reunify China in the Northern Expedition (1926–1928). The institution produced many prestigious commanders who fought during that conflict, as well as in the Sino-Japanese War (1937–1945) and the Chinese Civil War (1945–1949). Huang, *Politics of Depoliticization,* 25, 34–35, 108.

4. Huang, *Politics of Depoliticization,* 108.

5. Huang, *Politics of Depoliticization,* 109; Frederic Wakeman Jr., "A Revisionist View of the Nanjing Decade: Confucian Fascism," *China Quarterly,* no. 150 (June 1997): 421.

6. Huang, *Politics of Depoliticization,* 109.

7. Lloyd Eastman, Jerome Ch'en, Suzanne Pepper, and Lyman P. Van Slyke, *The Nationalist Era in China, 1927–1949* (Cambridge: Cambridge University Press, 1991), 27. Meanwhile, Maggie Clinton believes "CC" to represent "Central Committee." Maggie Clinton, *Revolutionary Nativism: Fascism and Culture in China, 1925–1937* (Durham, NC: Duke University Press, 2017).

8. Huang, *Politics of Depoliticization,* 108–109.

9. Chen, *Storm Clouds,* 147.

10. Wakeman, "Revisionist View," 422.

11. Huang, *Politics of Depoliticization,* 91; Wakeman, "Revisionist View," 421–422.

12. Huang, *Politics of Depoliticization,* 91; Wakeman, "Revisionist View," 396–397, 411–412, 417, 421.

13. Wakeman, "Revisionist View," 421.

14. Huang, *Politics of Depoliticization,* 91, fn. 35.

15. Wakeman, "Revisionist View," 423.

16. Wakeman, "Revisionist View," 426.

17. Wakeman, "Revisionist View," 428.

18. Wakeman, "Revisionist View," 428. See Gan Guoxun, "Guanyu suowei 'Fuxingshe' de zhenqing shikuang" [The true conditions and actual circumstances of the so-called Fuxingshe], *Zhuanji wenxue, shang* 35, no. 3 (1979): 32–38; *zhong* 35, no. 4 (1979): 68–73; *xia* 35, no. 5 (1979): 81–86.

19. Wakeman, "Revisionist View," 396.

20. Shepherd-Paxton Talk, in Records of the Department of State, Internal, China, 1930–1939, no. D130, 00/14127, cited in Wakeman, "Revisionist View," 430.

21. William C. Kirby, *Germany and Republican China* (Stanford, CA: Stanford University Press, 1984), 174.

22. Wakeman, "Revisionist View"; Kirby, *Germany and Republican China;* Clinton, *Revolutionary Nativism.*

23. Kirby, *Germany and Republican China,* 174. See A. James Gregor, "Fascism and Modernization: Some Addenda," *World Politics* 26, no. 3 (1974): 370–384; and A. James Gregor, *The Fascist Persuasion in Radical Politics* (Princeton, NJ: Princeton University Press, 1974).

24. Kirby, *Germany and Republican China,* 174.

170   Notes to Pages 37–41

25. Kirby, *Germany and Republican China,* 174.

26. Kirby, *Germany and Republican China,* 175.

27. Clinton, *Revolutionary Nativism,* 4.

28. Lloyd Eastman, "Fascism in Kuomintang China: The Blue Shirts," *China Quarterly,* no. 49 (January–March 1972): 1–31; Eastman, *Abortive Revolution,* 31–84; Lloyd E. Eastman, "The Kuomintang in the 1930s," in *The Limits of Change,* ed. Charlotte Furth (Cambridge, MA: Harvard University Press, 1976), 191–210; Lloyd Eastman, "Fascism and Modern China: A Rejoinder," *China Quarterly,* no. 80 (December 1979): 838–842; Lloyd Eastman, "The Rise and Fall of the 'Blue Shirts': A Review Article," *Republican China* 13, no. 1 (November 1987): 39–43. Support for Eastman has come from Lincoln Li, *Student Nationalism in China, 1924–1949* (Albany: State University of New York Press, 1994), 55, 72–74. Critique of Eastman's works has come from Maria Hsia-Chang, "'Fascism' and Modern China," *China Quarterly,* no. 79 (September 1979): 553–567; Maria Hsia-Chang, *The Chinese Blue Shirt Society: Fascism and Developmental Nationalism* (Berkeley: Institute of East Asian Studies, University of California, 1985).

29. Hsia-Chang, "'Fascism' and Modern China," 562–563.

30. Liu Liang-chan, "Faxisizhuyi jiu Zhongguo" [Fascism saves China], *Shehui xinwen* 8, no. 24 (June 12, 1933): 381, cited in Hsia-Chang, "'Fascism' and Modern China," 563.

31. Eastman, *Abortive Revolution,* 40–42.

32. Huang, *Politics of Depoliticization,* 192.

33. Huang, *Politics of Depoliticization,* 192.

34. Huang, *Politics of Depoliticization,* 40.

35. Huang, *Politics of Depoliticization,* 40–75; Culp, *Articulating Citizenship,* 235.

36. Huang, *Politics of Depoliticization,* 48–75; Howard Boorman, ed., *Biographical Dictionary of Republican China,* vol. 3 (New York: Columbia University Press, 1971), 295–299.

37. "Principles in Organizing Student Organizations," *Bulletin of the Ministry of Education* [Jiaoyu gongbao] 2, no. 6 (February 1930): 21, cited in Huang, *Politics of Depoliticization,* 74.

38. "Outline for the Organization of SSGAs," *Bulletin of the Ministry of Education* [Jiaoyu gongbao] 2, no. 6 (February 1930): 24–26, cited in Huang, *Politics of Depoliticization,* 74.

39. "Outline for the Organization of SSGAs," 24–26, cited in Huang, *Politics of Depoliticization,* 74.

40. Huang, *Politics of Depoliticization,* 192.

41. Eastman, *Abortive Revolution,* 64–65; Huang, *Politics of Depoliticization,* 93; Wakeman, "Revisionist View," 397.

42. Huang, *Politics of Depoliticization,* 183.

43. Huang, *Politics of Depoliticization,* 183.

44. Huang, *Politics of Depoliticization,* 183.

45. Huang, *Politics of Depoliticization,* 104; Chen, *Storm Clouds,* 143.

46. Jay Taylor, *The Generalissimo's Son: Chiang Ching-kuo and the Revolutions in China and Taiwan* (Cambridge, MA: Harvard University Press, 2000), 85.

47. Huang, *Politics of Depoliticization,* 104.

48. *Sanmin zhuyi qingniantuan tuanshi ziliao diyi chugao* [The first draft of volume one of historical materials on the Three People's Principles Youth Corps], part I (Nanjing, 1946), 1; also reprinted in *Geming wenxian* [Documents on revolution], vol. 62 (Taipei: Guomindang Historical Commission, 1973), 1, cited in Huang, *Politics of Depoliticization,* 104.

49. Eastman, *Seeds of Destruction,* 91.

Notes to Pages 41–44   171

50. Zhu Jiahua, *Qingnian tuanwu zhi jinzhan* [The development of Youth Corps affairs] (May 1939), 12; Kang Ze, "Sanmin zhuyi qingniantuan chengli de jingguo" [The process of forming the Three People's Principles Youth Corps], *Wenshi ziliao* [Literary and historical documents], vol. 40 (November 1963): 197, cited in Huang, *Politics of Depoliticization*, 104–105.

51. Chiang Kai-shek diaries, November 3, 1937, box 39, folder 17, Hoover Institution Archives.

52. Huang, *Politics of Depoliticization*, 105.

53. Chiang Kai-shek diaries, February 4, 1938, box 39, folder 21, Hoover Institution Archives. The Vigorously-Carry-Out Society (*Lixingshe*) was a clandestine agency of the Whampoa Clique.

54. Chiang Kai-shek diaries, February 4, 1938, box 39, folder 21, Hoover Institution Archives.

55. Chiang Kai-shek diaries, February 5, 1938, box 39, folder 21, Hoover Institution Archives; Huang, *Politics of Depoliticization*, 109; Chen, *Storm Clouds*, 143.

56. Huang, *Politics of Depoliticization*, 109.

57. Huang, *Politics of Depoliticization*, 109.

58. Taylor, *Generalissimo's Son*, 86.

59. "Speech for the Oath of Members Joining the Corps," *Speeches of the President of the Three People's Principles Youth Corps*, Three People's Principles Youth Corps Central Headquarters, April 1942; Chiang Kai-shek, *President Chiang Kai-shek's Selected Speeches and Messages, 1937–1945* (Taipei: China Cultural Service, 1949), 25–29.

60. Eastman, *Seeds of Destruction*, 91.

61. Taylor, *Generalissimo's Son*, 86.

62. Taylor, *Generalissimo's Son*, 86.

63. Eastman, *Seeds of Destruction*, 91.

64. Chiang Kai-shek diaries, May 19, 1945, box 44, folder 6, Hoover Institution Archives.

65. Chiang Kai-shek diaries, May 19, 1945, box 44, folder 6, Hoover Institution Archives.

66. Chiang Kai-shek diaries, May 19, 1945, box 44, folder 6, Hoover Institution Archives.

67. Chiang Kai-shek diaries, May 19, 1945, box 44, folder 6, Hoover Institution Archives.

68. Chiang Kai-shek diaries, May 26, 1945, box 44, folder 6, Hoover Institution Archives.

69. "Book Instructing the Entire Nation's Youth," *Speeches of the President of the Three People's Principles Youth Corps*, Three People's Principles Youth Corps Central Headquarters, April 1942, 2–4; Chiang, *Chiang Kai-shek's Selected Speeches*, 27–29.

70. Chen, *Storm Clouds*, 143.

71. Chen, *Storm Clouds*, 143.

72. Chen, *Storm Clouds*, 143.

73. Chen, *Storm Clouds*, 143.

74. Taylor, *Generalissimo's Son*, 85.

75. Chen, *Storm Clouds*, 143; Taylor, *Generalissimo's Son*, 85. Ms. Ai was head of the women's unit in the first class of the Youth Cadre School under Chiang Ching-kuo in 1944. Ai Ch'i-ming, interview conducted by Jay Taylor, June 15, 1996 (Nanjing), *Generalissimo's Son*, 459, fn. 44.

76. Chen, *Storm Clouds*, 144.

77. Chen, *Storm Clouds*, 144.

78. Chen, *Storm Clouds*, 143.

79. Huang, *Politics of Depoliticization*, 108.

172   Notes to Pages 44–47

80. *Amerasia Papers: A Clue to the Catastrophe of China,* vol. 1 (Washington, DC, 1970), 236. The estimate here has been attributed to Chen Lifu, cited in Huang, *Politics of Depoliticization,* 106.

81. Zhu Zishuang, *Zhongguo Guomindang lizi quanguo daibiao dahui yaolan* [Successive national party congresses of the Chinese Guomindang] (Chongqing, 1945), 70, cited in Eastman, *Seeds of Destruction,* 89.

82. Chiang Kai-shek, *China's Destiny,* trans. Wang Chung-hui (New York: Macmillan, 1947), 214, 220.

83. Wang Jingwei subsequently defected and went on to collaborate with the Japanese in setting up a puppet government in the occupied areas of China.

84. Huang, *Politics of Depoliticization,* 110.

85. Huang, *Politics of Depoliticization,* 113.

86. Chen Cheng, *Sanmin zhuyi qingniantuan zhi xingzhi ji qi zhanwang* [The nature and outlook of the Three People's Principles Youth Corps] (April 1939), 35–36, cited in Huang, *Politics of Depoliticization,* 112.

87. Sanmin zhuyi qingniantuan zhongyang tuanbu [The Central Corps of the Three People's Principles Youth Corps], *Dang yu tuan de guanxi* [The relationship between the party and the Corps] (May 1940), 51, cited in Huang, *Politics of Depoliticization,* 112.

88. Kang Ze, "Sanmin zhuyi qingniantuan chengli de jingguo" [The process of the Three People's Principles Youth Corps Establishment], 197–198, cited in Huang, *Politics of Depoliticization,* 112.

89. "The Rallying of Youth during the War of Resistance," *Geming wenxian* [Documents on revolution], vol. 62, 2, cited in Huang, *Politics of Depoliticization,* 112; Huang, *Politics of Depoliticization,* 113.

90. Chiang Kai-shek diaries, February 10, 1938, box 39, folder 21, Hoover Institution Archives.

91. Huang, *Politics of Depoliticization,* 118.

92. Chiang Kai-shek to Chen Lifu, February 6, 1938, and Ministry of Education, circular dispatched February 12, 1938, file 5-2/1420, SHAC, cited in Huang, *Politics of Depoliticization,* 116.

93. Letter from the Student Federation for the Salvation of China, March 15, 1938, file 5-2/1501, SHAC, cited in Huang, *The Politics of Depoliticization in Republican China,* 116.

94. Reply from Ministry of Education official Wu Junsheng, March 19, 1938, file 5-2/1501, SHAC, cited in Huang, *Politics of Depoliticization,* 116.

95. Huang, *Politics of Depoliticization,* 183.

96. Huang, *Politics of Depoliticization,* 183.

97. Huang, *Politics of Depoliticization,* 183.

98. Huang, *Politics of Depoliticization,* 120.

99. Huang, *Politics of Depoliticization,* 120.

100. Mulready-Stone, *Mobilizing Shanghai Youth,* 7.

101. Huang, *Politics of Depoliticization,* 123.

102. Huang, *Politics of Depoliticization,* 123.

103. Huang, *Politics of Depoliticization,* 123; David Macleod, *Building Character in the American Boy: The Boy Scouts, YMCA, and Their Forerunners, 1870–1920* (Madison: University of Wisconsin Press, 1983), 296.

Notes to Pages 47–53   173

104. Draft of the Three People's Principles Youth Corps, reproduced in Wang Liangqing, *Study of the Relationship*.

105. *Sanmin zhuyi qingniantuan tuanshi ziliao diyi chugao* [The first draft of volume one of historical materials on the Three People's Principles Youth Corps], part I (Nanjing, 1946), 4–5, cited in Huang, *Politics of Depoliticization*, 124.

106. Huang, *Politics of Depoliticization*, 124.

107. Huang, *Politics of Depoliticization*, 124.

108. "20% of China Youth Corps More Than 30 Years Old," *New York Times*, September 12, 1947, 10.

109. Chiang, *Chiang Kai-shek's Selected Speeches*, 34.

110. "The Organizational Work of 1940," *Tuanwu tongxun* [Communication on corps affairs] 2, no. 4 (April 1940): 21, cited in Huang, *Politics of Depoliticization*, 126.

111. *Sanmin zhuyi qingniantuan zhongyang tuanshi ziliao diyi chugao* [The first draft of volume one of historical materials on the Three People's Principles Youth Corps], part I (Nanjing, 1946), 208–209, cited in Huang, *Politics of Depoliticization*, 127.

112. Sanmin zhuyi qingniantuan zhongyang ganshi weiyuanhui [The Central Executive Committee of Three People's Principles Youth Corps], *Sanmin zhuyi qingniantuan qinianlai tuanwu gongzuo zongbaogao* [General work report on the previous seven years of the Three People's Principles Youth Corps] (ca. May 1945), 109–110; *Geming wenxian* [Documents on revolution], vol. 63 (Taipei: Guomindang Historical Commission, 1973), 4–5, cited in Huang, *Politics of Depoliticization*, 127–128.

113. Huang, *Politics of Depoliticization*, 127.

114. Guoli bianyi guan [National Institute of Compilation and Translation], *Tongzijun xunlian* [Scouts training], vol. 1 (Taipei: Guoli bianyi guan, 1972), 12.

115. Guoli bianyi guan, *Tongzijun xunlian*, 14.

116. Culp, *Articulating Citizenship*, 178.

117. Culp, *Articulating Citizenship*, 183.

118. Huang, *Politics of Depoliticization*, 130.

119. Te Fang Chou Ch'ien, interview by Thomas A. Brindley, December 23, 1991, Huntsville, AL, in Brindley, *China Youth Corps*, 20.

120. Chen Cheng, *Gao quantuan tuanyuan shu: lingdao qingnian de zhenglu* [Message to all corps members: The proper way of leading youth] (September 1939), 7; *Geming wenxian* [Documents on revolution], vol. 63, 83; "Policy on the Guidance of Social Youth," passed by the Standing Committee on September 5, 1939, in *Geming wenxian* [Documents on revolution], vol. 62, 48–51, cited in Huang, *Politics of Depoliticization*, 130–131.

121. Zhu Jiahua, *Qingniantuan tuanwu zhi jinzhan* [The development of Youth Corps affairs], May 1939, 23–25, cited in Huang, *Politics of Depoliticization*, 131–132.

122. *Sanmin zhuyi qingniantuan zhongyang tuanshi ziliao diyiji chugao* [The first draft of volume one of historical materials on the Three People's Principles Youth Corps], part I (Nanjing, 1946), 141, cited in Huang, *Politics of Depoliticization*, 132.

123. Huang, *Politics of Depoliticization*, 133.

124. Huang, *Politics of Depoliticization*, 133.

125. "The Way to Recruit Members in the Future: Part 1," *Speeches of the President of the Three People's Principles Youth Corps*, Three People's Principles Youth Corps Central Headquarters, April 1942, 59–71.

174 Notes to Pages 53–58

126. Boorman, *Biographical Dictionary*, vol. 1, 328.

127. Boorman, *Biographical Dictionary*, vol. 1, 437–440.

128. Zhongguo Guomindang zhongyang zhixing weiyuanhui [Central Executive Committee of the Guomindang], *Zhongguo Guomindang dangwu tongji jiyao* [Statistical abstracts on party affairs of the Guomindang] (July 1942), 1, 4, cited in Huang, *Politics of Depoliticization*, 135.

129. *Sanmin zhuyi qingniantuan tuanshi ziliao diyiji chugao* [The first draft of volume one of historical materials on the Three People's Principles Youth Corps], part I (Nanjing, 1946), 103–104, cited in Huang, *Politics of Depoliticization*, 137.

130. *Geming wenxian* [Documents on revolution], vol. 70 (Taipei: Guomindang Historical Commission, 1976), 78–79, 93–94, 133; Huang, *Politics of Depoliticization*, 137–138, fn. 45.

131. Hans J. Van de Ven, *From Friend to Comrade: The Founding of the Chinese Communist Party, 1920–1927* (Berkeley: University of California Press, 1991), 139.

132. "Zhongguo gongchandang Zhongguo gongan zuyi qingniantuan zhongyangju tonggao—guanyu hupai daibiao ji dangyuan jian tuanyuan deng ziguiding" [Chinese Communist Youth League's Central Bureau announcement], *Chinese Communist Central Committee Youth Movement Compilations, July 1921–September 1949* (Beijing: Zhongguo qingnian chubanshe 1988), 49.

133. "Work Program of the Three People's Principles Youth Corps," in *Sanmin zhuyi qingniantuan tuanshi ziliao diyiji chugao* [The first draft of volume one of historical materials on the Three People's Principles Youth Corps], part I (Nanjing, 1946), 136–138, cited in Huang, *Politics of Depoliticization*, 140.

134. "Method of Promoting Corps Affairs in Schools," *Sanmin zhuyi qingniantuan faling jiyao* [Abstracts on laws and regulations of the Three People's Principles Youth Corps] (March 1943), 117, cited in Huang, *Politics of Depoliticization*, 140.

135. "Method of Promoting Corps Affairs in Schools," *Sanmin zhuyi qingniantuan faling jiyao* [Abstracts on laws and regulations of the Three People's Principles Youth Corps], March 1943, 117, cited in Huang, *Politics of Depoliticization*, 140.

136. *Sanmin zhuyi qingniantuan tuanshi ziliao diyi chugao* [The first draft of volume one of historical materials on the Three People's Principles Youth Corps], part I (Nanjing, 1946), 439, cited in Huang, *Politics of Depoliticization*, 145.

137. Sanmin zhuyi qingniantuan zhongyang ganshi weiyuanhui [The Central Committee of the Three People's Principles Youth Corps], *Sanmin zhuyi qingniantuan diyijie zhongyang ganshihui gongzuo baogao* [Work report of the Central Executive Committee of the Three People's Principles Youth Corps], 52–53, cited in Huang, *Politics of Depoliticization*, 146.

138. "Method of Establishing Chiang Kai-shek Libraries at Directly Affiliated School Branch Corps," approved on April 16, 1941, in Sanmin zhuyi qingniantuan zhongyang tuanbu [The Central Corps of the Three People's Principles Youth Corps], *Sanmin zhuyi qingniantuan faling jiyao* [Abstracts on law and regulations of the Three People's Principles Youth Corps], March 1943, vol. 1, 33–34, cited in Huang, *Politics of Depoliticization*, 147.

139. "Method of Organizing Youth Essay Writing and Oratorical Contests at Various Levels of the Corps," approved on February 20, 1943, in *Sanmin zhuyi qingniantuan faling jiyao* [Abstracts on law and regulations of the Three People's Principles Youth Corps], March 1943, vol. 1, 29–30, cited in Huang, *Politics of Depoliticization*, 147.

140. "Method of Organizing Youth Essay Writing and Oratorical Contests at Various Levels of the Corps," approved on February 20, 1943, in *Sanmin zhuyi qingniantuan faling jiyao*

Notes to Pages 58–61   175

[Abstracts on law and regulations of the Three People's Principles Youth Corps], March 1943, vol. 1, 29–30, cited in Huang, *Politics of Depoliticization*, 147.

141. Huang, *Politics of Depoliticization*, 148.

142. Sanmin zhuyi qingniantuan zhongyang ganshi weiyuanhui [The Central Corps of the Three People's Principles Youth Corps], *Sanmin zhuyi qingniantuan zhongyang changwu ganshihui gongzuo baogao* [Work Report of the Standing Committee of the Three People's Principles Youth Corps], April 1940, 23; Sanmin zhuyi qingniantuan zhongyang ganshi weiyuanhui [The Central Corps of the Three People's Principles Youth Corps], *Sanmin zhuyi qingniantuan zhongyang tuanbu baogao* [Work report of the Central Corps of the Three People's Principles Youth Corps], November 1942, 4–5; Sanmin zhuyi qingniantuan zhongyang ganshi weiyuanhui [The Central Executive Committee of the Three People's Principles Youth Corps], *Sanmin zhuyi qingniantuan diyijie zhongyang ganshihui gongzuo baogao* [Work report of the First Central Executive Committee of the Three People's Principles Youth Corps], November 1939, 70–71, cited in Huang, *Politics of Depoliticization*, 148.

143. Sanmin zhuyi qingniantuan zhongyang ganshi weiyuanhui [The Central Corps of the Three People's Principles Youth Corps], *Sanmin zhuyi qingniantuan ershiba niandu Chongqing qingnian xialingying xunlian jishi* [A record of training events at the 1939 Chongqing Summer Youth Camp of the Three People's Principles Youth Corps], April 1940, 45–51, cited in Huang, *Politics of Depoliticization*, 148.

144. Speech by Kang Ze on "The Process and Reflections of Organizing Summer Camps," in Sanmin zhuyi qingniantuan zhongyang ganshi weiyuanhui [The Central Corps of the Three People's Principles Youth Corps], *Sanmin zhuyi qingniantuan ershiba niandu Chongqing qingnian xialingying xunlian jishi* [A record of training events at the 1939 Chongqing Summer Youth Camp of the Three People's Principles Youth Corps], April 1940, 23, cited in Huang, *Politics of Depoliticization*, 148.

145. Sanmin zhuyi qingniantuan zhongyang tuanbu [The Central Corps of the Three People's Principles Youth Corps], *Sanmin zhuyi qingniantuan zhongyang tuanbu gongzuo baogao* [Work report of the Central Corps of the Three People's Principles Youth Corps], November 1942, 4; Sanmin zhuyi qingniantuan zhongyang tuanbu [The Central Corps of the Three People's Principles Youth Corps], *Sanmin zhuyi qingniantuan sanshiyi niandu Guanxian qingnian xialingying xunlian jishi* [A record of training events at the 1942 Guan County Summer Youth Training Camp of the Three People's Principles Youth Corps], Chongqing, 1942, 24, cited in Huang, *Politics of Depoliticization*, 148.

146. Sanmin zhuyi qingniantuan zhongyang tuanbu [The Central Corps of the Three People's Principles Youth Corps], *Sanmin zhuyi qingniantuan zhongyang tuanbu gongzuo baogao* [Work report of the Central Corps of the Three People's Principles Youth Corps], November 1942, 4; Sanmin zhuyi qingniantuan zhongyang tuanbu [The Central Corps of the Three People's Principles Youth Corps], *Sanmin zhuyi qingniantuan sanshiyi niandu Guanxian qingnian xialingying xunlian jishi* [A record of training events at the 1942 Guan County Summer Youth Training Camp of the Three People's Principles Youth Corps], Chongqing, 1942, 24, cited in Huang, *Politics of Depoliticization*, 148.

147. Mulready-Stone, *Mobilizing Shanghai Youth*, 5, 139.

148. Mulready-Stone, *Mobilizing Shanghai Youth*, 189.

149. Huang, *Politics of Depoliticization*, 148.

150. Part II of Chiang Kai-shek speech, "Path for the Future Development of Corps Affairs," in *Sanmin zhuyi qingniantuan tuanshi ziliao diyiji chugao* [The first draft of volume one

176   Notes to Pages 61–62

of historical materials on the Three People's Principles Youth Corps], part I (Nanjing, 1946), 179, cited in Huang, *Politics of Depoliticization*, 149.

151. Order #16980 "Future Guiding Principles for the Student Movement" in Sanmin zhuyi qingniantuan zhongyang ganshi weiyuanhui [The Central Executive Committee of the Three People's Principles Youth Corps], *Sanmin zhuyi qingniantuan diyici quanguo daibiao dahui huiyi jilu* [Minutes of meetings of the First National Congress of the Three People's Principles Youth Corps], March–April 1943, 336–337; reprint available in *Geming wenxian* [Documents on revolution], vol. 62, 156–157, cited in Huang, *Politics of Depoliticization*, 149–150.

152. The Central Corps of the Three People's Principles Youth Corps, *Work Report of the Standing Committee of the Three People's Principles Youth Corps*, April 1940, 41; Sanmin zhuyi qingniantuan zhongyang tuanbu [The Central Corps of the Three People's Principles Youth Corps], *Sanmin zhuyi qingniantuan changwu ganshihui gongzuo baogao* [Work Report of the Standing Committee of the Three People's Principles Youth Corps], cited in Huang, *Politics of Depoliticization*, 152.

153. Huang, *Politics of Depoliticization*, 152.

154. Sanmin zhuyi qingniantuan zhongyang ganshi weiyuanhui [The Central Executive Committee of the Three People's Principles Youth Corps], ed., *Sanmin zhuyi qingniantuan qinianlai tuanwu gongzuo zongbaogao* [General Work Report on the Previous Seven Years of the Three People's Principles Youth Corps] (May 1945), 260–261, cited in Huang, *Politics of Depoliticization*, 152.

155. Republican Government (Ministry of Education), *A Survey of Important Work of the Ministry of Education for the Previous Year*, February 1939, 3, 36; Guomin zhengfu (jiaoyubu), Yinianlai jiaoyubu zhongyao gongzuo gaikuang [A survey of important work of the Ministry of Education for the previous year], cited in Huang, *Politics of Depoliticization*, 152.

156. Republican Government (Ministry of Education), *A Survey of the Nation's Higher Education* (March 1939), 74–75; Guomin zhengfu (jiaoyubu), Quanguo gaodeng jiaoyu gaikuang [A survey of the nation's tertiary education], cited in Huang, *Politics of Depoliticization*, 152.

157. Chiang Kai-shek diaries, May 27, 1945, box 44, folder 6, Hoover Institution Archives.

158. Chiang Kai-shek diaries, July 9, 1945, box 44, folder 8, Hoover Institution Archives.

159. See Table 2.1.

160. Huang, *Politics of Depoliticization*, 171.

161. For more information on Western Hunan, see Jeffrey C. Kinkley, *The Odyssey of Shen Congwen* (Stanford, CA: Stanford University Press, 1987), a biography on the May 4th Movement (1919) writer who wrote about his native region.

162. *Shanghai Wenhuibao*, May 13, 1947, cited in Wang, *Study of the Relationship*, 341–343.

163. Wang, *Study of the Relationship*, 361.

164. The February 28 Incident, also known as 2-28, was an anti-government, anti-Chinese uprising in Taiwan that began on February 28, 1947. Two years of GMD administration led to the widespread impression among Taiwanese that the government was plagued by nepotism, corruption, and economic failure. Tensions increased between the Taiwanese and the new regime. The straw that broke the camel's back came on February 27, 1947, in Taipei when a dispute between a female Taiwanese cigarette vendor and a GMD agent of the Office of Monopoly triggered civil disorder and open rebellion, lasting for several days. The GMD army violently suppressed the uprising, resulting in many civilian deaths. Estimates of the number of deaths vary widely from under one thousand to tens of thousands or more. The incident

Notes to Pages 63–64   177

marked the beginning of the White Terror period in Taiwan in which thousands more Taiwanese, including mainlanders who the GMD suspected were dissenters, either vanished, were killed, or were placed in prison. In the aftermath of the 2-28 Incident, martial law was declared in 1949 and stayed in effect until 1987.

165. Lai Tse-han, Ramon H. Myers, and Wei Wou, *A Tragic Beginning: The Taiwan Uprising of February, 1947* (Stanford, CA: Stanford University Press, 1991), 155.

166. Chen Cuilian, *Paixi douzheng yu quanmo zhengzhi* [Factional struggle and power politics: Another facet of the 2/28 tragedy] (Taipei: China Times Press, 1995), 254, 268–269, 271, 279–280.

167. Chen, *Storm Clouds,* 144.

168. Wang, *Study of the Relationship,* 347, fn. 25, 26.

169. Wang, *Study of the Relationship,* 347, fn. 25, 26.

170. Huang, *Politics of Depoliticization,* 172.

171. Qian Anyi, "Sanqingtuan Guiyang qutuanbu gaikuang" [General conditions of the Three People's Principles Youth Corps branch at Guiyang] in *Wenshi ziliao* [Literary and historical documents], Guiyang, 3 (April 1982), 98, cited in Huang, *Politics of Depoliticization,* 172; Suzanne Pepper, *Civil War in China: The Political Struggle, 1945–1949* (Berkeley: University of California Press, 1978), 60.

172. *Liujie zhongchanghui jilu* [Minutes of meetings of the Sixth Plenum of the Central Committee], May 14, 1947, 402–403, 419, 432, cited in Wang, *Study of the Relationship,* 348.

173. Chiang Kai-shek diaries, June 8, 1947, box 46, folder 9, Hoover Institution Archives.

174. Chiang Kai-shek diaries, June 20, 1947, box 46, folder 9, Hoover Institution Archives.

175. Cho-yun Hsu, "Historical Setting for the Rise of Chiang Ching-kuo," in *Chiang Ching-kuo's Leadership in the Development of the Republic of China on Taiwan,* ed. Shaochuan Leng (Lanham, MD: University Press of America, 1993), 9.

176. Chiang Kai-shek diaries, June 25, 1947, box 46, folder 9, Hoover Institution Archives.

177. Chiang Kai-shek diaries, June 25, 1947, box 46, folder 9, Hoover Institution Archives.

178. Chiang Kai-shek diaries, June 25, 1947, box 46, folder 9, Hoover Institution Archives.

179. Wang, *Study of the Relationship,* 351; Chiang Kai-shek diaries, June 28, 1947, box 46, folder 9, Hoover Institution Archives.

180. Chiang Kai-shek diaries, June 29, 1947, box 46, folder 9, Hoover Institution Archives.

181. Chiang Kai-shek diaries, August 9, 1947, box 26, folder 11, Hoover Institution Archives.

182. Chiang Kai-shek diaries, September 12, 1947, box 26, folder 12, Hoover Institution Archives; Chen, *Storm Clouds,* 144.

183. Chiang Kai-shek diaries, September 12, 1947, box 26, folder 12, Hoover Institution Archives.

184. Chiang Kai-shek diaries, September 12, 1947, box 26, folder 12, Hoover Institution Archives.

185. Sanmin zhuyi qingniantuan zhongyang ganshi weiyuanhui [The Central Executive Committee of the Three People's Principles Youth Corps], *Sanmin zhuyi qingniantuan dierjie zhongyang ganshihui gongzuo baogao* [Work report of the Second Central Executive Committee of the Three People's Principles Youth Corps], September 1947, 47–60, 49–50; *Geming wenxian* [Documents on revolution], vol. 69, 446–448, cited in Huang, *Politics of Depoliticization,* 173.

186. Huang, *Politics of Depoliticization,* 173.

187. Huang, *Politics of Depoliticization,* 174.

178   Notes to Pages 65–67

188. *Geming wenxian* [Documents on revolution], vol. 69, 446–448, cited in Huang, *Politics of Depoliticization*, 174.

189. Sanmin zhuyi qingniantuan zhongyang ganshi weiyuanhui [The Central Executive Committee of the Three People's Principles Youth Corps], *Sanmin zhuyi qingniantuan dierjie zhongyang ganshihui gongzuo baogao* [Work report of the Second Central Executive Committee of the Three People's Principles Youth Corps], September 1947, 72–76, 79, cited in Huang, *Politics of Depoliticization*, 174.

190. Huang, *Politics of Depoliticization*, 193.

191. Huang, *Politics of Depoliticization*, 193.

192. Huang, *Politics of Depoliticization*, 28–29.

193. Zhu Jiahua to Chiang Kai-shek, August 24, 1945, in Zhongguo kexueyuan lishi yanjiusuo disansuo, "Zhongguo xiandi zhengzhishi ziliao huibian," vol. 3, part 88. Chiang's reply is not available. Cited in Huang, *Politics of Depoliticization*, 174–175.

194. "SSGAs Regulations" issued by the Ministry of Education, in *Central Daily News* (*Zhongyang Ribao*), December 9, 1947, cited in Huang, *Politics of Depoliticization*, 175.

195. Huang, *Politics of Depoliticization*, 175.

196. Huang, *Politics of Depoliticization*, 175.

197. "SSGAs Regulations," cited in Huang, *Politics of Depoliticization*, 176.

198. Suzanne Pepper, "The KMT–CCP Conflict, 1945–1949," in *The Cambridge History of China*, ed. John Fairbank and Albert Feuerweker, vol. 13 (Cambridge: Cambridge University Press, 1986), 746–747.

199. Chiang Kai-shek diaries, June 1, 1947, box 46, folder 9, Hoover Institution Archives.

200. Pepper, "KMT–CCP Conflict," 746–747.

201. Pepper, "KMT–CCP Conflict," 746–746; Huang, *Politics of Depoliticization*, 176.

202. Pepper, "KMT–CCP Conflict," 747.

203. Doak A. Barnett, *China on the Eve of Communist Takeover* (New York: Praeger, 1963), 46. Born to missionary parents in Shanghai in 1922, Barnett became a leading scholar and government adviser on China during the Johnson and Nixon administrations.

204. "Students Strike in Kunming as Protest against Civil War," *Xinhua News*, November 29, 1945, *Chinese Press Review*, U.S. Information Service, Chongqing, 6–8. Lianda was the commonly abbreviated name for the National Southwest Associated University, the wartime union of China's three prestigious northern universities—Beijing, Tsinghua, and Nankai—which moved to Kunming, the capital of Yunnan province in the remote and mountainous southwest to escape Japanese occupation. When the war ended with victory over the Japanese, the Lianda community, which had entered the war fiercely loyal to Chiang Kai-shek's government, emerged in 1946 as a critic of the Guomindang Party. Within three years, the majority of the Lianda academics and intellectuals had returned to their north China campuses, and leaned towards accepting Communist rule. For more information on Lianda, see Israel, *Lianda*.

205. Shi Huiqun, *A History of Chinese Student Movements, 1945–1949* (Shanghai: Shanghai People Publishing Company, 1992), 28.

206. Shi, *Chinese Student Movements*, 29.

207. "Kunming Students Killed in Anti-Civil War Strike," *Xinhua News*, December 4, 1945, China Press Review, U.S. Information Service, Chongqing, 4; Shi, *Chinese Student Movements*, 30.

208. Shi, *Chinese Student Movements*, 49; Wasserstrom, *Student Protests*, 247.

209. Huang, *Politics of Depoliticization*, 176. Accounts of these student activists could be found in Beijing City Archives (Beijingshi danganguan), *Jiefang zhanzheng shiqi Beiping xuesheng*

yundong [Beiping student movement during the civil war], cited in Huang, *Politics of Depoliticization,* 177.

210. Huang, *Politics of Depoliticization,* 177.

211. Wasserstrom, *Student Protests,* 169–170.

212. Pepper, "KMT–CCP Conflict," 747.

213. Barnett, *China on the Eve,* 50. Chen Lifu expressed this view in an interview with Doak Barnett.

214. Pepper, "KMT–CCP Conflict," 747.

215. Beijing City Archives [Beijingshi danganguan], *Jiefang zhanzheng shiqi Beiping xuesheng yundong* [Beiping student movement during the civil war], 26, 222, cited in Huang, *Politics of Depoliticization,* 177. See also Pepper, "KMT–CCP Conflict," 747.

216. Pepper, "KMT–CCP Conflict," 747–748.

217. Jessie G. Lutz, "The Chinese Student Movement of 1945–1949," *Journal of Asian Studies* 31, no. 1 (November 1971): 90–91.

218. Taylor, *Generalissimo's Son,* 85.

219. Taylor, *Generalissimo's Son,* 85.

220. Taylor, *Generalissimo's Son,* 85.

221. Taylor, *Generalissimo's Son,* 97.

222. Lee Wei-song, "Jiang Jingguo yu Jiuguotuan zhi yanjiu" [The study of Chiang Ching-kuo and the China Youth Corps (1969–1988)] (Master's thesis, National Central University, 2005), 35, fn. 76.

223. Taylor, *Generalissimo's Son,* 97.

224. Lee, "Study of Chiang Ching-kuo," 35, fn. 76.

225. Lee, "Study of Chiang Ching-kuo," 35, fn. 76.

226. Hsu, "Historical Setting," 7; Lee, "Study of Chiang Ching-kuo," 35.

227. Lee, "Study of Chiang Ching-kuo," 35.

228. Lee, "Study of Chiang Ching-kuo," 35.

229. Hsu, "Historical Setting," 7–8.

230. Hsu, "Historical Setting," 7–8.

231. Taylor, *Generalissimo's Son,* 25.

232. Taylor, *Generalissimo's Son,* 26.

233. Hsu, "Historical Setting," 8.

234. Hsu, "Historical Setting," 8.

235. Hsu, "Historical Setting," 8.

236. Hsu, "Historical Setting," 8; Shi Ming, *Four Hundred Years History of Taiwanese* (Taipei, 1980), 527, cited in Lee, "Study of Chiang Ching-kuo," 36.

237. Wu Nai-teh, "The Politics of a Regime Patronage System: Mobilization and Control within an Authoritarian Regime" (PhD diss., University of Chicago, 1987), 158.

238. Lee, "Study of Chiang Ching-kuo," 64–69; Lee Huan and Lin Yin-ting, *Zhuisui ban shiji: Lee Huan yu Chiang Ching-kuo xiansheng* [Lee Huan: Half a century of following Chiang Ching-kuo] (Taipei: Commonwealth Press, 1997).

239. Lee, "Study of Chiang Ching-kuo," 69–77.

240. Hsu, "Historical Setting," 9.

241. Hsu, "Historical Setting," 8–9; Taylor, *Generalissimo's Son,* 137.

242. Taylor, *Generalissimo's Son,* 138–140.

243. Taylor, *Generalissimo's Son,* 140.

180   Notes to Pages 73–76

Chapter 3. The China Youth Corps in Taiwan, 1952–1960

1. Bullard, *Soldier and the Citizen,* 135.

2. Bullard, *Soldier and the Citizen,* 134.

3. James Pinckney Harrison, *The Long March to Power: A History of the Chinese Communist Party, 1921–1972* (New York: Praeger, 1972), 454.

4. Harrison, *Long March to Power,* 454.

5. Bullard, *Soldier and the Citizen,* 135; Allen Chun, "From Nationalism to Nationalizing: Cultural Imagination and State Formation in Postwar Taiwan," in *Chinese Nationalism,* ed. Jonathan Unger (Armonk, NY: M. E. Sharpe, 1996), 142; Jong Huh Huang, "A Configurational Study of the Nonprofit Learning Organization: A Case Study of China Youth Corps in Taiwan" (DPA diss., University of Southern California, 1994), 99. The CYC removed the term "anti-communist" from its Chinese-language name on October 25, 2000.

6. Henry R. Lieberman, "New Youth Legion Formed by Chiang," *New York Times,* November 9, 1952, 6.

7. Li Tai-han, "Cong qingnian lianhui dao Jiuguotuan chengli de guocheng: yijiuwushi niandai chuqi—Guomindang duiyu qingnian yundong de chouhua yu zhangkong" [The process from the Youth League to the establishment of the China Youth Corps: The Guomindang's plan and control of youth movements in the early 1950s], *Taiwan wenxian* 56, no. 3 (2005); Wu, "Politics of a Regime"; Wu's brother, Wu Nai-ren, was the former secretary-general of the Democratic Progressive Party, the main opposition party to the GMD. Wu Nai-ren had close ties to ex-Taiwan president Chen Shui-bian, former Democratic Progressive Party chairman, and therefore Wu Nai-teh remains understandably skeptical about Guomindang claims of success and spontaneous support.

8. Jiuguotuan zongbu [China Youth Corps Headquarters], *Lüqi piaoyang sanshinian* [Green flag waves for thirty years] (Taipei: China Youth Corps Headquarters, 1982) [Coauthors not credited are Hsueh P'ing-kuo and Chao Ch'ing-ho], 48.

9. Li Tai-han, "Cong qingnian lianhui," 132.

10. Li Tai-han, "Cong qingnian lianhui," 130.

11. Li Tai-han, "Cong qingnian lianhui," 133.

12. In 1949, Chiang Kai-shek imposed martial law, banning the formation of any new political parties. It gave the military censorship and was used by military courts to convict thousands of civilians of sedition and other crimes. Under Chiang Ching-kuo, the GMD government ended martial law in 1987.

13. In the 1950s, all secondary schools and some colleges fell under the aegis of the Jiaoyuting.

14. Li Tai-han, "Cong qingnian lianhui," 134.

15. "How to Serve in the Military," *Central Daily News* [*Zhongyang ribao*], May 10, 1952, 4, cited in Li Tai-han, "Cong qingnian lianhui," 135.

16. "Summer Military Service of Youth," *Central Daily News* [*Zhongyang ribao*], June 9, 1952, 5, cited in Li Tai-han, "Cong qingnian lianhui," 135.

17. "Military Service in Nantou" newsletter [Junzhong fuwu zai Nantou], September 16, 1952, cited in Li Tai-han, "Cong qingnian lianhui," 135.

18. Li Tai-han, "Cong qingnian lianhui," 133.

19. Wu, "Politics of a Regime," 128.

20. Karl Gerth, *China Made: Consumer Culture and the Creation of the Nation* (Cambridge, MA: Harvard University Press, 2003), 160–161.

Notes to Pages 76–79   181

21. Gerth, *China Made,* 178.

22. Wu, "Politics of a Regime," 158.

23. "Foreign News: Father Flayed," *Time,* April 25, 1927, 44. Debate still continues as to whether Chiang Ching-kuo had been forced to write the editorial criticizing his father's actions. Joseph Stalin held Ching-kuo as a "hostage" in the Soviet Union and used him as leverage in Sino-Soviet relations.

24. Wu, "Politics of a Regime," 158.

25. Hsu, "Historical Setting," 8.

26. Wu, "Politics of a Regime," 126–127.

27. Bullard, *Soldier and the Citizen,* 135.

28. Taylor, *Generalissimo's Son,* 195. It is noteworthy that Chiang Kai-shek also appointed Ching-kuo as director of the secret police (1950–1965). Throughout the years that martial law was enforced on Taiwan (1949–1987), political opponents of the GMD were routinely harassed, imprisoned, and even put to death. In 1949, Ching-kuo established a Political Action Committee in Kaohsiung, Taiwan, to coordinate the intelligence and secret police operations on the island. Some scholars estimate that the secret police arrested ten thousand Taiwanese for interrogation that year, while military courts sentenced many to long detentions, and execution squads put more than a thousand to death. In the first half of 1950, Ching-kuo took a more active leadership role in internal security. He and his father now focused every possible resource on preparing for the Chinese Communists' mass invasion of the island expected in early summer. Thus, the secret police began to focus almost entirely on uncovering CCP agents who had come over during the chaotic influx in 1949. In fact, Central Intelligence Agency reports indicate that Mao Zedong's intelligence units were concentrated heavily on infiltrating the GMD military. Those who were arrested by the GMD secret police were either executed or imprisoned at a re-education school, the New Life Institute (Xinsheng jiaosuo), located on Green Island off the east coast of Taiwan. The re-education school was reminiscent of the New Man rehabilitation school that Ching-kuo established in southern Jiangxi (Gannan) on the mainland. He frequently visited the New Life Institute to check on living conditions and treatment of the "students." Even to this day, his activities as director of the Political Action Committee and secret police have widely been criticized for violating human rights in Taiwan. Taylor, *Generalissimo's Son,* 191–192.

29. The CYC remained under the control of the Ministry of National Defense until 1960 when it was transferred to the Ministry of Education. In 1989 the corps registered with the Ministry of the Interior as an independent nonprofit civic group.

30. Wu, "Politics of a Regime," 127.

31. Li Tai-han, "Cong qingnian lianhui," 134.

32. Wu, "Politics of a Regime," 127.

33. "Our Corps' Major Events in Ten Years," in *The Ten-Year Existence of the China Youth Corps* (Taipei: China Youth Corps Headquarters, 1963), n.p.

34. Wu, "Politics of a Regime," 128.

35. Wu, "Politics of a Regime," 128–129.

36. Shao-chuan Leng, *Chiang Ching-kuo's Leadership in the Development of the Republic of China on Taiwan* (Lanham, MD: University Press of America, 1993), 8.

37. China Youth Corps, *A Brief Introduction of the China Youth Service Association* (Taipei: China Youth Corps Headquarters, n.d.), 6.

38. "Important Historical Pictures," in Jiuguotuan zongbu, *Lüqi piaoyang sanshinian,* n.p.

182 Notes to Pages 79–87

39. Bullard, *Soldier and the Citizen*, 139.

40. "Important Historical Pictures," in Jiuguotuan zongbu, *Lüqi piaoyang sanshinian*, n.p.

41. "The Manuscript of President Chiang's Message Concerning the Establishment of CYC," in *Ten-Year Existence*.

42. "Manuscript of President Chiang's Message," in *Ten-Year Existence*.

43. Brindley, *China Youth Corps*, 33.

44. *Ten-Year Existence*.

45. Tzen Shian-yung, *China Youth Warriors March* (Taipei: Youth Publishers, 1953).

46. "Important Historical Pictures," in Jiuguotuan zongbu, *Lüqi piaoyang sanshinian*, n.p.

47. Brindley, *China Youth Corps*, 22.

48. Lieberman, "New Youth," 6.

49. Brindley, *China Youth Corps*, 33.

50. Reprinted in Brindley, *China Youth Corps*, 32.

51. Jiuguotuan zongbu, *Lüqi piaoyang sanshinian*, 4.

52. Lieberman, "New Youth."

53. Lieberman, "New Youth."

54. Bullard, *Soldier and the Citizen*, 138.

55. Bullard, *Soldier and the Citizen*, 140.

56. Bullard, *Soldier and the Citizen*, 100.

57. Bullard, *Soldier and the Citizen*, 135.

58. Bullard, *Soldier and the Citizen*, 138.

59. Bullard, *Soldier and the Citizen*, 138.

60. Jiaoyubu junxunchu, *Xuesheng junxun wushinian*, 338, 356.

61. Wu, "Politics of a Regime," 129.

62. Lee Wei-song, "Study of Chiang Ching-kuo," 42. The reason for Wu Guozhen's opposition towards the CYC will be discussed later.

63. Jiuguotuan zongbu, *Lüqi piaoyang sanshinian*, 67, cited in Wu, "Politics of a Regime," 129.

64. Wu, "Politics of a Regime," 129–130.

65. Wu, "Politics of a Regime," 129–130.

66. Jiuguotuan zongbu, *Lüqi piaoyang sanshinian*, 105–106, cited in Wu, "Politics of a Regime," 130.

67. Brindley, *China Youth Corps*, 62.

68. Fu Zheng, "Qingnian fangong Jiuguotuan wenti" [The Youth Anti-Communist National Salvation Corps problem], *Ziyou Zhongguo* [Free China] 18, no. 1 (January 1, 1958): 6.

69. Bullard, *Soldier and the Citizen*, 140.

70. Lee Wei-song, "Study of Chiang Ching-kuo," 35–38.

71. Boorman, *Biographical Dictionary*, vol. 1, 160.

72. Lee Wei-song, "Study of Chiang Ching-kuo," 54.

73. Bullard, *Soldier and the Citizen*, 138.

74. "Li Accuses Chiang," *China World*, March 2, 1950, George Kerr Papers, file 7.20, Clippings Formosa—Chiang Kai-shek: activities, policies, history, rivals; Mme. Chiang 1950, Hoover Institution Archives.

75. John T. Woolley and Gerhard Peters "Statement by the President on the Situation in Korea, June 27, 1950," American Presidency Project, Santa Barbara, CA, accessed November 17, 2009, http://www.presidency.ucsb.edu/ws/?pid=13538 (information cited discontinued).

Notes to Pages 87–92   183

76. Bullard, *Soldier and the Citizen,* 5.

77. Jinmen, which is also known as Quemoy, is located off the port of Xiamen (Amoy), and Mazu (Matsu) is off the port of Fuzhou, also in Fujian province.

78. Brindley, *China Youth Corps,* 40–41.

79. Mao Cheng-how, in discussion with the author, July 21, 2009, and November 27, 2009, Princeton, NJ.

80. Brindley, *China Youth Corps,* 41.

81. Jiuguotuan zongbu, *Lüqi piaoyang sanshinian,* 287.

82. Wu, "Politics of a Regime," 136.

83. Bullard, *Soldier and the Citizen,* 141.

84. Bullard, *Soldier and the Citizen,* 141.

85. *Zenyang zhankai nongcun fuwu gongzuo* [How to develop rural service work] (Taiwan: Young Lion, 1954); Bullard, *Soldier and the Citizen,* 141.

86. Bullard, *Soldier and the Citizen,* 141–142.

87. *Zenyang zhankai nongcun fuwu gongzuo,* 16–17.

88. *Zenyang zhankai nongcun fuwu gongzuo,* 64.

89. *Zenyang zhankai nongcun fuwu gongzuo,* 64. The English translation is from the following passage in Taiwanese: "Jiang zhongtong youxi, chang jing jie de, gingna bua de qit tao, mo lun xi, bi yi ka buahan, yaxi ka xiehan, yi long mei ze gingna tao."

90. *Zenyang zhankai nongcun fuwu gongzuo,* 65. Zhang Zhidong was a late Qing statesman who wrote *Exhortation to Study* in 1898.

91. *Zenyang zhankai nongcun fuwu gongzuo,* 65.

92. Bullard, *Soldier and the Citizen,* 142.

93. Jiuguotuan zongbu, *Lüqi piaoyang sanshinian,* 289.

94. *Manual of Educational Statistics, the Republic of China—1961* (Taipei: National Educational Materials Center, 1961), 166, cited in Bullard, *Soldier and the Citizen,* 198.

95. Jiuguotuan zongbu, *Lüqi piaoyang sanshinian,* 69, cited in Wu, "Politics of a Regime," 134.

96. Huang, *Politics of Depoliticization,* 130–131.

97. Wu, "Politics of a Regime," 134.

98. *Manual of Educational Statistics,* 166, cited in Bullard, *Soldier and the Citizen,* 198.

99. Bullard, *Soldier and the Citizen,* 142.

100. C. P. Fitzgerald, "Review: Soviet Russia in China," *Pacific Affairs* 31 no. 1 (March 1958): 88.

101. Tzen, *China Youth Warriors March,* 1–2; Chiang Kai-shek, *Soviet Russia in China* (New York: Farrar, Straus, and Cudahy, 1957).

102. Tzen, *China Youth Warriors March,* 4, 9–10.

103. Tzen, *China Youth Warriors March,* 10.

104. Tzen, *China Youth Warriors March,* 4–15.

105. Tzen, *China Youth Warriors March,* 5.

106. Tzen, *China Youth Warriors March,* 5.

107. Tzen, *China Youth Warriors March,* 2.

108. Mao, discussion, November 27, 2009.

109. Mao, discussion, November 27, 2009.

110. Mao, discussion, November 27, 2009.

184   Notes to Pages 92–98

111. Mao, discussion, July 21, 2009.

112. Chiang Kai-shek, *Resistance and Reconstruction: Messages during China's Six Years of War, 1937–1943* (Freeport, NY: Harper & Row, 1970), 155.

113. Mao, discussion, July 21, 2009.

114. Mao, discussion, July 21, 2009, and November 27, 2009.

115. Brindley, *China Youth Corps,* 41.

116. Wu, "Politics of a Regime," 139; "Our Corps' Major Events in the Past Ten Years," *Ten-Year Existence,* n.p.

117. Wu, "Politics of a Regime," 139.

118. Wu, "Politics of a Regime," 139.

119. *Ten-Year Existence.*

120. Brindley, *China Youth Corps,* 41.

121. Brindley, *China Youth Corps,* 41.

122. Brindley, *China Youth Corps,* 42.

123. Bullard, *Soldier and the Citizen,* 126.

124. Wu Manjun, *Ziyou Zhongguo shijian kenan yundong* [Free China's practice of the Overcoming Difficulty Movement] (Taipei: Gaizao chubanshe, 1953), 3.

125. Wu, *Ziyou Zhongguo shijian kenan yundong,* 3

126. Wu, *Ziyou Zhongguo shijian kenan yundong,* 7.

127. Wu, *Ziyou Zhongguo shijian kenan yundong,* 7.

128. Wu, *Ziyou Zhongguo shijian kenan yundong,* 8.

129. Bullard, *Soldier and the Citizen,* 126.

130. Brindley, *China Youth Corps,* 42.

131. Chiang Ching-kuo, *Chiang Ching-kuo xiansheng quanji* [The complete works of Mr. Chiang Ching-Kuo], vol. 4 (Taipei: News Bureau of the Executive Yuan, 1991), 357.

132. Brindley, *China Youth Corps,* 5.

133. Brindley, *China Youth Corps,* 34, 74.

134. Lee Wei-song, "Study of Chiang Ching-kuo," 61.

135. Wu, "Politics of a Regime," 137.

136. "China Youth Anticommunist National Salvation Corps Laws and Regulations" (Republic of China, 1952), reprinted in Bullard, *The Soldier and the Citizen,* 195; Lieberman, "New Youth," 6.

137. *Demographic Yearbook, 1953* (New York: United Nations, 1953), 120.

138. Brindley, *China Youth Corps,* 46.

139. Mao, discussion, November 27, 2009; Li Tai-han, "Cong qingnian lianhui," 111.

140. Mao, discussion, July 21, 2009; Li Tai-han, "Cong qingnian lianhui," 111.

141. Mao, discussion, November 27, 2009.

142. Mao, discussion, November 27, 2009.

143. Brindley, *China Youth Corps,* 46.

144. Yu Jian-ye, in discussion with the author, July 25, 2008, Taipei, Taiwan.

145. Brindley, *China Youth Corps,* 46.

146. "Statistics on Summer Camp Programs," *Ten-Year Existence,* n.p.

147. Yu, discussion.

148. George H. Bowie, "The China Youth Corps: A Contributor to the Development of the Republic of China" (MA thesis, Brigham Young University, 1990), 11; Bullard, *Soldier and the Citizen,* 141–142.

Notes to Pages 98–105   185

149. Tzen, *China Youth Warriors March,* 4.

150. Tzen, *China Youth Warriors March,* 4.

151. Interviewees who reminisced about school and the CYC in the 1950s also recounted this situation. Wu Cai-e, in discussion with the author, August 24, 2008, Taipei, Taiwan.

152. Mao, discussion, November 27, 2009.

153. Henry R. Lieberman, "Overseas Chinese Back Chiang Policy," *New York Times,* October 31, 1952, 2.

154. Lieberman, "New Youth," 6.

155. "Chinese Visit City Hall," *New York Times,* September 24, 1957, 24. The MRA had a training center on Mackinac Island from 1942 to 1971.

156. "History of the MRA and Mission Point Resort," accessed December 19, 2009, http://www.mackinacfilms.com/mra.html (site discontinued). In 2001, the MRA was renamed Initiatives of Change.

157. "Location of Student Dormitories and Youth Hostels," *Ten-Year Existence,* n.p.

158. "Location of Student Dormitories," *Ten-Year Existence,* n.p.

159. "General Statistics of Various College Student Center and Youth Recreational Centers of Different Cities," *Ten-Year Existence,* n.p.

160. Brindley, *China Youth Corps,* 47.

161. Yang Zhen, in discussion with the author, August 28, 2008, Xindian, Taiwan.

162. Brindley, *China Youth Corps,* 45–46.

163. Brindley, *China Youth Corps,* 49.

164. Bullard, *Soldier and the Citizen,* 138.

165. Lee and Lin, *Zhuisui ban shiji,* 62, 115.

166. Jiuguotuan zongbu, *Lüqi piaoyang sanshinian,* 338.

167. "Our Corps' Major Events in Ten Years," *Ten-Year Existence,* n.p.; Brindley, *China Youth Corps,* 113.

168. Brindley, *China Youth Corps,* 114.

169. *Happy New Year, Merry Christmas* (Taipei: Young Lion, ca. 1950s).

170. Jiuguotuan zongbu, *Lüqi piaoyang sanshinian,* 62.

171. Lee Wei-song, "Study of Chiang Ching-kuo," 42.

172. K. C. Wu, "Your Money Has Built a Police State in Formosa," *Look* (June 29, 1954): 40.

173. "Militant Nationalist," *New York Times,* September 12, 1963.

174. Ma Zhisu, *Lei Zhen and Chiang Kai-shek* (Taipei: Zili wanbao she wenhua chuban bu, 1993), 113; Lei Zhen, *Wo de muqin: huiyilu* [My mother: Memoir] (Taipei: Guiguan tushu gufen youxian gongsi: Faxing jiu bo tushu gufen youxian gongsi, 1989), 81–82.

175. Marina Svensson, *Debating Human Rights in China: A Conceptual and Political History* (Lanham, MD: Rowman & Littlefield, 2002), 214.

176. Fu, "Qingnian fangong Jiuguotuan wenti," 5.

177. Jiaoyubu [Ministry of Education], *Zhonghua minguo zuijin liu nian lai jiaoyu tongji* [Republic of China's education statistics for the previous six years] (Taipei: Jiaoyubu, 1960), 13.

178. *Demographic Yearbook, 1957* (New York: United Nations, 1957), 141.

179. Fu, "Qingnian fangong Jiuguotuan wenti," 5.

180. Fu, "Qingnian fangong Jiuguotuan wenti," 5.

181. Fu, "Qingnian fangong Jiuguotuan wenti," 6.

182. Fu, "Qingnian fangong Jiuguotuan wenti," 6.

183. Fu, "Qingnian fangong Jiuguotuan wenti," 6.

186   Notes to Pages 105–110

184. Fu Zheng, "Zailun Qingnian fangong Jiuguotuan chexiao wenti," *Ziyou zhongguo* [Free China] 18, no. 11 (June 1, 1958): 3–6.

185. Chen San-jing, "Jiang Jingguo xiansheng yu Zhongguo qingnian fangong jiuguotua" [Mr. Chiang Ching-kuo and the China Youth Anti-Communist Save (Our) Country Corps], *Jindai Zhongguo* [Contemporary China]: 64; Svensson, *Debating Human Rights,* 214.

186. "Our Corps' Major Events in Ten Years," *Ten-Year Existence.*

187. Brindley, *China Youth Corps,* 64.

188. Yu Jian-ye, in discussion with the author, July 25, 2008, Taipei, Taiwan.

189. Yu, discussion.

Chapter 4. Military Training and Instructors, 1953–1960

1. Wen-hsin Yeh, *Provincial Passages: Culture, Space, and the Origins of Chinese Communism* (Berkeley: University of California Press, 1996).

2. Culp, *Articulating Citizenship,* 198.

3. Chun-peng Pao, Quanguo jiaoyuhui lianhehui xinxuezhi kecheng biaozhun qicao weiyuanhui [National Education Association, New school curriculum standard drafting committee], "Gaoji zhongxue kecheng zonggang" [Senior high school curriculum general outline], in *Xinxuezhi kecheng biaozhun gangyao* [Outline of the curriculum standards for the New School System], 4–7, cited in Culp, *Articulating Citizenship,* 198; Zhu Youhuan et al., eds., *Zhongguo jindai xuezhi shiliao* [Historical materials for the modern Chinese school system], part 3, I (Shanghai: East China Normal University Press, 1983–1992), 400, cited in Culp, *Articulating Citizenship,* 198.

4. Culp, *Articulating Citizenship,* 199.

5. Zhongguo di'er lishi dang'anguan [Second historical archives of China], *Zhonghua minguoshi dang'an ziliao huibian* [Compilation of archival materials for Chinese Republican history], series 5, part I, Jiaoyu, vol. 2 (Nanjing: Jiangsu guji chubanshe, 1994), 1239–1240, cited in Culp, *Articulating Citizenship,* 199. The University Council system was an attempt by Cai Yuanpei and other liberal educators within the Nationalist Party to set up an autonomous system for academic and educational administration under the aegis of the GMD government. The University Council soon succumbed to intraparty factionalism and was replaced in August 1928 by the Ministry of Education, which directed national educational policy for the rest of the Nanjing decade (1927–1937). Culp, *Articulating Citizenship,* 21, n. 8.

6. Israel, *Student Nationalism,* 22.

7. Jiaoyubu junxunchu [Ministry of Education, Military Training Department], *Xuesheng junxun wushi nian* [Fifty years of student military training] (Taipei: Youshi wenhua shiye gongsi, 1978), 39.

8. Zhongguo di'er lishi dang'anguan, *Zhonghua minguoshi,* vol. 2, 1239, cited in Culp, *Articulating Citizenship,* 199; Israel, *Student Nationalism,* 22.

9. Wasserstrom, *Student Protests,* 173.

10. Yeh, *Alienated Academy,* 224–225.

11. Yeh, *Alienated Academy,* 225.

12. Wang Min et al., eds., *Shanghai xuesheng yundong dashiji* [Major events in the Shanghai student movement] (Shanghai: Xuelin, 1981), 134, cited in Wasserstrom, *Student Protests,* 173.

13. Some scholars and many Taiwanese argue that the Qing empire colonized the island from 1683 to 1895, therefore they also regard the post-1945 era under the Nationalists as a colonial regime, especially from 1949 to 1987 during the martial-law period. See Andrew Morris, *Co-*

Notes to Pages 111–115   187

lonial Project, National Game: A History of Baseball in Taiwan (Berkeley: University of California Press, 2011).

14. Zongtongfu dang'an [Presidential Palace Archives], "Chengfu qie shi yanjiu Bai zong jiaoguan Hongliang yu Yi jiaoguan Zuoren, guanyu dongyuan yanxi hou zhi tanhua yao dian, bing ni ding shishi banfa you" [Submit in return thorough study of General Military Instructor Bai Hongliang and Military Instructor Yi Zuoren, regarding the key points of discussion after the mobilization drill, and draft the implementation plan], Buchong bing chu xun jihua [Reserve training plan], 10 March 1952, cited in Li Tai-han, "Dangtuan, junshi, yu jiaoyu," 49.

15. Bullard, *Soldier and the Citizen,* 166.

16. Li Tai-han, "Dang'an yunyong yu lishi yanjiu," 4–5.

17. Zongtongfu dang'an, *Buchong bing chuxun jihua* [Reserve army training plan], 2130307/7, December 1950 to May 1953, cited in Li Tai-han, "Dang'an yunyong yu lishi yanjiu," 5.

18. Guojun dang'an [National Military Archives], "Jianli houbei bing yuan an" [Establish the reserves], Zongzhang bangongshi [Director's office], 1622/1540, February–July 1952, cited in Li Tai-han, "Dang'an yunyong yu lishi yanjiu," 5.

19. Zongtongfu dang'an, *Buchong bing chuxun jihua,* cited in Li Tai-han, "Dang'an yunyong yu lishi yanjiu," 5.

20. Guojun dang'an [National Military Archives], "Putong xuexiao junxun shi shi an" [Regular school military implementation plan], 0600 8060.2, December 1951 to August 1955, cited in Li Tai-han, "Dang'an yunyong yu lishi yanjiu," 7.

21. Xu Liang, "Tan xuexiao shishi junshi xunlian" [Discussing the implementation of military training practice in schools], *Taiwan jiaoyu fudao yuekan* 2, no. 3 (March 1952): 6–7, cited in Li Tai-han, "Dangtuan, junshi, yu jiaoyu," 22.

22. Bullard, *Soldier and the Citizen,* 100.

23. Guofangbu zhengzhibu [General Political Warfare Department], *Guojun zhengzhan shigao* [Draft history of political warfare in the Chinese Armed Forces] (Taipei: Guofangbu Zhengzhibu, 1965), 183–189, cited in Bullard, *Soldier and the Citizen,* 100–101.

24. Zongtongfu dang'an [Presidential Palace Archives], "Taiwan sheng gaoji zhongdeng xuexiao xuesheng junxun shishi gaikuang baogao shu" [Taiwan province upper middle schools' student military training implementation general situation report book], *Gaozhong xuesheng junxun banfa* [Upper middle school students military training way], September 13, 1953, cited in Li Tai-han, "Dangtuan, junshi, yu jiaoyu," 133.

25. Chen San-jing, Chu Hong-yuan, and Wu Mei-hui (fangwen), Wu Mei-hui (jilu), *Nü qingnian dadui fangwen ji* [The reminiscences of the Women's Corps] (Taipei: Zhongyang yanjiu yuan jindai shi yanjiu suo, 1995); Bullard, *Soldier and the Citizen,* 147.

26. Bullard, *Soldier and the Citizen,* 147.

27. Chen et al., *Nü qingnian dadui fangwen ji,* 413.

28. Chen et al., *Nü qingnian dadui fangwen ji,* 28–29.

29. Cong, *Teachers' Schools,* 131, 134, 141, 154.

30. Jiaoyubu, "Jiaoguan de xinshui yu junjie yaoqiu" [Military instructors' salaries and rank eligibility requirements], Jiaoyuting, file 30895, November 2, 1951. The Jiaoyuting (Taiwan Province's Department of Education) director, Chen Xueping, sent this order to all provincial normal upper middle schools.

31. Jiaoyubu junxunchu, *Xuesheng junxun wushi nian,* 157.

32. Bullard, *Soldier and the Citizen,* 146–147.

33. Li Tai-han, "Dangtuan, junshi, yu jiaoyu," 139–140.

188   Notes to Pages 115–120

34. Li Tai-han, "Dangtuan, junshi, yu jiaoyu," 135.

35. Jiaoyubu junxunchu, *Xuesheng junxun wushi nian*, 309–312.

36. Jiaoyubu junxunchu, *Xuesheng junxun wushi nian*, 309–312.

37. Chen et al., *Nü qingnian dadui fangwen ji*, 2.

38. Chen et al., *Nü qingnian dadui fangwen ji*, 1.

39. Chen et al., *Nü qingnian dadui fangwen ji*, 3.

40. Chen et al., *Nü qingnian dadui fangwen ji*, 222, 224.

41. Chen et al., *Nü qingnian dadui fangwen ji*, 227.

42. Chen et al., *Nü qingnian dadui fangwen ji*, 227.

43. Chen et al., *Nü qingnian dadui fangwen ji*, 228.

44. Jiaoyuting [Taiwan's Provincial Government, Department of Education], file 3806, August 22, 1951. The document was sent by the Jiaoyuting to Provincial Governor Wu Guozhen. Copies were also sent to the Ministry of Education and the Ministry of National Defense.

45. Li Tai-han, "Dangtuan, junshi, yu jiaoyu," 123.

46. Chiang Ching-kuo, "Jianli junxun de xin guannian" [Establishing the new idea of military training], in *Chiang Ching-kuo xiansheng quanji*, vol. 4, 277, 279.

47. Chiang, "Jianli junxun de xin guannian," 279–280.

48. Li Tai-han, "Dangtuan, junshi, yu jiaoyu," 123–124.

49. Jiuguotuan zongbu [China Youth Corps Headquarters], *Gaozhong junxun keben* [Upper middle school military training textbook], vol. 1, 1957.

50. Li Tai-han, "Dangtuan, junshi, yu jiaoyu," 124.

51. Li Tai-han, "Dangtuan, junshi, yu jiaoyu," 126–130.

52. Guoshiguan [Academia Historica], "Zhongguo guomin shi shi jiyao, 1952" [Republic of China historical records summary, 1952] (Taipei: Guoshiguan, 1952), 651–652.

53. "Duiyu Jiuguotuan da ke wen, ke canjian Zhongguo qingnian fangong jiuguo da ke wen" [Questions and answers for the China Youth Corps], *Zhongyang ribao* [Central Daily News] 6, no. 3, February 14, 1953.

54. "Duiyu Jiuguotuan da ke wen."

55. Xiao Xiqing, "Junxun gongzuo jingyan tan" [Discussion of military training job experience], *Tuanwu gongzuo shilu* [Corps' work record] (Taipei: China Youth Corps Headquarters, 1982), 37–39, cited in Li Tai-han, "Dangtuan, junshi, yu jiaoyu," 144.

56. Zongtongfu dang'an, "Taiwan sheng gaoji zhongdeng," cited in Li Tai-han, "Dangtuan, junshi, yu jiaoyu," 144.

57. In 1978, the CYC's publishing company, Young Lion Cultural Enterprise, distributed five thousand copies of *Fifty Years of Student Military Training* (*Xuesheng junxun wushi nian*) to members of the Military Training Department and every military instructor in Taiwan.

58. Liu Yifu, *Zhandou qingnian de zhandou shenghuo* [Combat youth's combat life] (Taipei: n.p., n.d.), 36, cited in Li Tai-han, "Dangtuan, junshi, yu jiaoyu," 147.

59. Liu Yifu, "Fuxing de qiji, shengli de baozheng" [Revival's opportunity, victory's guarantee], in *Zhongguo qingnian de junxun shenghuo* [Chinese youth's military training life] (Taipei: Youshi wenhua shiye gongsi, 1955), 66.

60. Liu Yifu, "Fuxing de qiji," 58.

61. Liu Yifu, *Zhandou qingnian*, 42, cited in Li Tai-han, "Dangtuan, junshi, yu jiaoyu," 148.

62. Liu Yifu, "Fuxing de qiji."

63. Chiang Ching-kuo, "Jiaqiang sixiang lingdao zuo hao junxun gongzuo: minguo sishiwu nian shier yue si ri dui xuexiao junxun ganbu di ba qi xueyuan jiang" [Reinforce thought lead-

Notes to Pages 121–126   189

ership to do well military training work: Speech for schools' military training cadre of the eighth college class], in *Chiang Ching-kuo xiansheng quanji*, vol. 5, 352.

64. Mao, discussion, November 27, 2009.

65. Mao, discussion, July 21, 2009, and November 27, 2009.

66. Xu Fuguan, "Qingnian fangong Jiuguotuan de jianquan fazhan de shangque" [The discussion of the China Youth Anti-Communist National Salvation Corps' perfect development], *Ziyou zhongguo* [Free China] 7, no. 8 (October 16, 1952): 10.

67. Yuan Shi, "Daxue jiaoyu de beiai" [The tragedy of college education], *Ziyou zhongguo* [Free China] 16, no. 5 (February 1, 1957): 10.

68. Ramon H. Myers, "A New Chinese Civilization: The Evolution of the Republic of China on Taiwan," *China Quarterly*, no. 148 (December 1996): 1075.

69. Fu Zheng, "Qingnian fangong Jiuguotuan wenti," [China Youth Anti-Communist National Salvation Corps problem], *Ziyou zhongguo* [Free China] 18, no. 1 (January 1, 1958): 6.

70. Chiang Ching-kuo, *Chiang Ching-kuo xiansheng quanji*, vol. 6, 26–27.

71. Ching-kuo, "Jiaqiang sixiang lingdao zuo," in *Chiang Ching-kuo xiansheng quanji*, vol. 5, 348.

72. Fu Zheng, "Zai lun qingnian fangong Jiuguotuan chexiao wenti" [Another discussion of the problem of dismantling of China Youth Anti-Communist National Salvation Corps], *Ziyou zhongguo* [Free China] 18, no. 11 (June 1, 1958): 5.

73. Fu, "Zai lun qingnian fangong," 5.

74. Lu Di, "Jiuguotuan hai guo, hai qingnian" [China Youth Corps harms the country, harms the youth], *Ziyou zhongguo* 18, no. 12 (June 16, 1958): 30.

75. Bullard, *Soldier and the Citizen*, 151.

76. Greg MacGregor, "Taipei Riot Begun by Widow's Plea," *New York Times*, May 27, 1957.

77. "Taiwan Blow-Up," *New York Times*, May 26, 1957; "Memorandum from the Director of the Office of Chinese Affairs (McConaughy) to the Assistant Secretary of State for Far Eastern Affairs (Robertson), May 24, 1957," *Foreign Relations of the United States 1955–1957* (Washington, DC: Government Printing Office, 1955–1957), 524 (henceforth, *FRUS*).

78. MacGregor, "Taipei Riot."

79. MacGregor, "Taipei Riot"; Karl Lott Rankin, *China Assignment* (Seattle: University of Washington Press, 1964), 302.

80. MacGregor, "Taipei Riot."

81. "Taiwan Blow-Up," E1; "Anti-U.S. Riots in Taipei Curbed by Chiang Troops," *New York Times*, May 25, 1957.

82. Stephen G. Craft, *American Justice in Taiwan: The 1957 Riots and Cold War Foreign Policy* (Lexington: University Press of Kentucky, 2016), 14.

83. MacGregor, "Taipei Riot," 4; "Taiwan Blow-Up."

84. "Anti-U.S. Riots."

85. Taylor, *Generalissimo's Son*, 237–238.

86. Zheng Yiying, "Liu Ziran shijan" [The Liu Ziran Incident], *Zhongyang tongxun she* [Central News Agency], Guojia wenhua shuzi dangan, Taiwan xingzheng yuan wenhua jianshe weiyuanhui [National Culture Digital Archives, Taiwan Executive Yuan Council for Cultural Affairs], accessed February 12, 2010, http://km.cca.gov.tw/myphoto/h_main.asp?categoryid =35 (site discontinued).

87. Taylor, *Generalissimo*, 491.

88. Taylor, *Generalissimo's Son*, 237.

190 Notes to Pages 127–130

89. Lee and Lin, *Zhuisui ban shiji*, 79.

90. Lee and Lin, *Zhuisui ban shiji*, 80.

91. Taylor, *Generalissimo*, 491.

92. Ma Ying-jeou, interview by Jay Taylor, *Generalissimo's Son*, 238.

93. Robert Trumbull, "Riot Link Denied by Chiang Regime," *New York Times*, May 28, 1958.

94. "Taiwan Blow-Up."

95. "Memorandum," *FRUS*, vol. 3, 534.

96. Zheng Yiying, "Liu Ziran shijan."

97. Trumbull, "Riot Link Denied."

98. Zheng Yiying, "Liu Ziran shijan."

99. Rankin, *China Assignment*, 304.

100. "Letter from the Ambassador in the Republic of China (Rankin) to the President's Special Consultant (Nash), June 17, 1957," *FRUS*, vol. 3, 542–544.

101. Foreign Office Records, FO 371/127472/FCN10345/37, "Report by Mr. O. K. Yui, President of the Executive Yuan, on Actions Taken by the Government Regarding the Incident on May 24, 1957, in Taipei," PRO, Public Records Office, National Archives, Kew, UK (cited hereafter as "Report by Mr. O. K. Yui"), cited in Craft, *American Justice*, 132.

102. "Report by Mr. O. K. Yui," cited in Craft, *American Justice*, 132.

103. Summarized Report on Investigation by the Taipei Garrison Command of Persons Arrested on May 24, 1957, *524 shijian zhuanan jiantao* [Review of the May 24th Incident investigation], *danghao* 425.2/0014, Waijiao dang'an [Diplomatic Archives], Institute of Modern History, Academia Sinica, Nangang, Taiwan, cited in Craft, *American Justice*, 132.

104. "Report by Mr. O. K. Yui," cited in Craft, *American Justice*, 132.

105. Craft, *American Justice*, 132.

106. "Zi Lei Nuozi shenpan wuzui hou zhi May 24 shangban shishi zhi chuli qingxing" [Timeline of measures taken from the Reynolds acquittal until May 24th 10:00 a.m.], *524 shijian zhuanan jiantao* [Review of the May 24th Incident investigation], *danghao* 425.2/0013, Waijiao dang'an [Diplomatic Archives], Institute of Modern History, Academia Sinica, Nangang, Taiwan, cited in Craft, *American Justice*, 132.

107. "May 24 shangban shishi hou zai qingyun sheyun fangmian chuli qingxing" [Timeline of measures taken after 10:00 a.m. on May 24th to control youth and social groups], *524 shijian zhuanan jiantao* [Review of the May 24th Incident investigation], *danghao* 425.2/0013, Waijiao dang'an [Diplomatic Archives], Institute of Modern History, Academia Sinica, Nangang, Taiwan, cited in Craft, *American Justice*, 132.

108. "Report by Mr. O. K. Yui," cited in Craft, *American Justice*, 133.

109. "Report by Mr. O. K. Yui," cited in Craft, *American Justice*, 133.

110. "Memorandum from the President's Special Assistant (Richards) to the Secretary of State," October 9, 1957, *FRUS*, vol. 3, 626.

111. "Memorandum of Discussion, 325th National Security Council Meeting," May 27, 1957, *FRUS*, vol. 3, 541.

112. "Memorandum of Discussion," *FRUS*, vol. 3, 541.

113. Nancy Bernkopf Tucker, *Taiwan, Hong Kong, and the United States, 1945–1992: Uncertain Friendships* (New York: Twayne, 1994), 92.

114. Tucker, *Taiwan*, 92.

Notes to Pages 130–136   191

115. Robert Trumbull, "Chiang Expresses Regret Over Riot," *New York Times*, May 27, 1957, 4. The three officers were imprisoned on Green Island, where political dissidents were sent during the martial law period. Zheng Yiying, "Liu Ziran shijan."

116. Tucker, *Taiwan*, 92.

117. Taylor, *Generalissimo's Son*, 250.

118. Taylor, *Generalissimo's Son*, 259–260.

119. Jiaoyubu junxunchu, *Xuesheng junxun wushi nian*, 160.

Chapter 5. Civics Textbooks and Curricular Standards, 1937–1960

1. Zarrow, *Educating China*, 8–9.

2. Peter Zarrow, "The New Schools and National Identity: Chinese History Textbooks in the Late Qing," in Tze-ki Hon and Robert J. Culp, eds., *The Politics of Historical Production in Late Qing and Republican China* (Leiden: Brill, 2012), 23.

3. Zarrow, *Educating China*, 86.

4. Zarrow, *Educating China*, 77, fn. 2.

5. Zarrow, *Educating China*, 77, 80.

6. Zarrow, *Educating China*, 81–82.

7. Zarrow, *Educating China*, 82.

8. Zarrow, *Educating China*, 77.

9. Zarrow, *Educating China*, 82.

10. Zarrow, *Educating China*, 83.

11. Zarrow, *Educating China*, 84.

12. Zarrow, *Educating China*, 84–85.

13. Zarrow, *Educating China*, 86.

14. Zarrow, *Educating China*, 86–87.

15. Zarrow, *Educating China*, 113.

16. Culp, *Articulating Citizenship*, 42–43.

17. Zarrow, *Educating China*, 112.

18. Zarrow, *Educating China*, 123.

19. Robert Culp, "Setting the Sheet of Loose Sand: Conceptions of Society and Citizenship in Nanjing Decade Party Doctrine and Civics Textbooks," in *Defining Modernity: Guomindang Rhetorics of a New China, 1920–1970*, ed. Terry Bodenhorn (Ann Arbor: Center for Chinese Studies, University of Michigan, 2002).

20. Zarrow, *Educating China*, 88.

21. Zarrow, *Educating China*, 88–89.

22. Culp, *Power of Print*, 1–2.

23. Hu, "Politics and Higher Education," 62.

24. Hu, "Politics and Higher Education," 96.

25. Hu, "Politics and Higher Education," 96–97.

26. Hu, "Politics and Higher Education," 96–97. The GMD organized the Second Defense Advisory Meeting (Guofan canyi hui) to meet in the spring of 1938 to hear suggestions from the different strata of society in order to deal with the crisis after the outbreak of the Marco Polo Bridge Incident.

27. Chen Lifu, *Zhanshi jiaoyu xingzheng huiyi* [Recollections on wartime educational administration] (Taipei: Shangwu yingshuguan, 1973), 10.

192   Notes to Pages 136–143

28. Hu Kuo-tai, "Disputes on the Question of Wartime Education and the Formation of an Educational Policy for the Guomindang on the War," *Republican China* 14, no. 1 (November 1988): 48, from Jiang Jieshi (Chiang Kai-shek), *Xian zongtong Jianggong quanji* [The complete works of Jiang Jieshi], vol. 2 (Taipei: Zhongguo wenhua daxue, 1984), 1058.

29. Chan Wai-keung, "Contending Memories of the Nation: History Education in Wartime China, 1937–1945," in *The Politics of Historical Production in Late Qing and Republican China,* ed. Tze-ki Hon and Robert Culp (Leiden: Brill, 2012), 173.

30. Hu, "Politics and Higher Education," 48.

31. Chen, *Zhanshi jiaoyu xingzheng huiyi,* 9; Chan, "Contending Memories," 172.

32. Chen Lifu, *Chinese Education during the War, 1937–1942* (n.p.: Ministry of Education, 1942), 6.

33. Culp, "Setting the Sheet," 51.

34. Ou, "Education in Wartime China," 119.

35. Chen, *Zhanshi jiaoyu xingzheng huiyi,* 30.

36. Chan, "Contending Memories," 182.

37. Chen, *Zhanshi jiaoyu xingzheng huiyi,* 31.

38. Chen, *Zhanshi jiaoyu xingzheng huiyi,* 31.

39. Jenny Huangfu Day, "The War of Textbooks: Educating Children during the Second Sino-Japanese War, 1937–1945," *Twentieth-Century China* 46, no. 2 (May 2021): 108.

40. Day, "War of Textbooks," 117.

41. Schneider, *Keeping the Nation's House,* 130.

42. Schneider, *Keeping the Nation's House,* 130.

43. Schneider, *Keeping the Nation's House,* 130; Chan, "Contending Memories," 182.

44. Chan, "Contending Memories," 183.

45. Chan, "Contending Memories," 182.

46. Chan, "Contending Memories," 183–184.

47. Chan, "Contending Memories," 184.

48. Robert Culp, "Mass Production of Knowledge and the Industrialization of Mental Labor: The Rise of the Petty Intellectual," in *Knowledge Acts in Modern China: Ideas, Institutions, and Identities,* ed. Robert Culp, Eddy U, and Wen-hsin Yeh (Berkeley: Institute of East Asian Studies, University of California, Berkeley, 2016), 209–210.

49. Chen, *Zhanshi jiaoyu xingzheng huiyi,* 32.

50. Jiaoyubu [Ministry of Education], *Xiuding zhongxue gongmin guowen lishi dilike kecheng biaozhun* [Revised middle school civics, Chinese literature, history, and geography courses' curricular standards] (Taipei: Jiaoyubu, 1952), 1.

51. Culp, *Articulating Citizenship,* 160.

52. Culp, *Articulating Citizenship,* 160.

53. Zhou Gan et al., eds., *Gongmin keben* [Civics textbook], vol. 2 (Shanghai: Shangwu yinshuguan, 1937), 12.

54. Zhou Gan et al., *Gongmin keben,* vol. 2, 12.

55. Zhou Gan et al., *Gongmin keben,* vol. 2, 12.

56. Zhou Gan et al., *Gongmin keben,* vol. 2, 13–16.

57. Zarrow, *Educating China,* 121.

58. Zhou Gan et al., *Gongmin keben,* vol. 2, 37–38.

59. Zhou Gan et al., *Gongmin keben,* vol. 2, 42.

Notes to Pages 144–153   193

60. Guomin zhengfu, Jiaoyubu [National Government, Ministry of Education], "Jiaoyubu Sanmin zhuyi jiaoyu shishi yuanze" [How to put Three Principles of the People into practice], file 410-J-2941, vol. 1, sec. 5, Di'er lishi dang'anguan, Nanjing [SHAC].

61. Guomin zhengfu, Jiaoyubu, "Jiaoyubu Sanmin zhuyi jiaoyu shishi yuanze."

62. Guomin zhengfu, Jiaoyubu, "Jiaoyubu Sanmin zhuyi jiaoyu shishi yuanze."

63. Culp, *Articulating Citizenship*, 178–179.

64. Culp, *Articulating Citizenship*, 178.

65. Culp, *Articulating Citizenship*, 178.

66. Guomin zhengfu, Jiaoyubu, "Jiaoyubu Sanmin zhuyi jiaoyu shishi yuanze."

67. Guomin zhengfu, Jiaoyubu, "Jiaoyubu Sanmin zhuyi jiaoyu shishi yuanze."

68. Andres Rodriguez, "Building the Nation, Serving the Frontier: Mobilizing and Reconstructing China's Borderlands during the War of Resistance," *Modern Asian Studies* 45, no. 3 (2011): 347.

69. Sun Yat-sen promoted the notion of Chinese nationality transcending ethnic divisions. He described China's main ethnic groups—the Han, Manchu, Hui, Mongolian, and Tibetans—as the "five fingers" of China, noting that if one finger was missing, the Chinese would feel that the nation was not whole.

70. Thomas Mullaney, *Coming to Terms with the Nation: Ethnic Classification in Modern China* (Berkeley: University of California Press, 2011), 77.

71. Mullaney translates Chiang Kai-shek's *minzu* in these terms. Mullaney, *Coming to Terms*, 16.

72. Guomin zhengfu, Jiaoyubu, "Jiaoyubu Sanmin zhuyi jiaoyu shishi yuanze."

73. Guomin zhengfu, Jiaoyubu, "Jiaoyubu Sanmin zhuyi jiaoyu shishi yuanze."

74. Rodriguez, "Building the Nation, Serving the Frontier," 372.

75. Guomin zhengfu, Jiaoyubu, "Jiaoyubu Sanmin zhuyi jiaoyu shishi yuanze."

76. Chen, *Zhanshi jiaoyu xingzheng huiyi*, appendix 2, 67–86.

77. Chen, *Zhanshi jiaoyu xingzheng huiyi*, 80–81.

78. Culp, "Setting the Sheet," 66.

79. Jiaoyubu [Ministry of Education], *Zhongxue kecheng biaozhun* [Middle school curricular standards] (Nanjing: Minsheng Press, 1948); Jiaoyubu, *Xiuding zhongxue gongmin*.

80. Jiaoyubu, *Zhongxue kecheng biaozhun*.

81. Henrietta Harrison, "Changing Nationalities, Changing Ethnicities: Taiwan Indigenous Villages in the Years after 1946," in *In Search of the Hunters and Their Tribes: Studies in the History and Culture of the Taiwan Indigenous People*, ed. David Faure (Taipei: Shung Ye Museum of Formosan Aborigines, 2001), 60.

82. Harrison, "Changing Nationalities," 60–61.

83. Harrison, "Changing Nationalities," 61, 71.

84. Harrison, "Changing Nationalities," 71.

85. Harrison, "Changing Nationalities," 67.

86. Harrison, "Changing Nationalities," 68–69.

87. Harrison, "Changing Nationalities," 51.

Epilogue

1. Thomas Dewey, *Journey to the Far Pacific* (Garden City, NY: Doubleday, 1952), 132, cited in Chen, *Storm Clouds,* 218, fn. 1. In winter 1950, Chiang admitted to the Standing

194   Notes to Pages 153–161

Committee that he "held responsibility for the loss of the . . . country," cited in Taylor, *Generalissimo*, 422.

2. Chen, *Storm Clouds*, 218.

3. Chen, *Storm Clouds*, 158.

4. Sun Chen, "Investment in Education and Human Resource Development in Postwar Taiwan," in *Cultural Change in Postwar Taiwan*, ed. Steve Harrell and Huang Chün-chieh (Boulder, CO: Westview Press, 1994), 96.

5. *Education Statistics of the Republic of China, 1989* (Taipei: Ministry of Education, 1989), Tables 8, 9, and 10, cited in Sun, "Investment in Education," 97.

6. Chen, *Storm Clouds*, 159.

7. Chen, *Storm Clouds*, 159.

8. Jiaoyubu junxunchu, *Xuesheng junxun wushinian*, 157–160.

9. Jiaoyubu junxunchu, *Xuesheng junxun wushinian*, 157–160.

10. Guomin Xingzhengyuan [National Executive Yuan], "Sanmin zhuyi qingniantuan ji suo shu danwei: 1944–1947 niandu jingfei yusuan" [Sanmin Zhuyi Youth Corps and the belonging units: 1944–1947 budget], file 790, 16J-1748, vol. 2, sec. 3, Di'er lishi dang'anguan, Nanjing [SHAC].

11. See Tables 2.1 and 2.2.

12. Several student protests occurred from the 1970s and 1980s in Taiwan. See Teresa Wright, *The Perils of Protest: State Repression and Student Activism in China and Taiwan* (Honolulu: University of Hawai'i Press, 2001), 96–102.

13. Wright, *Perils of Protest*, 95.

14. Wright, *Perils of Protest*, 102–103.

15. Wright, *Perils of Protest*, 103.

16. Wright, *Perils of Protest*, 102–126.

17. Wright, *Perils of Protest*, 126.

18. Jeremy Taylor, "The Production of the Chiang Kai-shek Personality Cult, 1929–1975," *China Quarterly*, no. 185 (March 2006): 96–110.

19. Taylor, *Generalissimo*, 102.

20. Thomas A. Brindley, "The China Youth Corps: Democratization in Process," *American Journal of Chinese Studies* 2, no. 2 (October 1994): 201.

Bibliography

Primary Sources

Borg, Dorothy. "Students in Kuomintang China." *Far Eastern Survey* (January 14, 1948): 4–7.

Chen Cheng. *Sanmin zhuyi qingniantuan zhi xingzhi ji qi zhanwang* [The nature and prospects of the Three People's Principles Youth Corps]. N.p., April 1939.

Chen Lifu. *Chinese Education during the War, 1937–1942*. N.p.: Ministry of Education, 1942.

———. *Four Years of Chinese Education, 1937–1941*. Chongqing: China Information Committee, 1941.

———. *The Storm Clouds Clear Over China: The Memoir of Ch'en Li-fu, 1900–1993*, edited by Sidney H. Chang and Ramon H. Myers. Stanford, CA: Hoover Institution Press, 1994.

———. *Zhanshi jiaoyu xingzheng huiyi* [Recollections on wartime educational administration]. Taipei: Shangwu yinshuguan, 1973.

Chiang Ching-kuo. *Chiang Ching-kuo xiansheng quanji* [The complete works of Chiang Ching-kuo]. Vols. 3–6. Taipei: Xingzhengyuan xinwenju, 1991–1992.

Chiang Kai-shek. *China's Destiny*. Translated by Wang Chung-hui. New York: Macmillan, 1947.

———. *President Chiang Kai-shek's Selected Speeches and Messages, 1937–1945*. Taipei: China Cultural Service, 1949.

———. *Resistance and Reconstruction: Messages during China's Six Years of War, 1937–1943*. Freeport, NY: Harper & Row, 1970.

———. *Soviet Russia in China: A Summing-Up at Seventy*. New York: Farrar, Straus and Cudahy, 1957.

———. *Xian zongtong Jianggong quanji* [The complete works of Jiang Jieshi]. Taipei: Zhongguo wenhua daxue, 1984.

Chiang, Monlin. *Tides from the West: A Chinese Autobiography*. New Haven, CT: Yale University Press, 1947.

China Youth Corps. *A Brief Introduction of the China Youth Service Association*. Taipei: China Youth Corps Headquarters, n.d.

Chinese Ministry of Information. *China Handbook, 1937–1945: A Comprehensive Survey of Major Developments in China in Eight Years of War*. New York: Macmillan, 1947.

196   Bibliography

Chinese Press Review. U.S. Consulate General (and U.S. Office of War Information), Chongqing, China. January 3, 1945 to October 21, 1946.

Demographic Yearbook, 1949–1950. New York: United Nations, 1950.

Demographic Yearbook, 1953. New York: United Nations, 1953.

Demographic Yearbook, 1957. New York: United Nations, 1957.

Dewey, Thomas E. *Journey to the Far Pacific.* Garden City, NY: Doubleday, 1952.

Education Statistics of the Republic of China, 1989. Taipei: Ministry of Education, 1989.

Gu Shuxing, "Xuexiao junxun wenti de yantao" [Discussion on the issue of military training in schools]. *Jiaoyu tongxun fukan taiban* [Education newsletter] 2, no. 16 (July 20, 1951): 10–13.

Guofangbu Zhengzhibu [General Political Warfare Department]. *Guojun zhengzhan shigao* [Draft history of political warfare in the Chinese Armed Forces]. Taipei: Guofangbu Zhengzhibu, 1965.

Guojun dang'an [National Military Archives]. "Jianli houbei bing yuan an" [Establish the reserves], Zongzhang bangongshi [Director's office]. 1622/1540, February–July 1952.

———. "Putong xuexiao junxun shi shi an" [Regular school military implementation plan]. 0600 8060.2, December 1951 to August 1955.

Guoli bianyi guan [National Institute of Compilation and Translation]. *Tongzijun xunlian, diyice* [Scouts training]. Vol. 1. Taipei: Guoli bianyi guan, 1972.

Guomin xingzhengyuan [National Executive Yuan]. "Ge di zhongdeng xuexiao jiaozhiyuan beikong" [Secondary school staff from different locales accused of crimes]. File 5262, J-1275, vol. 2. Di'er lishi dang'anguan, Nanjing.

———. "Ge sheng shi jiaoyu shicha baogao" [Report on the investigation of education in each province and city]. File 2286, 16J-1621, vol. 2, sec. 2. Di'er lishi dang'anguan, Nanjing.

———. "Ge sili zhongxue qing buzhu fei" [Private middle schools applying for subsidies]. File 1951, 16J-1904, vol. 2, sec. 3. Di'er lishi dang'anguan, Nanjing.

———. "Guomindang zhongyang junxiao tebie xunlianban yuanbing cansha Hechuan xian Guoli di'er zhongxue xuesheng Zheng Xuepu deng jingguo qingxing" [The stages of events that led the GMD Central Special Military Training class member to murder Zheng Xuepu of Number Two Middle School from Hechuan County]. File 2300, 16J-1621, vol. 2, sec. 2, December 1942. Di'er lishi dang'anguan, Nanjing.

———. "Jiaoyubu qingnian fu xue jiu ye fudao weiyuanhui gongzuo gaikuang gaihui shi zi xunlian suo banfa" [Solution of Ministry of Education's Guidance Committee for youth returning to school to acquire jobs and teachers' training institute]. File 2294, 16J-1621, vol. 2, sec. 2, January 1946 to November 1947. Di'er lishi dang'anguan, Nanjing.

———. "Sanmin zhuyi qingniantuan ji suo shu danwei: 1944–1947 niandu jingfei yusuan" [Sanmin Zhuyi Youth Corps and the belonging units: 1944–1947 budget]. File 790, 16J-1748, vol. 2, sec. 3. Di'er lishi dang'anguan, Nanjing.

———. "Zhan di shixue qingnian zhao xun banfa gangyao jige fang zhi jianyi" [Proposal for registration and training solution for youth who do not have schools where war occurs]. File 2293, 16J-1621, vol. 2, sec. 2, April 1939 to July 1944. Di'er lishi dang'anguan, Nanjing.

Guomin zhengfu, Jiaoyubu [National Government, Ministry of Education]. "Jiaoyubu San-min zhuyi jiaoyu shishi yuanze" [How to put Three Principles of the People into practice]. File 410-J-2941, vol. 1, sec. 5. Di'er lishi dang'anguan, Nanjing.

Guomindang Historical Commission, ed. *Geming wenxian* [Documents on revolution]. Taipei: Guomindang Historical Commission, 1953–present.

Guoshiguan [Academia Historica]. "Zhongguo guomin shi shi jiyao, 1952" [Republic of China historical records summary, 1952]. Taipei: Guoshiguan, 1952.

Hook, Brian, ed. *The Individual and the State in China*. Oxford: Clarendon Press, 1996.

Jiaoyubu [Ministry of Education], ed. *Di'erci Zhongguo jiaoyu nianjian* [The second year-book of Chinese education]. Nanjing: Zhongqing, 1948; repr., Taipei: Zhongqing, 1981.

———. *Disanci Zhongguo jiaoyu nianjian* [The third yearbook of Chinese education]. Taipei: Zhongqing, 1957.

———. "Jiaoguan de xinshui yu junjie yaoqiu" [Military instructors' salaries and rank eligibility requirements]. Jiaoyuting, file 30895, November 2, 1951.

———. "Methods of the Ministry of Education to Manage Students Retreating from War Zones." Order #660 issued by the Ministry of Education on February 25, 1938 in *Jiaoyubu gongbao* [Bulletin of the Ministry of Education] 10, nos. 1–3 (March 1938).

———. "Methods to Unify the Management of Various Levels of Educational Institutions by Government Agencies," issued on January 20, 1938. In *Jiaoyubu gongbao* [Bulletin of the Ministry of Education] 10, nos. 1–3 (March 1938).

———. *Xiuding zhongxue gongmin guowen lishi dilike kecheng biaozhun* [Revised middle school civics, Chinese literature, history, and geography courses' curricular standards]. Taipei: Jiaoyubu, 1952.

———. *Xiuzheng chuji zhongxue lishi kecheng biaozhun* [The revised standard of the junior high school curriculum]. Chongqing: Jiaoyubu, 1940.

———. *Xiuzheng gaozhong zhongxue lishi kecheng biaozhun* [The revised standard of the upper middle school curriculum]. Chongqing: Jiaoyubu, 1940.

———. *Zhonghua minguo zuijin liu nian lai jiaoyu tongji* [Republic of China's education statistics for the previous six years]. Taipei: Jiaoyubu, 1960.

———. *Zhongxue kecheng biaozhun* [Middle school curricular standards]. Nanjing: Minsheng Press, 1948.

———. *Zuijin jiaoyu tongji jianbian* [A concise edition of the latest educational statistics], part of Table 10. Chongqing: Jiaoyubu, 1940.

Jiaoyubu junxunchu [Ministry of Education, Military Training Department]. *Xuesheng junxun wushinian* [Fifty years of student military training]. Taipei: Youshi wenhua shiye gongsi, 1978.

Jiaoyuting [Taiwan's Provincial Government, Department of Education]. File 3806, August 22, 1951.

Jiuguotuan zongbu [China Youth Corps Headquarters]. *Lüqi piaoyang sanshinian* [Green flag waves for thirty years]. Taipei: China Youth Corps Headquarters, 1982 [Coauthors not credited are Hsueh P'ing-kuo and Chao Ch'ing-ho].

———. *Senior High School Military Training Textbook*. Vol. 1. Taipei: Taiwan shudian yinshua gongchang, February 1957.

Bibliography

Kirby, William C., *Germany and Republican China*. Stanford, CA: Stanford University Press, 1984.

Lary, Diana, and Stephen MacKinnon. *Scars of War: The Impact of Warfare on Modern China*. Vancouver: University of British Columbia Press, 2001.

Lee Huan, and Lin Yin-ting. *Zhuisui ban shiji: Lee Huan yu Chiang Ching-kuo xiansheng* [Lee Huan: Half a century of following Chiang Ching-kuo]. Taipei: Commonwealth Press, 1997.

Lei Zhen. *Wo de muqin: huiyilu* [My mother: Memoir]. Taipei: Guiguan tushu gufen youxian gongsi: Faxing jiu bo tushu gufen youxian gongsi, 1989.

Liu Yifu. "Fuxing de qiji, shengli de baozheng" [Revival's opportunity, victory's guarantee]. In *Zhongguo qingnian de junxun shenghuo* [Chinese youth's military training life]. Taipei: Youshi wenhua shiye gongsi, 1955.

———. *Zhandou qingnian de zhandou shenghuo* [Combat youth's combat life]. Taipei: n.p., n.d.

Lu Liu. "Imagining the Refugee: The Emergence of a State Welfare System in the War of Resistance." In *Visualizing Modern China: Image, History, and Memory, 1750–Present*, edited by James A. Cook, Joshua Goldstein, Matthew D. Johnson, and Sigrid Schmalzer, 165–183. Lanham, MD: Lexington Books, 2014.

MacNair, Harley F., ed. *Voices from Unoccupied China*. Chicago: University of Chicago Press, 1943.

Manual of Educational Statistics, the Republic of China—1961. Taipei: National Educational Materials Center, 1961.

New York Times.

Pao Chun-peng. Quanguo jiaoyuhui lianhehui xinxuezhi kecheng biaozhun qicao weiyuanhui [National Education Association, New school curriculum standard drafting committee], "Gaoji zhongxue kecheng zonggang" [Senior high school curriculum general outline]. In *Xinxuezhi kecheng biaozhun gangyao* [Outline of the curriculum standards for the New School System]. 3rd ed. 1924.

———. Sanmin zhuyi qingniantuan [Three People's Principles Youth Corps]. *Tuanzhang xunshi* [Speeches of the president of the Three People's Principles Youth Corps]. Sanmin zhuyi qingniantuan zhongyang tuan yi yin, April 1942.

———. *Zhongguo qingnian fangong jiuguotuan zai zhandou zhong* [China Youth Corps in combat]. Taipei: Youth Press, 1955.

Sang Bing. *Wanqing xuetang xuesheng yu shehui bianqian* [Late Qing school students and social change]. Taipei: Daohe chubanshe, 1991.

Sassani, Abul Hassan K. *Education in Taiwan (Formosa)*. Washington, DC: United States Government Printing Office, 1956.

Taiwan sheng jiaoyu tongji [Taiwan province education statistics]. Taipei: Jiaoyuting, 1954.

The Ten-Year Existence of the China Youth Corps. Taipei: China Youth Corps Headquarters, 1963.

TIME.

Tzen Shian-yung. *China Youth Warriors March*. Taipei: Youth Publishers, 1953.

Wang Shijie. "Education." In *The Chinese Yearbook, 1937*. Shanghai: Commercial Press, 1937.

Wu, K. C. "Your Money Has Built a Police State in Formosa." *Look* (June 29, 1954): 39–43.

Wu Manjun, *Ziyou Zhongguo shijian kenan yundong* [Free China's practice of the Overcoming Difficulty Movement]. Taipei: Gaizao chubanshe, 1953.

Xiao Xiqing. "Junxun gongzuo jingyan tan" [Discussion of military training job experience]. *Tuanwu gongzuo shilu* [Corps' work record]. Taipei: China Youth Corps Headquarters, 1982.

Xu Liang. "Tan xuexiao shishi junshi xunlian" [Discussing the implementation of military training practice in schools]. *Taiwan jiaoyu fudao yuekan* 2, no. 3 (March 1952): 6–7.

Youshi [Young lion].

Zenyang zhankai nongcun fuwu gongzuo [How to develop rural service work]. Taipei: Youshi chubanshe, 1954.

Zhejiang Province Department of Education. *Zhejiang jiaoyu* [Zhejiang education] 3, no. 6 (December 1939).

Zhonggong Zhongyang qingnian yundong bianxuan [Chinese Communist Central Committee Youth Movement compilations, July 1921 to September 1949]. Beijing: Zhongguo qingnian chubanshe, 1988.

"Zhongguo gongchandang di'erci quanguo daibiao dahui wenjian" [Chinese Communist Party Second National Congress document]. *Chinese Communist Central Committee Youth Movement Compilations, July 1921–September 1949.* Beijing: Zhongguo qingnian chubanshe, 1988.

"Zhongguo gongchandang Zhongguo gongan zuyi qingniantuan zhongyangju tonggao—guanyu hupai daibiao ji dangyuan jian tuanyuan deng ziguiding" [Chinese Communist Youth League's Central Bureau announcement]. *Chinese Communist Central Committee Youth Movement Compilations, July 1921–September 1949.* Beijing: Zhongguo qingnian chubanshe 1988.

Zhongyang ribao [Central Daily News].

Zhou Gan et al., eds. *Gongmin keben* [Civics textbook]. Vol. 2. Shanghai: Shangwu yinshuguan, 1937.

Ziyou qingnian [Free Youth].

Ziyou zhongguo [Free China].

Zongtongfu dang'an [Presidential Palace Archives]. *Buchong bing chuxun jihua* [Reserve army training plan]. 2130307/7, December 1950 to May 1953.

———. "Chengfu qie shi yanjiu Bai zong jiaoguan Hongliang yu Yi jiaoguan Zhuoren, guanyu dongyuan yanxi hou zhi tanhua yao dian, bing ni ding shishi banfa you" [Submit in return thorough study of General Military Instructor Bai Hongliang and Military Instructor Yi Zhuoren, regarding the key points of discussion after the mobilization drill, and draft the implementation plan]. March 10, 1952.

———. "Feng jun zuo jiu Jiuguotuan sishisan nian gaozhong yishang xuexiao junxun gaikuang baogao heshi si dian jin jiang banli qingxing chengfu" [Submit and return, Your Excellency, China Youth Corps, 1954 Upper Middle School and above military training implementation report examining four points carefully to handle condition]. *Gaozhong xuesheng junxun banfa* [Upper middle school students military training way]. July 4, 1955.

———. "Taiwan sheng gaoji zhongdeng xuexiao xuesheng junxun shishi gaikuang baogao shu" [Taiwan province upper middle schools' student military training

200   Bibliography

implementation general situation report book]. *Gaozhong xuesheng junxun banfa* [Upper middle school students military training way]. September 13, 1953.

Secondary Sources

Alitto, Guy. "Chiang Kai-shek in Western Historiography." *Sino-American Relations* 27, no. 4 (Winter 2001): 40–81.

Bailey, Paul J. "Active Citizen or Efficient Housewife? The Debate over Women's Education in Early Twentieth-Century China." In *Education, Culture, and Identity in Twentieth-Century China,* edited by Glen Peterson, Ruth Hayhoe, and Yongling Lu, 318–347. Ann Arbor: University of Michigan Press, 2001.

———. *Reform the People: Changing Attitudes towards Popular Education in Early Twentieth Century China.* Vancouver: University of British Columbia Press, 1990.

Barnett, A. Doak. *China on the Eve of Communist Takeover.* New York: Praeger, 1963.

Bedeski, Robert E. *State Building in Modern China: The Kuomintang in the Prewar Period.* Berkeley: University of California, Institute of East Asian Studies, 1981.

Bian, Morris L. *The Making of the State Enterprise System in Modern China: The Dynamics of Institutional Change.* Cambridge, MA: Harvard University Press, 2005.

Bodenhorn, Terry, ed. *Defining Modernity: Guomindang Rhetorics of a New China, 1920–1970: A Neotraditional Scientism?* Ann Arbor: Center for Chinese Studies, University of Michigan, 2002.

Boorman, Howard, ed. *Biographical Dictionary of Republican China.* 4 vols. New York: Columbia University Press, 1971.

Bowie, George H. "The China Youth Corps: A Contributor to the Development of the Republic of China." Master's Thesis, Brigham Young University, 1990.

Brindley, Thomas A. "The China Youth Corps: Democratization in Process." *American Journal of Chinese Studies* 2, no. 2 (October 1994): 195–217.

———. *The China Youth Corps in Taiwan.* New York: Peter Lang, 1999.

Brown, Melissa J. *Is Taiwan Chinese? The Impact of Culture, Power, and Migration on Changing Identities.* Berkeley: University of California Press, 2004.

———. ed. *Negotiating Ethnicities in China and Taiwan.* Berkeley: Institute of East Asian Studies, University of California Press, 1996.

Bullard, Monte R. *The Soldier and the Citizen: The Role of the Military in Taiwan's Development.* Armonk, NY: M. E. Sharpe, 1997.

Chan, Wai-keung. "Contending Memories of the Nation: History Education in Wartime China, 1937–1945." In *The Politics of Historical Production in Late Qing and Republican China,* edited by Tze-ki Hon and Robert Culp, 169–210. Leiden: Brill, 2007.

Chang Jui-the. "Technology Transfer in Modern China: The Case of Railway Enterprise (1876–1937)." *Modern Asian Studies* 27, no. 2 (1993): 281–296.

Chauncey, Helen R. *Schoolhouse Politicians: Locality and State during the Chinese Republic.* Honolulu: University of Hawai'i Press, 1992.

Chen Cuilian. *Paixi douzheng yu quanmou zhengzhi: ererba beiju de ling yi mianxiang* [Factional struggle and power politics: Another facet of the 2/28 tragedy]. Taipei: China Times Press, 1995.

Bibliography 201

Chen, Edward I-te. "Formosan Political Movements under Japanese Colonial Rule, 1914–1937." *Journal of Asian Studies* 31, no. 3 (May 1972): 477–497.

Chen, Janet Y. *Guilty of Indigence: The Urban Poor in China, 1900–1953*. Princeton, NJ: Princeton University Press, 2012.

Chen Jinjin. *Kangzhan qian jiao yu zhengce zhi yanjiu: Min guo shi qi nian zhi er shi liu nian* [Pre-war educational policies of the ROC: 1928–1937]. Taipei: Jindai Zhongguo chubanshe, 1997.

Chen San-jing. "Jiang Jingguo xiansheng yu Zhongguo qingnian fangong jiuguotua" [Mr. Chiang Ching-kuo and the China Youth Anti-Communist Save (Our) Country Corps]. *Jindai Zhongguo* [Contemporary China] 92 (December 1, 1992): 35–50.

Chen San-jing, Chu Hong-yuan, and Wu Mei-hui (fangwen), Wu Mei-hui (jilu). *Nü qingnian dadui fangwen ji* [The reminiscences of Women's Corps]. Taipei: Academia Sinica, Institute of Modern History, 1995.

Ching, Leo T. S. *Becoming "Japanese": Colonial Taiwan and the Politics of Identity Formation*. Berkeley: University of California Press, 2001.

Chun, Allen. "From Nationalism to Nationalizing: Cultural Imagination and State Formation in Postwar Taiwan." In *Chinese Nationalism*, edited by Jonathan Unger, 126–147. Armonk, NY: M. E. Sharpe, 1996. Reprinted in *Australian Journal of Chinese Affairs* 30 (1994): 49–69.

Clinton, Maggie. *Revolutionary Nativism: Fascism and Culture in China, 1925–1937*. Durham, NC: Duke University Press, 2017.

Cogan, John J., Paul Morris, and Murray Print, eds. *Civic Education in the Asia-Pacific Region: Case Studies across Six Societies*. New York: RoutledgeFalmer, 2002.

Cohen, Paul A. "The Post-Mao Reforms in Historical Perspective." *Journal of Asian Studies* 43, no. 3 (1988): 519–541.

———. "Reflections on a Watershed Date: The 1949 Divide in Chinese History." In *Twentieth-Century China: New Approaches*, edited by Jeffrey N. Wasserstrom, 27–36. London: Routledge, 2003.

Cong Xiaoping. "Localizing the Global, Nationalizing the Local: The Role of Teachers' Schools in Making China Modern, 1897–1937." PhD diss., UCLA, 2001.

———. *Teachers' Schools and the Making of the Modern Chinese Nation-State, 1897–1937*. Vancouver: University of British Columbia Press, 2007.

Corcuff, Stephane, ed. *Memories of the Future: National Identity Issues and the Search for a New Taiwan*. Armonk, NY: M. E. Sharpe, 2002.

Craft, Stephen G. *American Justice in Taiwan: The 1957 Riots and Cold War Foreign Policy*. Lexington: University Press of Kentucky, 2016.

Crossley, Pamela K. "Thinking about Ethnicity in Early Modern China." *Late Imperial China* 11, no. 2 (June 1990): 1–36.

Crozier, Ralph C. *Koxinga and Chinese Nationalism: History, Myth, and the Hero*. Cambridge, MA: East Asian Research Center, Harvard University Press, 1977.

Culp, Robert. *Articulating Citizenship: Civic Education and Student Politics in Southeastern China, 1912–1940*. Cambridge, MA: Harvard University Asia Center, 2007.

———. "China—'The Land and Its People': Fashioning Identity in Secondary School History Textbooks, 1911–1937." *Twentieth-Century China* 26, no. 2 (April 2001): 17–62.

202 Bibliography

———. "Elite Association and Local Politics in Republican China: Educational Institutions in Jiashan and Lanqi Counties, Zhejiang, 1911–1937." *Modern China* 20, no. 4 (October 1994): 446–477.

———. "Mass Production of Knowledge and the Industrialization of Mental Labor: The Rise of the Petty Intellectual." In *Knowledge Acts in Modern China: Ideas, Institutions, and Identities,* edited by Robert Culp, Eddy U, and Wen-hsin Yeh, 207–241. Berkeley: Institute of East Asian Studies, University of California, Berkeley, 2016.

———. *The Power of Print in Modern China: Intellectuals and Industrial Publishing from the End of Empires to Maoist State Socialism.* New York: Columbia University Press, 2019.

———. "Research Note: Shanghai's Lexicographical Publishing House Library's Holdings on Republican Period Popular Culture and Education." *Republican China* 22, no. 2 (April 1997): 104–109.

———. "Rethinking Governmentality: Training, Cultivation, and Cultural Citizenship in Nationalist China." *Journal of Asian Studies* 65, no. 3 (August 2006): 529–554.

———. "Self-Determination or Self-Discipline? The Shifting Meanings of Student Self-Government in 1920s Jiangnan Middle Schools." *Twentieth-Century China* 23, no. 2 (April 1998): 1–39.

———. "Setting the Sheet of Loose Sand: Conceptions of Society and Citizenship in Nanjing Decade Party Doctrine and Civics Textbooks." In *Defining Modernity: Guomindang Rhetorics of a New China, 1920–1970,* edited by Terry Bodenhorn, 45–90. Ann Arbor: Center for Chinese Studies, University of Michigan, 2002.

———. "Zhongguo tongzijun: Nanjing shinian tongzijun shouce zhong de gongmin xunlian yu shehui yishi" [Scouting for Chinese boys: Civic training and social consciousness in Nanjing Decade Boy Scout handbooks]. *Xinshixue* 11, no. 4 (December 2000): 17–63.

Curran, Thomas D. *Educational Reform in Republican China: The Failure of Educators to Create a Modern Nation.* Lewiston, NY: Edwin Mellen, 2005.

Day, Jenny Huangfu. "The War of Textbooks: Educating Children during the Second Sino-Japanese War, 1937–1945." *Twentieth-Century China* 46, no. 2 (May 2021): 105–129.

De Hart, Jane Sherron. "Oral Sources and Contemporary History: Dispelling Old Assumptions." *Journal of American History* 80, no. 2 (September 1993): 582–595.

Dickson, Bruce J. "The Lessons of Defeat: The Reorganization of the Kuomintang on Taiwan, 1950–52." *China Quarterly,* no. 133 (March 1993): 56–84.

Eastman, Lloyd. *The Abortive Revolution: China under Nationalist Rule, 1927–1937.* Cambridge, MA: Harvard University Press, 1974.

———. "China under Nationalist Rule, Two Essays: The Nanking Decade, 1927–1939 and the War Years, 1937–1945." Urbana, IL: Center for Asian Studies, University of Illinois. Volume I of Papers in Asian Studies, 1981.

———. "Fascism and Modern China: A Rejoinder." *China Quarterly,* no. 80 (December 1979): 838–842.

———. "Fascism in Kuomintang China: The Blue Shirts." *China Quarterly,* no. 49 (January–March 1972): 1–31.

———. "The Rise and Fall of the 'Blue Shirts': A Review Article." *Republican China* 13, no. 1 (November 1987): 25–48.

Bibliography   203

———. *Seeds of Destruction: Nationalist China in War and Revolution, 1937–1949.* Stanford, CA: Stanford University Press, 1984.

Eastman, Lloyd, Jerome Ch'en, Suzanne Pepper, and Lyman P. Van Slyke. *The Nationalist Era in China, 1927–1949.* Cambridge: Cambridge University Press, 1991.

Eastman, Lloyd E. "The Kuomintang in the 1930s." In *The Limits of Change: Essays on Conservative Alternatives in Republican China,* edited by Charlotte Furth, 191–210. Cambridge, MA: Harvard University Press, 1976.

Ebrey, Patricia. "Surnames and Han Chinese Identity." In *Negotiating Ethnicities in China and Taiwan,* edited by Melissa J. Brown, 19–36. Berkeley: University of California Press, 1996.

Edmondson, Robert. "The February 28 Incident and National Identity." In *Memories of the Future: National Identity Issues and the Search for a New Taiwan,* edited by Stephane Corcuff, 25–47. Armonk, NY: M. E. Sharpe, 2002.

Fenby, Jonathan. *Generalissimo: Chiang Kai-shek and the Nation He Lost.* London: Free Press, 2003.

Fitzgerald, C. P. "Review: Soviet Russia in China." *Pacific Affairs* 31, no. 1 (March 1958): 88–89.

Fitzgerald, John. *Awakening China: Politics, Culture and Class in the Nationalist Revolution.* Stanford, CA: Stanford University Press, 1996.

Gan Guoxun, "Guanyu suowei 'Fuxingshe' de zhenqing shikuang" [The true conditions and actual circumstances of the so-called Fuxingshe]. *Zhuanji wenxue, shang* 35, no. 3 (1979): 32–38.

Gerth, Karl. *China Made: Consumer Culture and the Creation of the Nation.* Cambridge, MA: Harvard University Press, 2003.

Glosser, Susan. *Chinese Visions of Family and State, 1915–1953.* Berkeley: University of California Press, 2003.

Greene, J. Megan. "Looking toward the Future: State Standardization and Professionalization of Science in Wartime China." In *Knowledge Acts in Modern China: Ideas, Institutions, and Identities,* edited by Robert Culp. Eddy U, and Wen-hsin Yeh, 275–303. Berkeley: Institute of East Asian Studies, University of California, 2016.

———. *The Origins of the Developmental State in Taiwan: Science Policy and the Quest for Modernization.* Cambridge, MA: Harvard University Press, 2008.

Gregor, A. James. "Fascism and Modernization: Some Addenda." *World Politics* 26, no. 3 (1974): 370–384.

———. *The Fascist Persuasion in Radical Politics.* Princeton, NJ: Princeton University Press, 1974.

Hansen, Valerie. *The Open Empire: A History of China to 1600.* New York: W. W. Norton, 2000.

Harp, Stephen L. *Learning to Be Loyal: Primary Schooling as Nation Building in Alsace and Lorraine, 1850–1940.* DeKalb: Northern Illinois University Press, 1998.

Harrison, Henrietta. "Changing Nationalities, Changing Ethnicities: Taiwan Indigenous Villages in the Years after 1946." In *In Search of the Hunters and Their Tribes: Studies in the History and Culture of the Taiwan Indigenous People,* edited by David Faure, 50–78. Taipei: Shung Ye Museum of Formosan Aborigines, 2001.

204   Bibliography

———. *The Making of the Republican Citizen: Political Ceremonies and Symbols in China, 1911–1929.* Oxford: Oxford University Press, 2000.

Harrison, James Pinckney. *The Long March to Power: A History of the Chinese Communist Party, 1921–1972.* New York: Praeger, 1972.

Harrison, Mark. *Legitimacy, Meaning and Knowledge in the Making of Taiwanese Identity.* New York: Palgrave Macmillan, 2006.

Herschatter, Gail. *Dangerous Pleasures: Prostitution and Modernity in Twentieth-Century Shanghai.* Berkeley: University of California Press, 1999.

Hsia-Chang, Maria. *The Chinese Blue Shirt Society: Fascism and Developmental Nationalism.* Berkeley: Institute of East Asian Studies, University of California, 1985.

———. "'Fascism' and Modern China." *China Quarterly,* no. 79 (September 1979): 553–567.

Hsiung, James C., and Steven I. Levine, eds. *China's Bitter Victory: The War with Japan, 1937–1945.* New York: M. E. Sharpe, 1992.

Hsu, Chiu-mei. "A Historical Study of the China Youth Corps' Summer Camps in Taiwan, 1953–1990." Master's thesis, University of Kansas, 1993.

Hsu, Cho-yun. "Historical Setting for the Rise of Chiang Ching-kuo." In *Chiang Ching-kuo's Leadership in the Development of the Republic of China on Taiwan,* edited by Shao-chuan Leng, 1–30. Lanham, MD: University Press of America, 1993.

Hsueh Hua-yuan, ed. *The Contents and Index of Free China Semimonthly.* Taipei: Yuan-Liou Publishing Co., 2000.

Hu Kuo-tai. "Disputes on the Question of Wartime Education and the Formation of an Educational Policy for the Guomindang in the War." *Republican China* 14, no. 1 (November 1988): 30–56.

———. "The Impact of War on Higher Education in China, 1937–1945." *Bulletin of Academia Historica* 1 (December 2001): 77–126.

———. "Politics and Higher Education in China: The Control and Development Policies of the Guomindang, 1937–1945." PhD diss., Griffith University, 1987.

———. "The Struggle between the Kuomintang and the Chinese Communist Party on Campus during the War of Resistance: 1937–1945." *China Quarterly,* no. 118 (June 1989): 300–323.

Huang Jianli. *The Politics of Depoliticization in Republican China: Guomindang Policy towards Student Political Activism, 1927–1949.* Bern: Peter Lang, 1996.

Huang, Jong Huh. "A Configurational Study of the Nonprofit Learning Organization: A Case Study of China Youth Corps in Taiwan." DPA diss., University of Southern California, 1994.

Huang, Ray. *Chiang Kai-shek and His Diary as a Historical Source.* Armonk, NY: M. E. Sharpe, 1996.

Hung, Chang-tai. *War and Popular Culture: Resistance in Modern China, 1937–1945.* Berkeley: University of California Press, 1994.

Israel, John. *Lianda: A Chinese University in War and Revolution.* Stanford, CA: Stanford University Press, 1998.

———. *Student Nationalism in China, 1927–1937.* Stanford, CA: Stanford University Press, 1966.

Bibliography 205

Israel, John, and Donald W. Klein. *Rebels and Bureaucrats: China's December 9ers*. Berkeley: University of California Press, 1976.

Jian, Min-yuan. "Junxun jiaoguan tuiwu hou zaijiuye zhi yanjiu" [A study of reemployment of retired military training instructor]. Master's thesis, National Defense University, 2007.

Kater, Michael H. *Hitler Youth*. Cambridge, MA: Harvard University Press, 2004.

Keenan, Barry. *The Dewey Experiment in China: Educational Reform and Political Power in the Early Republic*. Cambridge, MA: Harvard University Press, 1977.

———. *Imperial China's Last Classical Academies: Social Change in the Lower Yangzi, 1864–1911*. Berkeley: University of California Press, 1994.

———. "Lung-men Academy in Shanghai and the Expansion of Kiangsu's Educated Elite, 1865–1911." In *Education and Society in Late Imperial China, 1600–1900*, edited by Benjamin A. Elman and Alexander Woodside, 493–524. Berkeley: University of California Press, 1994.

Kerr, George H. *Formosa Betrayed*. Boston: Houghton Mifflin, 1965.

Kinkley, Jeffrey C. *The Odyssey of Shen Congwen*. Stanford, CA: Stanford University Press, 1987.

Kirby, William C. "The Chinese War Economy." In *China's Bitter Victory: The War with Japan, 1937–1945*, edited by James C. Hsiung and Steven I. Levine, 185–212. Armonk, NY: M. E. Sharpe, 1992.

———. "Continuity and Change in Modern China: Economic Planning on the Mainland and on Taiwan, 1943–1958." *Australian Journal of Chinese Affairs* 24 (1990): 121–141.

———. "Engineering China: Birth of the Developmental State, 1928–1937." In *Becoming Chinese: Passages to Modernity and Beyond*, edited by Wen-hsin Yeh, 137–160. Berkeley: University of California Press, 2000.

———. *Germany and Republican China*. Stanford, CA: Stanford University Press, 1984.

Lai Tse-han, Ramon H. Myers, and Wei Wou. *A Tragic Beginning: The Taiwan Uprising of February, 1947*. Stanford, CA: Stanford University Press, 1991.

Lall, Marie, and Edward Vickers, eds. *Education as a Political Tool in Asia*. New York: Routledge, 2009.

Lang, Olga. *Chinese Family and Society*. North Haven, CT: Archon Books, 1968.

Lee, Ger-bei. "Values, Tradition, and Social Change: A Study of School Textbooks in Taiwan and in China." PhD diss., UCLA, 1987.

Lee, Thomas H. "Chinese Education and Intellectuals in Postwar Taiwan." In *Postwar Taiwan in Historical Perspective*, edited by Chun-Chieh Huang and Feng-fu Tsao, 135–157. Bethesda: University Press of Maryland, 1998.

Lee Wei-song. "Jiang Jingguo yu Jiuguotuan zhi yanjiu" [The study of Chiang Ching-kuo and the China Youth Corps (1969–1988)]. Master's thesis, National Central University, 2005.

Leng, Shao-chuan. *Chiang Ching-kuo's Leadership in the Development of the Republic of China on Taiwan*. Lanham, MD: University Press of America, 1993.

Lévesque, Stephane. "Becoming Citizens: High School Students and Citizenship in BC and Québec." *Encounters on Education* 4 (2003): 107–126.

Li, Danke. *Echoes of Chongqing: Women in Wartime China.* Urbana-Champaign: University of Illinois Press, 2010.

Li Huaxing, Zhou Yongxiang, Chen Zuhuai, and Zhang Yuanlong, eds. *Minguo jiaoyushi* [Republican education history]. Shanghai: Shanghai jiaoyu chubanshe, 1997.

Li, Lincoln. *Student Nationalism in China, 1924–1949.* Albany: State University of New York Press, 1994.

Li Tai-han. "Cong qingnian lianhui dao Jiuguotuan chengli de guocheng—yijiuwushi niandai chuqi—Guomindang duiyu qingnian yundong de chouhua yu zhangkong" [The process from the Youth League to the establishment of the China Youth Corps: The Guomindang's plan and control of youth movements in the early 1950s]. *Taiwan wenxian* 56, no. 3 (2005): 130–156.

———. "Dang'an yunyong yu lishi yanjiu: yi xuesheng junxun zai zhanhou Taiwan shi shi de yiti wei li" [Archive research and history study: Issues on the implication of student military training in postwar Taiwan]. *Dangan jikan* 56, no. 4 (June 2004): 1–13.

———. "Dangtuan, junshi, yu jiaoyu: yijiu wuling niandai xuesheng junxun jinru xiaoyuan zhi yanjiu" [Party corps, the military, and education: The study of 1950s student military training entering the campus]. Master's thesis, National Central University, 2002.

Li Tongshi, trans. *Shanghai Shangwu yinshuguan, 1897–1949* [Shanghai Commercial Press, 1897–1949]. Beijing: Commercial Press, 2000.

Lin Jinsheng, ed. *Feiyue qingchun sishinian: Zhongguo qingnian fangong jiuguotuan chengli 40 zhounian tuanqing tekan* [Fly youth 40 years: China Youth Anti-Communist National Salvation Corps 40th anniversary special edition]. Taipei: Zhongguo qingnian fangong jiuguotuanbu, 1992.

Linden, Allen B. "Politics and Education in China: The Case of the University Council, 1927–1928." *Journal of Asian Studies* 27, no. 4 (August 1968): 763–777.

———. "Politics and Higher Education in China: The Kuomintang and the University Community, 1927–1937." PhD diss., Columbia University, 1969.

Liu Huixuan. *Kangzhan shiqi xinan diqu daxue xunyu wenti zhi yanjiu* [A study of the issue of discipline in southwest region colleges during the War of Resistance, 1937–1945]. Taipei: Wenshizhe chubanshe yinxing, 1992.

Liu, Meihui. "Civic Education at the Crossroads: Case Study of Taiwan." In *Civic Education in the Asia-Pacific Region: Case Studies across Six Societies,* edited by John J. Cogan, Paul Morris, and Murray Print, 93–117. New York: RoutledgeFalmer, 2002.

———. "Teachers' Perspectives toward the Issues-centered Instructional Approach: A Study of Taipei Senior High School Civics Teachers." PhD diss., University of Minnesota, 1995.

Loh, Pichon P. Y. "The Politics of Chiang Kai-shek: A Reappraisal." *Journal of Asian Studies* 25, no. 3 (May 1966): 431–451.

Lu Fangshang. *Cong xuesheng yundong dao yundong xuesheng, Minguo banian zhi shibanian* [From student movements to mobilizing students, 1919–1929]. Taipei: Academia Sinica, Institute of Modern History, 1994.

Lung, Ying-tai. *Da Jiang Da Hai 1949* [Big river, big sea: Untold stories of 1949]. Taipei: CommonWealth Magazine, 2009.

Lutz, Jessie G. *China and the Christian Colleges, 1850–1950*. Ithaca, NY: Cornell University Press, 1971.

———. "The Chinese Student Movement of 1945–1949." *Journal of Asian Studies* 31, no. 1 (November 1971): 89–110.

———. "Comments." In *Nationalist China during the Sino-Japanese War, 1937–1945*, edited by Paul K. T. Sih, 124–130. Hicksville, NY: Exposition Press, 1977.

Ma Zhisu. *Lei Zhen and Chiang Kai-shek*. Taipei: Zili wanbao she wenhua chuban bu, 1993.

Mackerras, Colin. *China's Minorities: Integration and Modernization in the Twentieth Century*. Oxford: Oxford University Press, 1994.

———. *China's Minority Cultures: Identities and Integration since 1912*. New York: St. Martin's Press, 1995.

MacKinnon, Stephen R. "Conclusion: Wartime China." In *China at War: Regions of China, 1937–1945*, edited by Stephen R. MacKinnon, Diana Lary, and Ezra F. Vogel, 338–339. Stanford, CA: Stanford University Press, 2007.

———. *Wuhan, 1938: War, Refugees, and the Making of Modern China*. Berkeley: University of California Press, 2008.

MacKinnon, Stephen R., Diana Lary, and Ezra F. Vogel. *China at War: Regions of China, 1937–1945*. Stanford, CA: Stanford University Press, 2007.

Macleod, David. *Building Character in the American Boy: The Boy Scouts, YMCA, and Their Forerunners, 1870–1920*. Madison: University of Wisconsin Press, 1983.

Martin, Roberta. "The Socialization of Children in China and on Taiwan: An Analysis of Elementary School Textbooks." *China Quarterly*, no. 62 (1975): 242–262.

McElroy, Sarah Coles. "Forging a New Role for Women: Zhili First Women's Normal School and the Growth of Women's Education in China, 1901–21." In *Education, Culture, and Identity in Twentieth Century China*, edited by Glen Peterson, Ruth Hayhoe, and Yongling Lu, 348–374. Ann Arbor: University of Michigan Press, 2001.

———. "Transforming China through Education: Yan Xiu, Zhang Boling, and the Effort to Build a New School System, 1901–1927." PhD diss., Yale University, 1996.

Meyer, Mahlon. *Remembering China from Taiwan: Divided Families and Bittersweet Reunions after the Chinese Civil War*. Hong Kong: Hong Kong University Press, 2012.

Mitchell, Brian R. *International Historical Statistics: Africa, Asia & Oceania, 1750–2000*. New York: Palgrave Macmillan, 2003.

Mitter, Rana. *A Bitter Revolution: China's Struggle with the Modern World*. Oxford: Oxford University Press, 2004.

———. "Classifying Citizens in Nationalist China during World War II, 1937–1941." *Modern Asian Studies* 45, no. 2 (2011): 243–275.

———. *Forgotten Ally: China's World War II, 1937–1945*. New York: Houghton Mifflin Harcourt, 2013.

Mitter, Rana, and Aaron William Moore, eds. "China in World War II, 1937–1945: Experience, Memory and Legacy." Special issue, *Modern Asian Studies* 45, no. 2 (2011).

Mitter, Rana, and Helen M. Schneider. "Introduction: Relief and Reconstruction in Wartime China." *European Journal of East Asian Studies* 11, no. 2 (2012): 179–186.

Bibliography

Morris, Andrew. *Colonial Project, National Game: A History of Baseball in Taiwan.* Berkeley: University of California Press, 2011.

Mullaney, Thomas. *Coming to Terms with the Nation: Ethnic Classification in Modern China.* Berkeley: University of California Press, 2011.

Mulready-Stone, Kristin. *Mobilizing Shanghai Youth: CCP Internationalism, GMD Nationalism and Japanese Collaboration.* New York: Routledge, 2015.

Myers, Ramon H. "Economic Policy and Moral Principles of Chiang Kai-shek." *Sino-American Relations* 27, no. 1 (Spring 2001): 14–37.

———. "A New Chinese Civilization: The Evolution of the Republic of China on Taiwan." China Quarterly, no. 148 (December 1996): 1072–1090.

Nedostup, Rebecca. *Superstitious Regimes: Religion and the Politics of Chinese Modernity.* Cambridge, MA: Harvard University Press, 2009.

Ou Tsiun-chen [Wu Junsheng]. "Education in Wartime China." In *Nationalist China during the Sino-Japanese War, 1937–1945,* edited by Paul K. T. Sih, 89–123. Hicksville, NY: Exposition Press, 1977.

Peake, Cyrus H. *Nationalism and Education in Modern China.* New York: Columbia University Press, 1932.

Peng, Mingmin. *A Taste of Freedom: Memoirs of a Formosan Independence Leader.* Irvine, CA: Taiwan Publishing Company, 1994.

Pepper, Suzanne. *Civil War in China: The Political Struggle, 1945–1949.* Berkeley: University of California Press, 1978.

———. *Civil War in China: The Political Struggle, 1945–1949.* Lanham, MD: Rowman & Littlefield, 1999.

———. "The KMT–CCP Conflict, 1945–1949." In *The Cambridge History of China,* edited by John Fairbank and Albert Feuerweker, vol. 13, 746–747. Cambridge: Cambridge University Press, 1986.

———. *Radicalism and Education Reform in 20th-Century China: The Search for an Ideal Development Model.* Cambridge: Cambridge University Press, 1996.

Peterson, Glen, Ruth Hayhoe, and Yongling Lu, eds. *Education, Culture, and Identity in Twentieth-Century China.* Ann Arbor: University of Michigan Press, 2001.

Phillips, Steven E. *Between Assimilation and Independence: The Taiwanese Encounter Nationalist China, 1945–1950.* Stanford, CA: Stanford University, 2003.

Qi Hongshen. *Liuwang: Dongbei xuesheng* [Refugees: The northeast students]. Zhengzhou: Daxiang chubanshe, 2008.

Rankin, Karl Lott. *China Assignment.* Seattle: University of Washington Press, 1964.

Rankin, Mary. *Early Chinese Revolutionaries: Radical Intellectuals in Shanghai and Chekiang, 1902–1911.* Cambridge, MA: Harvard University Press, 1971.

Rawski, Evelyn S. *Education and Popular Literacy in Ch'ing China.* Ann Arbor: University of Michigan Press, 1979.

Rodriguez, Andres. "Building the Nation, Serving the Frontier: Mobilizing and Reconstructing China's Borderlands during the War of Resistance (1937–1945)." *Modern Asian Studies* 45, no. 3 (2011): 345–376.

Roy, Denny. *Taiwan: A Political History.* Ithaca, NY: Cornell University Press, 2003.

Schneider, Helen M. *Keeping the Nation's House: Domestic Management and the Making of Modern China.* Vancouver: University of British Columbia Press, 2012.

Schneider, Laurence A. *Ku Chieh-kang and China's New History: Nationalism and the Quest for Alternative Traditions.* Berkeley: University of California Press, 1971.

Schoppa, R. Keith. *In a Sea of Bitterness: Refugees during the Sino-Japanese War.* Cambridge, MA: Harvard University Press, 2011.

Shi Huiqun. *A History of Chinese Student Movements, 1945–1949.* Shanghai: Shanghai People Publishing Company, 1992.

Sih, Paul K. T., ed. *Nationalist China during the Sino-Japanese War, 1937–1945.* Hicksville, NY: Exposition Press, 1977.

Spence, Jonathan. *The Search for Modern China.* New York: W. W. Norton, 1999.

Su Bing [Shih Ming]. *Taiwan's 400 Year History: The Origins and Continuing Development of the Taiwanese Society and People.* Washington, DC: Taiwanese Grassroots Association, 1986.

Sun Chen, "Investment in Education and Human Resource Development in Postwar Taiwan." In *Cultural Change in Postwar Taiwan,* edited by Steve Harrell and Huang Chün-chieh, 91–110. Boulder, CO: Westview Press, 1994.

Svensson, Marina. *Debating Human Rights in China: A Conceptual and Political History.* Lanham, MD: Rowman & Littlefield, 2002.

Synott, John P. *Teacher Unions, Social Movements and the Politics of Education in Asia: South Korea, Taiwan and the Philippines.* Burlington, VT: Ashgate, 2002.

Taylor, Jay. *The Generalissimo: Chiang Kai-shek and the Struggle for Modern China.* Cambridge, MA: Belknap Press of Harvard University Press, 2009.

———. *The Generalissimo's Son: Chiang Ching-kuo and the Revolutions in China and Taiwan.* Cambridge, MA: Harvard University Press, 2000.

Taylor, Jeremy. "The Production of the Chiang Kai-shek Personality Cult, 1929–1975." *China Quarterly,* no. 185 (March 2006): 96–110.

Thogerson, Stig. *A County of Culture.* Ann Arbor: University of Michigan Press, 2002.

Tillman, Margaret Mih. *Raising China's Revolutionaries: Modernizing Childhood for Cosmopolitan Nationalists and Liberated Comrades, 1920s–1950s.* New York: Columbia University Press, 2018.

Tsang, Chiu-sam. *Nationalism in School Education in China.* Hong Kong: Progressive Education Publishers, 1967.

Tsurumi, E. Patricia. *Japanese Colonial Education in Taiwan, 1895–1945.* Cambridge, MA: Harvard University Press, 1977.

Tucker, Nancy Bernkopf. *Taiwan, Hong Kong, and the United States, 1945–1992: Uncertain Friendships.* New York: Twayne, 1994.

Tyson, Thomas. "Rendering the Unfamiliar Intelligible: Discovering the Human Side of Accounting's Past through Oral History Interviews." *Accounting Historians Journal* (December 1996): 1–14.

Van de Ven, Hans J. *From Friend to Comrade: The Founding of the Chinese Communist Party, 1920–1927.* Berkeley: University of California Press, 1991.

Vanderven, Elizabeth R. *A School in Every Village: Educational Reform in a Northeast China County, 1904–1931.* Vancouver: University of British Columbia Press, 2012.

Bibliography

Wakeman, Frederic, Jr. *Policing Shanghai, 1927–1937.* Berkeley: University of California Press, 1995.

———. "A Revisionist View of the Nanjing Decade: Confucian Fascism." *China Quarterly*, no. 150 (June 1997): 395–432.

Wang Liangqing. *Sanmin zhuyi qingniantuan yu Zhongguo Guomindang guanxi yanjiu: 1938–1949* [A study of the relationship between the San-min Chu-I Youth Corps and the Kuomintang, 1938–1949]. Taipei: Kuomintang History Library No. 4, Historical Commission, Central Committee of the Kuomintang, Modern China Publishers, 1998.

Wang Min, Wang Suifang, Zhang Huiying, Ren Yuxiong, Lu Huaming, Lin Xintai, Shi Yu, et al., eds. *Shanghai xuesheng yundong dashiji* [Major events in the Shanghai student movement]. Shanghai: Xuelin, 1981.

Wang, Pi-Lang. "Civics and Morality among Thirteen and Fifteen Year Olds: A Study in the Republic of China on Taiwan." PhD diss., University of Maryland at College Park, 1996.

Wang, Q. [Qingjia] Edward. "China's Search for National History." In *Turning Points in Historiography: A Cross-Cultural Perspective,* edited by Q. Edward Wang and Georg G. Iggers, 185–207. Rochester, NY: University of Rochester Press, 2002.

———. *Inventing China through History: The May Fourth Approach to Historiography.* New York: State University of New York Press, 2001.

Wang Zheng. *Women in the Chinese Enlightenment: Oral and Textual Histories.* Berkeley: University of California Press, 1999.

Wasserstrom, Jeffrey N. *Student Protests in Twentieth-century China: The View from Shanghai.* Stanford, CA: Stanford University Press, 1991.

———. ed. *Twentieth-Century China: New Approaches.* London: Routledge, 2003.

Wilson, Richard W. *Learning to Be Chinese: The Political Socialization of Children in Taiwan.* Cambridge, MA: MIT Press, 1970.

Woolley, John T., and Gerhard Peters. "Statement by the President on the Situation in Korea, June 27, 1950." American Presidency Project, Santa Barbara, CA. Accessed November 17, 2009, http://www.presidency.ucsb.edu/ws/?pid=13538 (post discontinued).

Wright, Teresa. *The Perils of Protest: State Repression and Student Activism in China and Taiwan.* Honolulu: University of Hawai'i Press, 2001.

Wu Nai-teh. "The Politics of a Regime Patronage System: Mobilization and Control within an Authoritarian Regime." PhD Diss., University of Chicago, 1987.

Yang, Ying-kuei. "A Study of Employees' Cognition of Organization Change, Role Stress and Job Satisfaction: A Case of Military Training Instructors" [Yuangong zuzhi biange renzhi, jiaose yali yu gongzuo manzu zhi yanjiu: yi junxun jiaoguan weili]. Master's thesis, Da-Yeh University, 2007.

Ye Wa and Joseph W. Esherick. *Chinese Archives: An Introductory Guide.* Berkeley: University of California, China Research Monograph, no. 45, 1996.

Yeh, Wen-hsin. *The Alienated Academy: Culture and Politics in Republican China, 1919–1937.* Cambridge, CA: Harvard University Press, 1990.

———. *Provincial Passages: Culture, Space, and the Origins of Chinese Communism.* Berkeley: University of California Press, 1996.

Bibliography   211

Zarrow, Peter. *Educating China: Knowledge, Society and Textbooks in a Modernizing World, 1902–1937.* New York: Cambridge University Press, 2015.

———. "The New Schools and National Identity: Chinese History Textbooks in the Late Qing." In *The Politics of Historical Production in Late Qing and Republican China,* edited by Tze-ki Hon and Robert J. Culp, 21–54. Leiden: Brill, 2012.

Zhejiang jiaoyu jianzhi [A brief chronicle of Zhejiang education]. Hangzhou: Zhejiang renmin chubanshe, 1988.

Zheng Yiying, "Liu Ziran shijan" [The Liu Ziran Incident]. *Zhongyang tongxun she* [Central News Agency]. Guojia wenhua shuzi dangan, Taiwan xingzheng yuan wenhua jianshe weiyuanhui [National Culture Digital Archives, Taiwan Executive Yuan Council for Cultural Affairs]. Accessed February 12, 2010, http://km.cca.gov.tw/myphoto/h_main.asp?categoryid=35 (site discontinued).

Zhongguo di'er lishi dang'anguan [Second Historical Archives of China]. *Zhonghua minguoshi dang'an ziliao huibian* [Compilation of archival materials for Chinese Republican history], Series 5, Part I, Jiaoyu, Vol. 2: 1239–1240. Nanjing: Jiangsu guji chubanshe, 1994.

Zhou, Shuzhen. *Sanqingtuan shimo* [The whole story of the Three People's Principles Youth Corps]. Nanchang: Jiangxi remin chubanshe, n.d.

Zhou Yuwen, "Xuesheng junxun zhi guoqu xianzai yu jianglai" [Discussion on the issue of military training in schools]. *Jiaoyu tongxun fukan* [Education Newsletter] 1 (n.d.): 4–5.

Zhu Youhuan et al., eds. *Zhongguo jindai xuezhi shiliao* [Historical materials for the modern Chinese school system, part 3, I]. Shanghai: East China Normal University Press, 1983–1992.

Index

Academia Sinica, 39, 53
Anti-Communist and Anti-Russia League of the Chinese Youth, 74–76, 86, 98
Aristotle, 141

Battle of Dachen Archipelago, 78, 87
Blue Shirts. *See* Whampoa Clique
Boy Scouts of America, 47, 100, 147. *See also* scouting
Buddhism, 1, 12, 19, 27–30

Cai Yuanpei, 39–40, 133–134, 186n5
camps, 58–59, 61, 76, 88–92. *See also* recreation
CC Clique, 36–44, 62–63
Central Cadre School (CCS), 70–71, 77
Chen Cheng, 7, 42–44, 50, 63–64, 79, 85–86, 130
Chen Guofu, 36, 42–43
Chen Lifu, 153–154; and civics curriculum, 136–138, 140, 146; and GMD factionalism, 12, 36–37, 42–44; and relocation, 17, 20, 24, 166n11; and SQT, 51, 63–64; and student protests, 68. *See also* Ministry of Education (MOE)
Chen Shui-bian, 158, 180n7
Cheng Tianfang, 112, 118. *See also* Ministry of Education (MOE)
Chiang Ching-kuo, 6, 157, 181n23; and critics, 103–106; as head of CYC, 84–86, 94–95, 97; and Liu Ziran Incident, 126–130; and military training, 14, 97, 108, 114, 116–117, 120–123, 131, 154; and origins of CYC, 74, 76–83; political rise, 7, 181n28; and SQT, 44, 69–72

Chiang Kai-shek: and the Anti-Communist and Anti-Russia League of Chinese Youth, 75; and civics education, 17, 135–136, 142, 145–146; and critics, 103–106, 140; and CYC, 79–86, 88–90, 92, 94, 96; and fascism, 37–39; and GMD factionalism, 7, 35–43, 45–46; legacy, 153, 158–162; and Liu Ziran Incident, 128, 130; and military training, 13, 108, 110, 112; relationship with Chiang Ching-kuo, 69–71, 77–78, 181n23; and SQT, 41–51, 53, 61–65; and student protest, 66, 181n28; on war, 5; on youth, 1; and youth camps, 58
Chiang Kai-shek libraries, 57
China Democratic Party, 106, 130
China Youth Corps (CYC), 3–4, 57; campaigns, 92–95; camps, 87–92; criticism, 8, 103–107, 123; ideology, 95–96; legacy, 156–157, 161–162, 181n29; and Liu Ziran Incident, 126–131; membership, 96–102, 104; and military instruction, 113–116, 118–122; mission, 83–84; organization, 84–87; origins, 13, 73–74, 78–83
Chinese Communist Party (CCP), 3, 5, 17, 45–46, 51, 67–68. *See also* Communist Youth League (CYL)
Churchill, Winston, 80
civics, 14, 17, 96; curriculum standards, 132; early curriculum, 133–135; textbook examples, 141–143; wartime reforms, 135–138. *See also* textbooks
civil service examination, 1

214   Index

Communist Youth League (CYL), 4–5, 13, 56, 73–74. *See also* Chinese Communist Party (CCP)
Confucianism, 2, 71, 88–89, 95–96, 133–134, 146, 148, 151
corruption, 16, 31–32
curriculum. *See* civics; Ministry of Education (MOE); textbooks

Dai Jitao, 39–40, 63
Democratic Progressive Party (DPP), 102, 107, 158, 160–161, 180n7
Development and Relief Commission (DRC), 16
Dewey, Thomas, 153
Donglin Academy, 1
Dulles, John Foster, 128–130

Eisenhower, Dwight D., 128–129

fascism, 36–41. *See also* Hitler Youth
females, 47, 50, 168n79; and civics curriculum, 147; in CYC, 96–97, 100–101; as military instructors, 113–116; and military training, 6, 13–14, 117, 161; and relocated schools, 31–32; in SQT, 58, 60. *See also* Women's Corps
First Sino-Japanese War, 1, 89
Free China (Ziyou Zhongguo), 8, 103–106, 121–125, 130. *See also* Lei Chen
Fu Sinian, 75, 136
Fu Zheng, 85, 104–106, 122–123

General Political Warfare Department (GPWD), 13, 75–77, 84
Green Gang, 32
Guomindang (GMD): and civics education, 134–137; corruption, 32; critics, 103–106; education policy, 40–41, 95–96, 112–113, 132, 139, 146, 148; factionalism, 12, 35–41, 43, 45–46; and fascism, 37–41; and Liu Ziran Incident, 124–130; Northern Expedition, 2, 36, 70, 73, 79, 86, 109, 169n3; propaganda, 26–27, 33, 51, 81, 87, 93–94, 103, 161; relocation, 15–27; and

textbooks, 138, 140–145. *See also* Chiang Ching-kuo; Chiang Kai-shek; China Youth Corps (CYC); General Political Warfare Department (GPWD); Ministry of Education (MOE); Ministry of National Defense (MND); Ministry of National Defense Political Department (MNDPD); Three People's Principles Youth Corps

Hitler Youth, 4, 13, 47, 103. *See also* fascism

Indigenous Taiwanese, 149–151
iron curtain, 79–80

Japan: invasion of Manchuria, 2, 15, 21, 109–110, 167n30; occupation of China, 26
Jiaoguan. *See* military instructors

Kang Ze, 43–44
Kuomintang (KMT). *See* Guomindang (GMD)

Lee Huan, 71, 78, 126, 158. *See also* China Youth Corps (CYC)
Lee Teng-hui, 157–158
Lei Chen, 103–104, 121–122, 130. See also *Free China (Ziyou Zhongguo)*
Liu Ziran Incident, 109, 123–131

Ma Ying-jeou, 127
Mao Zedong, 69, 73, 84, 181n28
Marco Polo Bridge Incident, 15, 42, 135, 191n26
May 4th Movement, 2, 39, 73, 75
May 30th Movement, 2
military instructors, 13–14, 107, 108–109, 154; critics, 118–123; legacy, 159–160; recruitment and training of, 112–117, 131; and student protest, 127, 157. *See also* military training
military training, 6, 11, 150; and Chiang Ching-kuo, 154; criticism, 14, 118–123; in CYC, 97; curriculum, 116–118, 146; and females, 50; justification, 110–112,

119–120, 130–131; legacy, 155, 157, 159–161; and Liu Ziran Incident, 123–130; and Ministry of Education (MOE), 144; origins, 109–110. *See also* military instructors

Ministry of Education (MOE), 3, 5–6, 19, 137, 153; and CYC, 84–85, 105–106; curriculum reform, 137, 144–146; and military training, 112, 114, 118, 161; and relocation, 8, 20–25; and SQT, 62; and SSGAs, 66; and student protest, 46, 129; and textbooks, 138–141. *See also* Chen Lifu; Cheng Tianfang

Ministry of National Defense (MND), 75, 78, 84, 111, 114–115, 118–119, 121. *See also* Chiang Ching-kuo; Ministry of National Defense Political Department (MNDPD)

Ministry of National Defense Political Department (MNDPD), 7, 108, 112–114, 116, 121. *See also* Ministry of National Defense (MND)

Mongolia, 16–17, 144–146, 151

Month of March Movement, 157–158

Moral Re-Armament, 99–100

music, 102–103, 147

Nanjing Massacre, 21

National Institute of Compilation and Translation, 7, 138–139

Nationalists. *See* Guomindang (GMD)

"national middle schools" (*guoli zhongxue*), 20–25, 31–33

National Taiwan University, 75, 91, 102

New Life Movement, 38, 53

New School System, 19

Overcoming Difficulty Movement, 93–94, 155

Pan Zhenqiu, 71

Peking University, 2–3, 39, 53, 136

Rankin, Karl, 128

recreation, 6, 14, 78, 84, 98–100, 147, 156, 162. *See also* camps

Reynolds, Robert. *See* Liu Ziran Incident

Sanqingtuan (SQT). *See* Three People's Principles Youth Corps

scouting, 21, 29, 49–50, 107, 144, 147. *See also* Boy Scouts of America

Social Darwinism, 142–143

Socialist Youth League (SYL). *See* Communist Youth League (CYL)

student protests, 1–3, 7, 10, 24–25, 39, 65–69, 82–83. *See also* Liu Ziran Incident; Month of March Movement; Tiananmen Square protest

student self-governing association (SSGA), 40, 65, 67

Sun Liren, 7, 115

Sun Yat-sen, 5, 30, 39, 64, 159; in civics curriculum, 135, 137, 141, 143, 146–149; and CYC, 79, 100; and SQT, 57. *See also* Three People's Principles

Sun Yat-sen Hall, 75, 79

Sun Yat-sen University, 53, 70–71

Taiwan Straits Crisis, 87, 92–93. *See also* Battle of Dachen Archipelago

textbooks, 9–10, 14, 132, 158; and CYC, 96, 102; publishers, 135, 138–140. *See also* civics; Three People's Principles

Three People's Principles: in curriculum, 7, 16, 33, 71, 134–136, 139, 144–149; and CYC, 57, 84, 87, 89, 92, 96; and GMD ideology, 39–40; and Three People's Principles Youth Corps, 45–46. *See also* Sun Yat-sen

Three People's Principles Youth Corps, 4–5, 104–105; activities, 57–62; and Chiang Ching-kuo, 63, 69–72, 77; composition, 47–57; and GMD factions, 7, 35, 43, 45–46; legacy, 156; merger with GMD, 62–65; origins, 12, 41–43; purpose, 43–47; and relocation, 49; and student protest, 24–25, 65–69

Tiananmen Square protest, 157–158

Tibet, 16–17, 28, 93, 144–146, 151

216   Index

Truman, Harry, 87
Tsai Ing-wen, 155
2-28 Incident, 62–63, 78, 176n164

Uighurs, 102
uniforms, 21, 79, 110, 112, 118, 126–127, 129, 154–155
United States Reserve Officers' Training Corps (ROTC), 111

Wang Jingwei, 45, 172n83
Whampoa Clique, 36–42, 44, 62
Women's Corps, 50, 115–116
Wu Guozhen, 85, 103–106

Zhang Zhizhong, 42, 58
Zhou Enlai, 46
Zhu De, 73, 84, 86
Zhu Jiahua, 41–42, 50, 53, 65–66

About the Author

JENNIFER LIU is associate professor of East Asian history at Central Michigan University. She received her BA from UCLA and MA and PhD from the University of California, Irvine. She has served as a Foreign Scholar at the Center for Chinese Studies at the National Central Library (Taipei) and the Peking University Exchange Program. In 2021, she was a Fulbright Senior Scholar in Taiwan. She teaches courses in Chinese, East Asian, world, and transnational history.